Economics and Other Disciplines

T0383130

During the second half of the twentieth century, economics exported its logic – utility maximization – to the analysis of several human activities or realities: a tendency that has been called "economic imperialism". This book explores the concept termed by John Davis as "reverse imperialism", whereby economics has been seen in recent years to have taken in elements from other disciplines.

Economics and Other Disciplines sheds light on the current state and possible future development of economics by focusing on it from a philosophical perspective, broadening the concept of rationality in economic theory. The beliefs that prevail in the world today make up a physicalist worldview. This book argues that this pervasive view is harmful for economics as a social science. Do new economic currents like behavioral economics, evolutionary economics, neuroeconomics, institutional economics, happiness economics, the capability approach and civil economy, escape this widespread mentality? What would be an adequate underlying economic *ethos*? Do these approaches fit into this *ethos*?

Ricardo F. Crespo appraises the contributions from a classical philosophy angle, emphasizing their implications regarding practical reason. This volume is of great importance to those who are interested in political economy, economic theory and philosophy, as well as philosophy of social science.

Ricardo F. Crespo is Professor of Philosophy of Economics in IAE (Universidad Austral) and in Universidad Nacional de Cuyo, Argentina. He is a researcher at the National Council of Scientific Research (CONICET, Argentina) and has published extensively in his field.

Routledge Advances in Social Economics

Edited by John B. Davis, *Marquette University*

This series presents new advances and developments in social economics thinking on a variety of subjects that concern the link between social values and economics. Need, justice and equity, gender, cooperation, work poverty, the environment, class, institutions, public policy and methodology are some of the most important themes. Among the orientations of the authors are social economist, institutionalist, humanist, solidarist, cooperatist, radical and Marxist, feminist, post-Keynesian, behaviouralist, and environmentalist. The series offers new contributions from today's most foremost thinkers on the social character of the economy.

Publishes in conjunction with the Association of Social Economics.

For a full list of titles in this series, please visit www.routledge.com/Routledge-Advances-in-Social-Economics/book-series/SE0071

Economics and Other Disciplines

Assessing New Economic Currents

Ricardo F. Crespo

Routledge
Taylor & Francis Group

LONDON AND NEW YORK

First published 2017
by Routledge

2 Park Square, Milton Park, Abingdon, Oxfordshire OX14 4RN
52 Vanderbilt Avenue, New York, NY 10017

Routledge is an imprint of the Taylor & Francis Group, an informa business

First issued in paperback 2020

British Library Cataloguing-in-Publication Data
A catalogue record for this book is available from the British Library

Library of Congress Cataloging-in-Publication Data
Names: Crespo, Ricardo F., author.
Title: Economics and other disciplines : assessing new economic currents /
Ricardo F. Crespo.
Description: 1 Edition. | New York : Routledge, 2017. | Includes index.
Identifiers: LCCN 2017000639 | ISBN 9781138642447 (hardback) |
ISBN 9781315629971 (ebook)
Subjects: LCSH: Economics--Philosophy. | Evolutionary economics. |
Institutional economics.
Classification: LCC HB72 .C737 2017 | DDC 330--dc23
LC record available at https://lccn.loc.gov/2017000639

ISBN: 978-1-138-64244-7 (hbk)
ISBN: 978-0-367-66781-8 (pbk)

Typeset in Times New Roman
by Taylor & Francis Books

Contents

Foreword

In this book Ricardo F. Crespo has asked questions and raised issues that have gone largely neglected in economics despite their fundamental importance to future development. He suggests economics is in the midst of a change in character and its possible future direction driven by the influences of other disciplines and also changes from within economics. His view is that heretofore economics has traveled into a *cul-de-sac* brought about by its commitment to a form of rationality that is determinist and makes choice illusory. Modeling itself on the natural sciences, economics has essentially eliminated freedom from its understanding of behavior, and the question this produces at this point in its historical development is: will the influence of other disciplines on economics – a reverse imperialism – and change from within economics redirect economics in such a way as to give freedom a role in explanations of economic behavior?

He labels his vision of economics as a non-determinist social science as "liberal naturalism." His focus is the nature of rationality, and his argument is that the standard view of rationality in economics, the instrumental rationality of means and given ends, falls well short of and should be encompassed within a broader, classical view of rationality as practical reason, in which people think not only in terms of means but also about their ends – indeed, they always think in terms of the relationship between means and ends. Instrumental rationality is a mechanical rationality, and optimization is the expression of a deterministic account of behavior in which people behave according to natural laws, a conception labeled "restrictive or scientific naturalism."

Needless to say, postwar economics has only deepened and strengthened its commitment to instrumental rationality. But more recently it has drawn increasingly on other disciplines in ways that may affect its existing direction. At the same time, the influences of other disciplines on economics are varied, some implicitly sharing a "scientific naturalist" worldview and some more compatible with a "liberal naturalism." So these influences, including how changes from within are influencing economics, place economics at a cross-roads regarding the way in which it will develop. Ricardo accordingly assesses the new currents within economics from this vantage point. The great contribution of the book is that it develops and explains how practical reason ought to be the benchmark by which economics marks its future progress. The book will be a success if it puts this issue on the agenda in economics. I am optimistic that economics will ultimately adopt this more expansive vision of its domain, and happy to see this thoughtful reflection appears at this important time in economics' on-going development.

John B. Davis
Marquette University and University of Amsterdam

Acknowledgments

My gratitude goes first to John B. Davis. John has completely read, revised and commented on the entire book manuscript, providing extensive and excellent feedback and contributing with relevant central ideas. In addition, he also wrote the foreword. My debt to John, however, goes beyond this because John, along with Marcel Boumans, supervised my PhD thesis defended at the University of Amsterdam.

The day of the defense, after dinner and already out on the street, after saying goodbye, John turned around and humorously told me, "Ricardo, for your next PhD, look for another supervisor." I simply replied, "That's impossible, John – you will always be my supervisor." In fact, that was a kind of prophesy because when I proposed the idea of this book to, its editor, Emily Kindleysides, she said that it would be best suited for the *Routledge Advances on Social Economy* series, headed by John.

I am also grateful to Pedro Rivas. After a lecture on "reverse imperialist" economic currents that I delivered at a University Residence in Buenos Aires, Pedro asked me, "But do these currents effectively overcome economics' narrow conceptions of rationality?" That was how the idea for this book came about.

D. Wade Hands read Chapter 3 on psychology and economics, offering some much appreciated comments. Huei-chun Su read Chapter 1 and suggested some nuances about my considerations on Mill's thought. Félix-Fernando Muñoz read and recommended more bibliography and new ideas for Chapter 4 on evolutionary currents. Stefano Zamagni provided me with interesting advice concerning bibliography on civil economy (Chapter 9). I have worked extensively with Belén Mesurado on happiness and flourishing: part of Chapter 6 derives from an article written with her. Ivana Anton Mlinar reads my works on the philosophy of neurosciences and teaches me about this booming field. Geoffrey Hodgson read and commented the chapter on institutionalism (Chapter 7). The contents of several chapters have been presented in seminars and conferences and have been enriched with useful comments from the attendants. Emily at Routledge has enthusiastically supported this book project, and Laura Johnson has diligently managed the process. I am also grateful to the anonymous reviewers of this work and of published parts of the book,

x *Acknowledgments*

who offered valuable advice. Mariana Donadini, Carmen Bordeu and Monique Vaughan revised the style. However, I am solely responsible for any shortcomings and oversights. Finally, Liliana Luchi and Fernanda Cid at IAE Business School's library efficiently handled my bibliography demands.

Some parts of the book draw from previous published works. I appreciate the permission granted by publishers to use excerpts or lengthy parts of these works:

Theoretical and Practical Reason in Economics: Capacities and Capabilities. Springer, Dordrecht, 2013.
"Neurosciences, Neuroeconomics, and Metaphysics," in P. A. Gargiulo and H. L. Mesones (eds.), *Neurosciences and Psychiatry Update: Bridging the Differences*, Springer, Dordrecht, 2015, pp. 39–48.
"Happiness Economics, Eudaimonia and Positive Psychology: From Happiness Economics to Flourishing Economics," co-authored with Belén Mesurado, *Journal of Happiness Studies*, 16, 2015, pp. 931–946.
"Aristotle on Agency, Habits and Institutions," *Journal of Institutional Economics*, DOI: http://dx.doi.org/10.1017/S1744137416000059.

The institutions where I work and from which I receive support are IAE Business School (Universidad Austral, Argentina), Universidad Nacional de Cuyo's School of Philosophy (Mendoza, Argentina), and Argentina's National Council for Scientific and Technical Research (Consejo Nacional de Investigaciones Científicas y Técnicas, CONICET).

Lastly, it is only fair that my deepest gratitude goes to my family, to whom I dedicate this book. It would not have become a reality without my family's support.

Mar del Plata, December 15, 2016

Abbreviations

CA	capability approach
CH	continuity hypothesis
EUT	expected utility theory
MBE	modern behavioral economics
NE	Nicomachean Ethics
PT	prospect theory
RCT	rational choice theory
SEUT	subjective expected utility theory
SWB	subjective well-being

1   Introductory overview

This book intends to shed light on the current state and possible future development of economics by focusing on it from a philosophical perspective. These are interesting, exciting times for economics. On the one hand, standard economics has become increasingly sophisticated – current micro and macroeconomics bear little resemblance to their 1970s counterparts. Asymmetrical information; industrial organization; new developments in game theory, econometrics and uncertainty management; rational expectations, and dynamic stochastic general equilibrium are all revamping economics. On the other hand, economic crises and laboratory and natural experiments show that there is something wrong with standard economics. The traditionally considered economic rationality, the "economic principle," appears to be erroneous or at least insufficient to explain economic facts. Economics is consequently opening up to other forms of rationality: psychological, biological, sociological, ethical. Valuable inputs from other sciences and some revisited classical political economy ideas are enriching economic approaches. New ideas are booming, and it is very hard to anticipate what economics will look like in 20 years. As new scenarios unfold, we urgently need to rely on philosophy, in its role as orchestra conductor whose basic function is to combine all instruments to create one harmonious melody. The philosopher, in his/her capacity as conductor, can detect what is going on, what could happen in the future, and suggest better ways of dealing with problems.

This book aims to appraise the contributions to economics of these new and emerging forms and to provide options for their development from a particular philosophical view. In fact, the greatest economists started off as philosophers. Adam Smith was a professor of moral philosophy at the University of Glasgow, and his close friend and colleague, philosopher David Hume, also wrote remarkable essays on economics. A list of other outstanding "economist-philosophers" notably includes John Stuart Mill, Karl Marx, Carl Menger, Frank Knight, Ludwig von Mises, John Maynard Keynes, Friedrich von Hayek, Joseph Schumpeter, Herbert Simon, Albert Hirschman, and Amartya Sen. These names are associated with varying positions.

Let me first address the question about where economics is going to in terms of the history of its relationship to other sciences. After having exported its view of rationality to other social sciences – a process called "imperialism of economics" – new approaches within economics, which "import" insights from other sciences like psychology, sociology, neuroscience, biology, anthropology and ethics, have recently emerged – giving rise to a new process that has been called "reverse imperialism." How are we to understand these two imperialisms? The aim of this book is to assess these new "reverse imperialist" approaches and other economic currents that revive political economy old traditions from a specific philosophical viewpoint, particularly, whether or not the possible incorporation of "classical practical rationality" and its related commitment to a "liberal naturalist" conception which, as I will later explain, is not a materialistic perspective, could broaden the concept of rationality in economic theory.

"Ideas rule the world." Indeed, throughout the ages, a set of philosophical ideas, that is, a "metaphysical worldview" or *ethos* has greatly influenced our conceptions of life and science. The beliefs that prevail today in the world make up a materialistic worldview. I believe that this pervasive view is harmful for economics as a social science. Do these new currents escape this widespread mentality? What would be an adequate underlying economic *ethos*? Do these approaches fit into this *ethos*?

The recognition of the influence of theory on data selection and interpretation has currently led to the widely accepted notion that scientific theories' content, formulation and method largely depend on the contemporary metaphysical worldview. Given the present materialistic perspective, the current "metaphysics of science" is also materialistic (or "physicalist").[1] According to this view, underlying and embedded into the development of sciences, everything that exists or happens is physical and can ultimately be explained by reducing it down to the categories of the natural sciences. As Thomas Nagel describes it, "among the scientists and philosophers who do express views about the natural order as a whole, reductive materialism is widely assumed to be the only serious possibility" (2012: 4).

Craig Dilworth (2006) argues that modern science is based on specific, fundamental metaphysical principles: first, uniformity of nature; second, substance; and, finally, causality. These principles determine what is ontologically necessary or possible within every discipline: they provide the structure of scientific rationality, set guidelines for pursuing science, and define basic concepts. Also, they are often unconscious: as Alfred N. Whitehead ([1926] 1948: 49) asserts:

> There will be some fundamental assumptions which adherents of all variant systems within the epoch unconsciously presuppose. Such assumptions appear so obvious that people do not know what they are assuming because no other way of putting things has ever occurred to them.

According to Dilworth, these principles drive modern science to support a physicalist, deterministic (albeit not always rigid) view of reality. However, many scientific disciplines have reservations about this notion. This resistance or tension in the applicability of this physicalist metaphysical commitment is especially present in the social sciences. Dilworth (2006: 130) explains:

> Some of the basic problems regarding their applicability in the social sciences are those of synthesizing uniformity and free will, the vagueness apparently inherent in the notion of a social substance, and the dominant position occupied in social thought by the notion of final causes.

John Searle (2007: 5) describes an analogue tension:

> We have a conception of ourselves as conscious, intentionalistic, rational, social, institutional, political, speech-act performing, ethical and free will possessing agents. Now, the question is, How can we square this self-conception of ourselves as mindful, meaning-creating, free, rational, etc. agents with a universe that consists entirely of mindless, meaningless, unfree, nonrational, brute physical particles?

An "easy fix" for this dilemma is to "boldly" admit that, ultimately, we are a set of physical particles, but, deep down, only a few individuals are satisfied with this answer. A similar tension is present in economics, as, once again, Dilworth points out (2006: 135):

> [T]here is a particular tension in the economist's conception of human nature. On the one hand the notion of free will is integral to it, since without free will the rationality principle would make no sense. On the other hand, however, no economic actor has the freedom not to follow the rationality principle, which itself determines how he or she is to act.[2]

It would prove useful to find out whether this tension stems from an underlying metaphysical view of economics. No doubt, science needs to simplify, to idealize, as Galileo Galilei has taught us. Science has immensely progressed by doing so. However, idealization should not imply setting aside essential factors for the analysis of science's subject-matter. These factors must be incorporated if science is to truly explain, accurately predict and adequately prescribe.

John Stuart Mill ([1844] 2006: 321), one of the modern founders of the scientific method, specifically speaking about political economy, considers the need for idealization:

> What is now commonly understood by the term "Political Economy" is not the science of speculative politics, but a branch of that science. It does not treat of the whole of man's nature as modified by the social state, nor of the whole conduct of man in society. It is concerned with him solely as

a being who desires to possess wealth, and who is capable of judging of
the comparative efficacy of means for obtaining that end.

The last part of the last sentence anticipates the prevailing current definition
of economics: the allocation of scarce means in order to satisfy given ends:
"the scarcity definition" of economics promoted by Lionel Robbins (1935:
Chapter 2). However, Mill ([1844] 2006: 322) is aware that this description of
political economy involves a simplifying abstraction:

> All these operations, though many of them are really the result of a
> plurality of motives, are considered by Political Economy as flowing
> solely from the desire of wealth [...] Not that any political economist
> was ever so absurd as to suppose that mankind are really thus
> constituted.

And, consequently, he finally emphasizes the need to consider additional
motives for these "operations" in order to reach a correct explanation and
prediction – a de-idealization process:[3]

> So far as it is known, or may be presumed, that the conduct of mankind
> in the pursuit of wealth is under the collateral influence of any other of
> the properties of our nature than the desire of obtaining the greatest
> quantity of wealth with the least labor and self-denial, the conclusions of
> Political Economy will so far fail of being applicable to the explanation or
> prediction of real events, until they are modified by a correct allowance for
> the degree of influence exercised by the other causes.
>
> (Mill, [1844] 2006: 323, see also 326–327)

Mill is inclined towards a determinist position within the free-will versus
determinism debate. Consistent with this stance is the belief that, if we have
all the information we need, we will eventually be able to determine all possible
motives influencing economic actions and thus achieve an exact explanation
and prediction. For Mill, the complexity of the human realm makes this
impossible in practice, but not in theory. He explicitly states that he accepts
the "doctrine commonly called Philosophical Necessity," and he proceeds to
explain it in the following way:

> Given the motives which are present to an individual's mind, and given
> likewise the character and dispositions of the individual, the manner in
> which he will act might be unerringly inferred: [...] we could foretell his
> conduct with as much certainty as we can predict any physical event.
>
> (Mill 1882: 581–582).

We only have a "feeling of freedom" (Mill 1882: 582) because we do not
know all the factors involved in determining our conduct.

Mill, like many pro-freedom economists, holds a weak notion of freedom, emphasizing external freedom, freedom from coercion, which is not internal freedom. Internal freedom is also called "free-will." It entails having the capacity to deliberate and decide (i.e., a power to choose) independently of the actual possibility of doing what has been decided: even when restricted by external factors, we still have the capacity to make a decision. External freedom is the absence of restrictions to carry out our decisions. Correlatively, philosophers distinguish between freedom of the will and freedom of action (see O'Connor 2010: 1). The classical concept of positive freedom derives from internal freedom, whereas negative freedom results from external freedom (Carter 2016: 1).

Consequently, for Mill (and other economists), there is no essential methodological divide between natural and social sciences, because the ontological nature of their subject matters (physical, biological and human reality) are explained by efficient causes, and for many contemporary thinkers, they are ultimately reducible to material stuff and to relations between material entities. The difference between these sciences is only a matter of degree of complexity. However, simultaneously holding external freedom and denying or devaluing internal freedom is itself a tensioning position.[4] That is, Mill acknowledges that there is a plethora of motives driving economic actions, but, at the same time and albeit with some tensions, he "naturalizes" these motives. We will find the same scenario in some of the currents that I will analyze in this book.

The alternative metaphysical position that I will defend concerning the difficult topic of free-will or determinism is that human beings, though conditioned and determined by biological, psychological and sociological factors, still have the capacity to act independently of these conditioning factors. This does not imply that people never act automatically, but rather that, in the first place, there is free decision at the root of their automatic conducts and, second, they can freely alter or consent to their automatic conducts. In other words, in the free-will versus determinism debate, I am taking the side of free-will. This is, of course, a metaphysical position that, though suggested by internal experience and several empirical experiments, cannot be definitively proved. However, there is a longstanding tradition of free-will supporters starting with Aristotle and including Augustine, most medieval scholastics, Immanuel Kant, William James, Henri Bergson, Elizabeth Anscombe and many others, up until the present.[5] For Joseph Schumpeter's theory of development, based on the entrepreneur's performance, "freedom of the will" [sic] was "obviously visible" ([1912] 2002: 122). Still, I am aware that, given today's predominant materialistic metaphysical vision, my position is not very popular.

However, this does not seem to be unreasonable, at least in our field. As I will later explain, and as Dilworth emphasizes, economists face a tension between the requirements of science and their feeling about the importance of freedom. Even if freedom seems to risk suffocation in the current materialistic atmosphere, it is still alive. This can be understood in terms of the view of rationality economists employ. The logic of standard economics – an optimal allocation of given means to satisfy given ends – is a form of "instrumental rationality," or maximizing instrumental rationality, also called "the economic principle." This rationality tends to strictly define a specific course of action enclosing freedom into brackets, as in physics. Today, however, behavioral and experimental economics have empirically challenged this narrow form of rationality. This raises the question I have posed above regarding whether reverse imperialistic and other new approaches are changing the metaphysical view underlying economics. The reasons for the failure of "the economic principle" could be attributed to Millian complexity, freedom, irrationality (as different from economics' specific form of rationality), or a combination of them. However, regardless of the position we adopt, instrumental rationality seems to have failed, and we thus need to complement it with another kind of rationality different from physicalist rationality.

Let's return to the history of economics' relationships to other sciences. During the second half of the 20th century, economics exported its instrumental maximizing rationality to other social sciences: a tendency that, as already mentioned, has been called "economic imperialism." However, we are now witnessing a slow reverse process that yields an emerging "mainstream pluralism" consisting of different approaches that draw elements from different sciences outside economics (Davis 2008 and 2011).[6] As Bruno Frey and Matthias Benz (2004: 68) put it, the time has come for a change in direction, with new emphasis placed on *importing* insights from other social [and natural] sciences rather than on *exporting* the logic of economics. This tendency shares the same purpose that drove Wilhelm Röpke many years ago: to broaden the scope of economics, opening the doors to wider fields of research (cf. 1942: 18). However, it could still ultimately fail to expand the logic of rationality in economic theory. John Davis (2008: 365) has asserted:

> … economics, as other sciences, has regularly imported other science contents in the past, and having subsequently "domesticated" them, remade itself still as economics. In the current situation, for example, behavioral economics – a research program in economics, not in psychology – employs imports from psychology but frames them in terms of economic concerns.

Daniel Aromí (2013) has described how the connection of economics with other disciplines has evolved over the past 122 years, relying on word search tools in the main economic journals. In the late 19th century and early 20th century, there was a strong connection with psychology, sociology, history, ethics, philosophy, and political science. Aromí (2013: 205) explains how this connection shifted in later years:

> … this study reports quantitative evidence that suggests that the evolution of the prevailing approach in economics experienced two regimes. There was a first regime of decreasing connectedness with other disciplines, a

focus on a narrower set of aspects and increasing embrace of mathematical tools. According to our observations, the stage of massive adoption of a more mathematical approach seems to have occurred after an important fraction of the decline in the connections with other disciplines already occurred. The second stage is characterized by a high degree of adherence to a formal approach together with increasing openness toward other disciplines and the consideration of a broader set of aspects.

This may be a sign of the "domestication" noted by Davis, and it is not good news. What steps, then, could be taken to prevent economics from taming the logic of other sciences?

I suggest that we re-consider other springs of action in economics. Most classical political economists – for example, Adam Smith – believed there are different reasons behind economic decisions and actions – broadly matching Max Weber's (1978: 24–25) four motivations for human actions: instrumental, ethical (value-rational), sociological (traditional) and psychological (affective). But modern economics has gradually reduced these motivations to only one: instrumental maximizing, the logic of the rational choice theory (RCT) and the expected utility theory (EUT). However, though important and sometimes prevalent, this is just one among many springs of economic actions. It predominantly deals with the allocation of means to given ends. Sociological and psychological motives can concern both means and ends. Instead, value rationality, which largely corresponds to the classical notion of "practical rationality," is a rationality of ends, and of means with a view to the ends they produce. It is an inexact rationality sometimes called "reasonability" which entails the existence of freedom. Escaping materialism will only be possible when this kind of rationality is accommodated. Only practical rationality cannot be reduced to materialistic explanations, because it involves free intuition and reasoning about ends and about means from the point of view of ends. Reinstating these reasons behind economic decisions and actions does not mean abandoning instrumental rationality, but rather supplementing it.

In his book *Ethics and Economics*, Amartya Sen begins the first chapter by arguing that economics has stemmed from two different origins. One of them is the ethics-related tradition that dates back to Aristotle (Sen 1987: 2–4). For Sen, "[t]his 'ethics-related view of social achievement' cannot stop the evaluation short at some arbitrary point like satisfying 'efficiency.' The assessment has to be more fully ethical, and take a broader view of 'the good'" (1987: 4). He mentions Smith, Mill and Karl Marx as members of this tradition. The other origin is engineering-related, and Sen (1987: 5) characterizes it as follows:

> This approach is characterized by being concerned with primarily logistic issues rather than with ultimate ends and such questions as what may foster "the good of man" or "how should one live." The ends are taken as fairly straightforwardly given, and the object of the exercise is to find

the appropriate means to serve them. Human behaviour is typically seen as being based on simple and easily characterizable motives.

Sen lists William Petty, Francois Quesnay, David Ricardo, Augustin Cournot, and Leon Walras as specially concerned with the logistic problems in economics (1987: 6). He notes that both ethical and the engineering-related origins should be complementary, but modern economics leans towards the latter, thus impoverishing gradually (1987: 7). Accordingly, he suggests reconsidering the ethical origin, which takes an array of motivations of economic actions into account. He upholds that economics "can be made more productive by paying greater and more explicit attention to the ethical considerations that shape human behavior and judgment. It is not my purpose to write off what has been or is being achieved, but definitely to demand more" (1987: 9). In the next chapter, I will further explore the 20th century's evolution of economics and will also show how economics has shifted from dealing with economic reality as influenced for very different motivations to looking at human reality as determined by a very specific logic.

Sen's classification brings another possibility for the future of economics suggested in this book: the revival of the old ethical-related tradition. So, the broadening of the conception of rationality in economics could stem from the "reverse imperialism" currents – that is, from outside economics – and from within economics – by the reinstatement of former economic notions encompassing a collection of motivations for economic events.

Assessing these new approaches in economics from the point of view of practical rationality and identifying the role they play regarding the nature of rationality proves essential, and are the main objectives of this book. At this juncture, I argue that practical rationality plays a decisive role.

Practical rationality was recognized and explored by Aristotle in ancient times. The past two centuries have seen the rise of new views of practical reasoning which differ from the Aristotelian or classical view that I will adopt here. When discussing it, I will be specifically referring to the classical conception. Strong support for its inclusion in social sciences emerged in the second half of the past century, mainly in Germany. The collective work edited by Manfred Riedel (1972–1974) entitled *Rehabilitierung der praktischen Philosophie* can be considered a hallmark of this trend. These views regard the practical paradigm as a reaction against the modern prevailing requirement of value-freedom or value-neutrality in the social sciences. For value-freedom supporters, scientific reason is only applicable to means. Goals or ends of action are for them a matter of private choice, and are beyond the boundaries of science. Supporters of practical reason argue that any science whose subject is an aspect or part of human action must include practical reason considerations as well. A different interpretation of the value-neutrality postulate becomes necessary: values should not be "officially" set aside but "impartially" pondered. This is a task for practical reason, as the neutral description of social facts is only achievable through the scientific definition of the standards of practical reasonableness (see Finnis 1980: 12). In other words, practical reason is used to determine the set of values that should be sought; thus, values are not discarded but reasoned. Hence, we cannot discard evaluation. John Finnis explains: "a theorist cannot give a theoretical description and analysis of social facts, unless he also participates in the work of evaluation, of understanding what is really good for human persons and what is really required by practical reasonableness" (1980: 3). Without evaluation we cannot determine what is significant. This exercise consequently does not annul value-neutrality because it looks for an unavoidable rational – neither emotivist nor consequentialist – evaluation which is part of the social science. Werner Güth and Halmut Kliemt (2013: 15), quoting H. L. A. Hart (1961), note that understanding a decision presupposes modeling its underlying intentions from an "internal point of view." In economics, Sen has heavily based his capability approach and theory of justice on practical reason (see 2002 and 2009).

Besides, for some practical science supporters, value-neutrality is a pedagogical and not an epistemological postulate (see Y. Simon 1991: 130–131). The widely recognized champion of value-freedom is Weber and his *Wertfreiheit* mandate of value impartiality (cf. Weber 1949).[7] However, this requirement has been misunderstood. Wilhelm Hennis, in a thorough and documented study, concludes "that one cannot comprehend the passion with which Weber held to the postulate of value-freedom if it is seen as having primarily a 'logical-methodological' foundation" (1991: 34). It is mainly a question of freedom from academic judgments. The value-freedom principle has a primarily pedagogical intention, provided by Weber"s fight against the arbitrary German academic policies of his time: "in Germany *'freedom of science' exists within the bounds of political and ecclesiastical acceptability* – and not outside these bounds" (Hennis, 1991). "Value-freedom" is seen as "impartiality."[8]

The purpose of this book is thus to analyze the new economic approaches from the point of view of their consideration of practical rationality. The next chapter will present the philosophical concepts and positions involved in this analysis: I will expand and reinforce the general claims made in this chapter and will explain the main concepts involved, especially practical rationality. The book will devote separate chapters to present and assess the influence of sciences on economics. Each chapter might make up an entire book! Thus, they will provide a summary of these new approaches as related to the point of view adopted in the book, specifically, their position regarding practical reason.

It is worth noting that physicalist-oriented sciences, reflecting the materialistic *ethos* of our time, also have an influence on economics. Actually, I will first address some almost entirely "physicalist" approaches from other sciences, and will then continue with other approaches that have escaped physicalism. The first group includes behavioral, evolutionary and neuroeconomics, while the second group comprises happiness economics, institutionalism, the capability approach, and civil economy. From the standpoint of the source of the change, in the first group it comes from the contact with other social sciences. Concerning the second group, we should make a number of distinctions: happiness economics is influenced by psychology, but it also revisits classical elements – namely, the concern with happiness; institutional economics is connected with sociology, but the interest in institutions was also present in classical ethical-related authors, like Smith and old institutionalists. Finally, the capability approach and civil economy can be more completely associated with the ethical-related tradition.

The final conclusion will provide an evaluation of the pros and cons of this movement. Its approaches evidently contribute new perspectives that broaden the range of possible motives behind economic action. However, do they all escape the metaphysical materialistic worldview? Do they consider practical reason, free will and final causes? Can they be modified or supplemented in this regard? New versions of behavioral, evolutionary and institutional economics, neuroeconomics and happiness economics cover diverse branches and sometimes hold very different positions under a common label. Besides, things in these fields are rarely black or white, but an ample gamut of greys. Consequently, this book will inevitably provide a limited evaluation of them. However, the common perspective of analysis, – physicalism and practical reason – is meant to gear us towards the development of an economics grounded on different metaphysical foundations. I contend that these foundations give us a realistic view of the human being: incarnated into matter but being more than matter, free, and capable of rational, moral thinking. I believe these approaches offer valuable contributions towards a new, richer and broader economics, adjusted to the requirements of non-physicalist, metaphysical fundamentals.

Notes

1 I will use these terms – materialism and physicalism – as lexical equivalents.
2 This last utterance calls for some nuances, as will be seen further along in the book.
3 On "idealization," see Ernan McMullin (1985).
4 I want to extend my thanks to Huei-chun Su for some corrections regarding Mill's thought on freedom and the methodology of social sciences. The responsibility remains mine.
5 Anscombe ([1971] 1981: 146) asserts: "The truth of physical indeterminism is thus indispensable if we are to make anything of the claim to freedom. But certainly it is insufficient. The physically undetermined is not thereby "free." For freedom at least involves the power of acting according to an idea, and no such thing is ascribed to whatever is the subject (what would be the relevant subject?) of unpredetermination in indeterministic physics."
6 For an assessment of the relation between this new trend and recent developments in economic methodology, see D. Wade Hands (2015).
7 Value-freedom, ethical neutrality or value-neutrality. On the translation to English of this German word, cf. Wolfgang Schluchter (1979: 65–66, note).
8 See also Hennis (1988: 161).

References

Anscombe, G. E. M. ([1971] 1981). "Causality and Determination," in *The Collected Philosophical Papers of G.E.M. Anscombe, Volume Two, Metaphysics and the Philosophy of Mind*. Oxford: Basil Blackwell.

Aromí, J. D. (2013). "The (Formal) Return to Openness: A Quantitative Contribution to the History of Economic Thought," *Journal of Applied Economics* 16/2: 203–222.

Carter, I. (2016). "Positive and Negative Liberty", *Stanford Encyclopedia of Philosophy*, ed. E. Zalta, online, https://plato.stanford.edu/entries/liberty-positive-negative/, retrieved April 6, 2017.

Davis, J. B. (2008). "The turn in recent economics and the return of orthodoxy," *Cambridge Journal of Economics*. 32: 349–366.

Davis, J. B. (2011). *Individuals and Identity in Economics*. Cambridge and New York: Cambridge University Press.

Dilworth, C. (2006). *The Metaphysics of Science*, second edition. Dordrecht: Springer.

Finnis, J. M. (1980). *Natural Law and Natural Rights*. Oxford: Oxford University Press.

Frey, B. and M. Benz (2004). "From Imperialism to Inspiration: a Survey of Economics and Psychology." In John B. Davis, Alain Marciano and Jochen Runde (eds.), *The Elgar Companion to Economics and Philosophy*. Cheltenham and Northampton: Elgar.

Güth, W. and H. Kliemt (2013). "Behaviorism, optimization and policy advice," Unpublished manuscript of a talk held at the Radein Workshop, 2013.

Hands, D. W. (2015). "Orthodox and heterodox economics in recent economic methodology," *Erasmus Journal for Philosophy and Economics*, 8/1: 61–81, http://ejpe.org/pdf/8-1-art-4.pdf, retrieved October 30, 2015.

Hart, H. L. A. (1961). *The Concept of Law*. Oxford: Clarendon Press.

Hennis, W. (1988). *Max Weber. Essays in Reconstruction*. London: Allen & Unwin.

Hennis, W. (1991). "The pitiless 'sobriety of judgment': Max Weber between Carl Menger and Gustav von Schmoller – the academic politics of value freedom," *History of the Human Sciences* 4/1: 27–59.

McMullin, E. (1985). "Galilean Idealization," *Studies in History and Philosophy of Science*. 16/3: 247–273.

Mill, J. S. ([1844] 2006). *Essays on Some Unsettled Questions of Political Economy* (Essay V: "On the Definition of Political Economy; and on the Method of Investigation Proper to It"). In *Collected Works of John Stuart Mill*, Volume 4. Indianapolis: Liberty Fund.

Mill, J. S. (1882). *A System of Logic, Ratiocinative and Inductive*, eighth edition. New York: Harper & Brothers.

Nagel, T. (2012). *Mind and Cosmos*. Oxford and New York: Oxford University Press.

O'Connor, T. (2010). "Free Will," *The Stanford Encyclopedia of Philosophy* (Summer 2016 edition), Edward N. Zalta (ed.), online, http://plato.stanford.edu/archives/sum2016/entries/freewill/, retrieved July 18, 2016.

Riedel, M. (ed.) (1972–1974), *Rehabilitierung der praktischen Philosophie*. Freiburg: Rombach.

Robbins, L. (1935). *Essay on the Nature and Significance of Economic Science*. London: MacMillan, second edition.

Röpke, W. (1942). "A Value Judgment on Value Judgment," *Extrait de la Revue de la Faculté des Sciences Economique d'Istanbul* III/1–2: 1–19.

Schluchter, W. (1979). "Value-neutrality and the ethic of responsibility." In G. Roth and W. Schluchter (eds.) *Max Weber's Vision of History. Ethics and Methods.* Berkeley, Los Angeles, London: University of California Press.

Schumpeter, J. A. ([1912] 2002). "The Economy as a Whole. Seventh Chapter of The Theory of Economic Development," translated by Ursula Backhaus, *Industry and Innovation* 9/1–2: 93–145.

Searle, J. (2007). *Freedom and Neurobiology. Reflections on Free Will, Language, and Political Power.* New York: Columbia University Press.

Sen, A. (1987). *On Ethics and Economics.* Oxford: Basil Blackwell.

Sen, A. (2002). *Rationality and Freedom.* Cambridge, MA: Belknap Press, Harvard.

Sen, A. (2009). *The Idea of Justice.* Cambridge, MA: Belknap Press, Harvard.

Simon, Y. R. (1991). *Practical Knowledge*, ed. by R. J. Mulvaney. New York: Fordham University Press.

Weber, M. (1949). *The Methodology of the Social Sciences*, translated and edited by E. A. Shields and H. A. Finch. New York: The Free Press.

Weber, M. (1978). *Economy and Society. An Outline of Interpretive Sociology.* Berkeley, Los Angeles, London: University of California Press.

Whitehead, A. N. ([1926] 1948). *Science and the Modern World.* New York: Pelican Mentor Books.

2 The theoretical and metaphysical foundations of sciences

The aim of this chapter is to build on some of the notions introduced in the previous chapter that set up the philosophical framework serving as the cornerstone for this book. The first section will elaborate on the argument about the influence and role of metaphysical worldviews on science development. Next, the notions associated with the contemporary worldview – namely, physicalism – will be explained, followed by a more comprehensive look at practical rationality – a central concept in this book – and its ties with this metaphysic worldview. This chapter will close with a quick review of the history of different conceptions of the nature of economics and their underlying metaphysical views up to the time when reverse imperialism began.

The impact of metaphysical worldviews on the content and methodology of contemporary sciences is well known. Economics is not an exception: it is heavily influenced by today's materialist worldview. However, the subject-matter of economics, a social science, calls for another metaphysical groundwork. It is possible to uphold a broad form of naturalism that includes practical reason and freedom. These ideas – a broad naturalism, practical reason and freedom – are, in my view, the key components for an appropriate framework for economics. This chapter will argue this thesis, and the rest of the book will assess the new economic views based on that thesis.

The influence and role of metaphysical worldviews in sciences

The idea that metaphysical notions influence the meaning and perception of scientific evidence has garnered widespread acceptance in the history and philosophy of science. As a first step in this influencing process, contemporary philosophers of science believe that there are no "neutral" data because a scientific theory always stands "behind" them, guiding the selection of and the method used to analyze or measure data. Second, on a deeper level, a metaphysical preconception "supports" scientific theory, influencing its perspective and formulation. Concerning the presuppositions of underlying data – that is, theories – French scientist Pierre Duhem is one of the earliest thinkers to note the theoretical commitments behind empirical scientific investigation – dubbed theory-ladenness. For him, the result of any experiment in physics is the fruit of observations interpreted on the bases of the theories held by the observer. When using their instruments, physicists, chemists, and physiologists "implicitly admit the accuracy of the theories, justifying the use of these pieces of apparatus as well as of the theories giving meaning to the abstract ideas of temperature, pressure" ([1906, 1954] 1998: 259–260).

In *The Logic of Scientific Discovery* (1934), Karl Popper wrote that "even for even singular statements, there are always *interpretations of the 'facts' based on theories*" ([1959] 2000: 423, italics in the original). Popper states that any descriptive statement contains universals, which are hypotheses or conjectures; indeed, for him, "universals cannot be correlated with any specific sense-experience" (95) – because "they transcend experience" (424); these propositions cannot be verified. Then, a scientific community's convention is required to establish an empirical basis (Popper [1959] 2000: Chapter 5).

In 1958, Norwood Russell Hanson coined the expression *theory-ladenness* in his well-known statement: "seeing is a 'theory-laden' undertaking" (1958: 19). Thomas Kuhn and Paul Feyerabend also uphold this view. Much has been said about the meaning and scope of this notion and the concept of incommensurability set forth by them. Since both thinkers underwent an intellectual evolution over the years, a moderate interpretation of their theses may be considered. While relevant differences separate the ideas of all the authors mentioned above (see, e.g., Heildelberger 2003), a certain influence of theory in observations and experiments remains undisputed and clear. This influence may be conceptual or semantic – the meaning of observational terms is (partially) determined by theory – or "perceptual," stemming from the cognitive theory biases of the observers.

More recently, empiricist Bas van Fraasen (1980: 81) has also supported theory-ladenness (see Monton and Mohler 2012). Jim Bogen explains that "by Bayes' theorem, the conditional probability of the claim of interest will depend on part upon that claim's prior probability ... One's use of evidence to evaluate a theory depends in part upon one's theoretical commitments" (2003: 11). Additionally, Julian Reiss complains that evidence theories fail to take into account that evidence about "a hypothesis is dependent on how the world works and our knowledge thereof" (2014: 302). In sum, as James Ladyman points out, "the degree of confirmation of a scientific theory is heavily theory-dependent, in the sense that background theories inform judgments about the extent to which different theories are supported by the available evidence" (2002: 214).

In 1951, Willard van Orman Quine challenged the analytic-synthetic distinction, arguing that empirical propositions cannot be isolated from their associated theories. His position takes a further step, implying that theory is linked to a metaphysical ground, when he states that there is "a blurring of the supposed boundary between speculative metaphysics and natural science" (1951: 20). Hans-Georg Gadamer, affiliated to a different tradition (hermeneutics), refers to the "horizon": "the range of vision that includes everything that can be seen from a particular vantage point" ([1960] 1996: 302).

As discussed in the previous chapter, Dilworth (2006), furthering this line of thought, underscores that modern science applies specific, fundamental metaphysical principles (uniformity of nature, substance, and causality), which outline a physicalist, deterministic (though not rigid) view of reality that is accepted by sciences. This creates some tensions within sciences, as has been argued in the last chapter and will be shown in upcoming chapters for the cases of the new reverse imperialist economic schools of thought. These principles determine what is ontologically necessary or possible within every discipline, providing the structure of scientific rationality, setting the guidelines for scientific work, and establishing basic concepts. They are not necessarily true but are assumed as if they were.

Evandro Aggazi (1988: 19, as quoted by Dilworth 2006: 71), states:

> Science [...] cannot be pursued without one's using certain criteria of intelligibility which are prior to the specific tasks it involves. In fact, every advancement of some science which has been presented as a "liberation from metaphysics" has actually been tantamount to discarding a *particular* metaphysical framework and accepting (often unconsciously) a different one [...] Therefore it is much more reasonable to be aware of the metaphysics one has than to have a metaphysics without knowing it.

Dilworth shows how these metaphysical criteria or principles have shaped the methodology of the empirical aspects of science. For him, we should thus speak of "principle-laden" (cf. 2006: 94) concepts rather than theory-laden notions. "Neither these principles," Dilworth argues, "nor the physicalist interpretation they have been given by modern science are inviolable, however, and to a large extent both have been adopted" (2006: 193). In other words, he refers directly to the metaphysical presuppositions and to the specific contemporary prevailing metaphysical view: physicalism.

John Dupré shares this view but criticizes its narrowness. He asserts, "[s]pecifically, it is supposed that canonical science must work by disclosing the physical or chemical mechanisms that generate phenomena. Together these ideas imply a narrow and homogeneous set of answers to the most diverse imaginable set of questions" (2001: 2). This is a particular form of monistic materialism (cf. 5ff.), the metaphysical presupposition that will be detected, albeit with tensions, in most of the approaches that will be studied in this book.

Summing up, metaphysics – construed as a worldview – is always present in science, and the current metaphysics of science is materialistic. As Maurice Schouten and Huib Looren de Jong simply put it, "science and philosophy have turned materialist: all that exist exists in space and time and must be considered fundamentally physical" (2007: 1). This is considered as an almost unquestionable truth. Daniel Stoljar (2015) states:

> The first thing to say when considering the truth of physicalism is that we live in an overwhelmingly physicalist or materialist intellectual culture.

The result is that, as things currently stand, the standards of argumentation required to persuade someone of the truth of physicalism are much lower than the standards required to persuade someone of its negation. (The point here is a perfectly general one: if you already believe or want something to be true, you are likely to accept fairly low standards of argumentation for its truth.)

However, this "truth" cannot be taken for granted. The next section will explore some distinctions that undermine this view.

Physicalism, materialism and naturalism

Let me explain the purpose of this section. The chapter in which it is included intends to build the intellectual backdrop for this book, and the second step to complete this setting is to introduce the notions of physicalism, materialism and naturalism that will be used and that provide a connection to the notion of practical reason. This step requires making some distinctions between these three concepts. I will argue that physicalism is very close to materialism but different from naturalism. I will then make a distinction between two kinds of naturalism and argue that adopting one of these kinds as the real meaning of naturalism will leave room to freedom and practical reason in a naturalist view that avoids the limitations of physicalism and materialism.

Some philosophers distinguish physicalism from materialism for specific reasons (Stoljar 2015: 1): there are some physical entities that do not seem to be material – for example, waves, energies and so on. However, "while 'physicalism' is no doubt related to 'physics,' it is also related to 'physical object,' and this in turn is very closely connected with 'material object,' and via that, with 'matter' (ibid). In fact, today, these terms are regularly used interchangeably" (Stoljar 2015: 1) – as I do in this book. This use can probably be accepted, and, therefore, I will consider physicalism and materialism as synonyms.

However, an identification *tout court* between physicalism or materialism and "naturalism" is not acceptable. First, within naturalism, we can distinguish naturalism both as an ontological subject and as a methodological or epistemic doctrine. On the one hand, ontological naturalism asserts that: first, there is no room for supernatural entities – "reality has no place for 'supernatural' or 'spooky' kinds of entity" (Papineau 2015: 1; cf. Stroud 1996: 44) – and, second, all that exists is material. There is a "causal closure" in the physical realm "according to which all physical effects have fully physical causes" (Papineau 2015: 4).

On the other hand, methodological or epistemic naturalism equates all science with natural science and upholds that the methods of natural sciences are applicable to the explanation of any reality. This position actually slides into a reduction of all that is natural to a physical realm: in fact, it implies an ontological naturalism. As Georg Gasser points out, "[a] consequence of the explanatory closure is that all entities reside within the spatiotemporal world as well" (Gasser 2007: 5). He also states (2007: 4), linking ontological and methodological naturalism, that for an explanatory closure:

> ... each entity within the spatiotemporal world owes its existence, continuity, and end to the operation of causal forces within the spatio-temporal world. We never go outside the spatiotemporal world for explaining anything which takes place within it. The empirical world which is investigated and explained paradigmatically by the sciences is intelligible in its own right.

Let us take a look at ontological and methodological naturalism. Concerning the former, it can be said, first, that there is no reason to affirm or to deny the existence of supernatural entities. Supernatural entities (if they exist) are, by definition, outside nature, and, consequently, they cannot be reached by the methods of natural sciences. Thus, we cannot legitimately affirm or deny the existence of supernatural entities using natural science methods. Second, ontological naturalism cannot be equated with physicalism because we can maintain the existence of non-physical natural realities. For example, though supported by matter, structures, forms, actions, and thoughts are non-material things, but they are natural.

Concerning methodological naturalism, some voices have claimed that not all natural entities or processes, especially human and biological ones (Dupré 2001; Nagel 2012), can be explained by the methods and concepts of physical sciences. For John McDowell (2002 and 2004: 92), modern natural science has evolved as a mechanistic approach to natural processes – "a disenchanted conception of the natural world" (2002: 174) – in which the knowing subject (the human being) threatens to withdraw from the natural world. It is tempting to identify nature with the subject matter of modern natural sciences (2004: 92), but McDowell views this as a mistake. He makes a distinction between a "restrictive naturalism," aiming "to naturalize the concepts of thinking and knowing by forcing the conceptual structure in which they belong into the framework of the realm of law [as opposed to the realm of reason, expressions taken from Sellars (1956)]" (2004: 95), and a "liberal naturalism" that does not require to integrate our capacities of thinking into this narrow scientific framework – "our capacities to acquire knowledge are natural powers" (2004: 95). For him, "knowledge and intentions can be in view only in the framework of the space of reasons" (2004: 93). Hence, "we can bring practical reason back into nature" (2002: 184). That is, nature provides for more than what natural sciences consider: it leaves room for practical reason, the human ability to rationally choose ends (a notion that will be addressed in the next section). "Scientific Naturalism," as "restrictive naturalism" is also often called, "interprets the natural strictly in terms of the scientific image of the world, narrowly or broadly conceived, whereas Liberal Naturalism – or some versions of it – offers a broader, more expansive conception of nature that makes room for a class of nonscientific, but nonetheless non supernatural, entities" (De Caro and Macarthur 2010: 3–4).[1] Mario De Caro and David Macarthur (2004: 14) consider that John Dupré, Jennifer Hornsby, Barry Strout and Hilary Putnam develop naturalist positions in the same "liberal" spirit. McDowell"s view on methodological naturalism is also expressed – rather independently, I think – by Nagel (2012: 8):

> The great advances in the physical and biological sciences were made possible by excluding the mind from the physical world. This has permitted a quantitative understanding of that world, expressed in timeless, mathematically formulated physical laws. But at some point it will be necessary to make a new start on a more comprehensive understanding that includes the mind.

Nagel favors "a pervasive conception of natural order, very different from materialism" (2012: 15) – that is, a non-materialist naturalism, including mind, consciousness, meaning and value as fundamental parts of nature that cannot be reduced to matter (2012: 20; 44). In other words, Nagel stands against physicalism and also against a restrictive or scientific naturalism.[2] He believes that teleology is "a naturalistic alternative" (2012: 91, 122, 124), a conception that has old classical overtones.[3] In the human consciousness field, teleology entails the use of practical reason to direct actions towards an end. Nagel asserts that human action "is explained not only by physiology or by desires, but by judgments" (2012: 114) made by practical reason. For a reductive materialist naturalism – that is, McDowell's "restrictive or scientific naturalism" – the adequate rationality to explain human action is instrumental rationality, because it is a specific rationality that fits with the supposedly deterministic work of the physical world. "Liberal naturalism," instead, makes use of both instrumental and practical rationality. That is, there is an intrinsic link between this "liberal" non-materialist naturalism, teleology, practical reason and freedom.[4]

In a nutshell, the argument proven here, which is the goal of this section, is that the distinction, within methodological naturalism, between a scientific or restrictive naturalism and a liberal naturalism leaves room within the latter for freedom and practical reason at a methodological level, and it also implies their ontological existence. This conclusion is important to economics because assuming that economic reality includes more than material stuff paves the way to an analysis that goes beyond standard economic rationality, which is an instrumental maximizing rationality.

Two steps more will be taken in this chapter: first, to develop the meaning of classical practical reason in relation to science and in relation to instrumental (or technical) reason (section 3), and, second, to show how economics, which was initially a practical science, evolved into a technical science. This evolution limited the scope of economics to instrumental rationality, with a corresponding methodology that fits with a scientific naturalist conception (section 4).

Practical and instrumental reason

Understanding the meaning of these two uses of reason and why I favor the Aristotelian version of practical reason in social science is relevant to the argument presented in this book that holds that economics is a liberal naturalist discipline which must recognize the reality of freedom and approach its subject-matter using practical reason. To explain this, we need to go back to Aristotle, who has developed an understanding of practical reason that fulfills the requirements of a liberal naturalist approach to science.

At the beginning of the *Politics* (I, 2), Aristotle describes the human person as a *zoon echon logon* – "man alone is furnished with the faculty of language [*logos* also means reason and order]." Aristotle there sustains that human beings can know what is good and evil, morally just and unjust, technically expedient and inexpedient. He distinguished between three uses of reason: theoretical, practical and *poietic* (technical or instrumental), paving the way for the three types of corresponding sciences. Each of these distinctions corresponds to a respective subject of study (*Metaphysics* VI, 1, 1025b 20–21 and XI, 7, 1063b 36–1064a):

1   For Aristotle, metaphysics, physics and mathematics comprise the theoretical sciences.
2   Practical sciences study objects stemming from human choices and have a practical end (*Nicomachean Ethics* I, 2, 1095a 6 and II, 2, 1103b 27–28).
3   Technical sciences are concerned with artifacts and rules for their production.

The theoretical use of reason points at understanding the essence and cause underlying anything that can be observed empirically or through experiments. Following in the footsteps of his predecessors, Aristotle asserted, "Plainly we are seeking the cause. And this is the essence, which in some cases is the end [...], and in some cases is the first mover" (*Metaphysics* VII, 17 1041a 27–30; see also 1041b 10ss). He made a distinction among real causes (efficient, formal, material and final) (*Metaphysics* I, 3–10; *Physics,* II, 3), leading to four different types of explanations known as "a doctrine of four 'becauses'" that answer the following questions: Who made it? Why this object and not another? What is it made of? And to what end was it made? (Ackrill 1981: 36) Theoretical knowledge is the path to these causes.

According to Aristotle's *Nicomachean Ethics* and *Politics,* on the other hand, the use of practical reason deals with the choice of ends of human actions and the best way to achieve them in order for the agent to strive for fulfillment. Practical reason is human reason itself that guides people to live according to what they are. Philosophy or practical science is a reflection on practical reason, its process and ends. This study on how to behave and why stems from practical experience: individuals always assume an end when they act, that is, human action is teleological. Rational people naturally ask themselves why they should seek one end as opposed to another, and what means are needed to secure them. This question and its answer are present in all human actions, at least tacitly.

Finally, technical or instrumental reason explores the way to allocate means to achieve a given set of predetermined ends. Though not necessarily, it could also strive for "maximization" – that is, the best way to achieve this allocation. This shows the difference between pure technical thinking (allocation only) and economic thinking (the best allocation).

Human sciences, then, have both a practical and a technical aspect. Law, for example, seeks justice as an end – it is a practical matter – but its own determination and its specific means to accomplish justice follow a technical process. The end of politics – in classical terms – is the common good, but it also requires an endless number of techniques to achieve it. Sociology deals with social ends, but it also makes use of a series of technical processes, like statistics and surveys, to conduct its work. Economics, by establishing a development index, for example, sets development as an end, defining its dimensions and their respective weights. Yet, construction of an index and its calculation are also the product of the application of technical reason. Similarly, firms set out ends and specific objectives that are achieved through a technical process. Therefore, neglecting ends and practical reason, as well as the technical procedures they involve, leads to an incomplete human or social science.[5] Practical reason is absent in natural sciences but cannot be set aside in the human realm. During the 20th century, economics has evolved into a set of techniques, leaving practical reason aside, under the influence of physicalism. I will analyze this process in the next section.

Before doing this, however, let me briefly discuss other conceptions of practical reason to highlight the advantages of the classical Aristotelian conception. It is indeed necessary to perform a brief introduction of these other approaches because, as Elijah Millgram notes, we are currently being witness to a huge profusion of competing views on this topic (2001: 1). Millgram defines practical reasoning as "reasoning directed towards action: figuring out what to do, as contrasted with figuring out how the facts stand [a task of theoretical reason]" (Millgram 2001). For Garrett Cullity and Berys Gaut, practical reason poses "questions about what one has reason to do" (1997: 1). R. Jay Wallace (2014) states that practical reason:

> … typically asks, of a set of alternatives for action none of which has yet been performed, what one ought to do, or what it would be best to do. It is thus concerned not with matters of fact and their explanation, but with matters of value, of what it would be desirable to do. In practical reasoning, agents attempt to assess and weigh their reasons for action, the considerations that speak for and against alternative courses of action that are open to them. Moreover they do this from a distinctively first-personal point of view, one that is defined in terms of a practical predicament in which they find ourselves (either individually or collectively – people sometimes reason jointly about what they should do together).

These definitions make room for both the Aristotelian practical and technical or instrumental reason. However, the most influential views, upheld by David Hume and Kant, each focus on only one of them.

First, let's consider the contemporary Humean view of practical reason. In effect, Hume reduces practical reason to instrumental reason. For him, reason is only instrumental: it allocates means based on goals determined by desires. Reason depends on and obeys these motivational tendencies. Hume sees no rational deliberation about ends and views deliberation on means as unconnected to any rational consideration of ends. His well-known statement reads: "Reason is and ought only to be the slave of passions and can never pretend to any other office than to serve and obey them" (Hume [1739–1740] 1968: 415 -II, iii, 3). For Hume, actions are motivated by ends determined by passions, not by reason (415). In other words, the sole role of reason in human behavior is instrumental. However, according to Hume, this role of reason cannot be normative because reason only aims at the truth – it is only theoretical – while desires are not rational or irrational. Given that desires are the only normative forces of actions, actions are not rational or irrational but laudable or not, or simply "non-rational." In Hume's opinion, as noted by Hampton, "reason is a purely informational faculty" (1995: 65). For Hampton (1995: 70), Hume rejects the idea of normativity of reason because it would prove problematic for a naturalist: it would violate the distinction between "is" and "ought." This is why Millgram asserts that Hume's position concerning practical reason is "nihilist": "there is no mental activity that counts as figuring out what to do" (2001: 3; see also Millgram 1995). Neo-Humeans, relaxing Hume's strict is-ought distinction, support the normativity of instrumental rationality but consider it "hypothetical" because it depends upon our desires.

Bertrand Russell (1954: 8) influentially put the Humean idea of the reduction of reason to instrumental reason in paradigmatic terms: "Reason has a perfectly clear and precise meaning. It signifies the choice of the right means to an end that you wish to achieve. It has nothing whatever to do with the choice of ends." As Robert Sugden explains it, "reason is to be seen as an instrument to achieve ends that are not themselves given by reason. We may say that an act is irrational if it is not the best means of achieving the ends that the actor himself had a view when choosing the act" (Sugden 1991: 753).

This Humean conception of practical reason reduced to instrumental reason has been the focus of some criticism. Millgram (2001: 9), for example, asserts:

> A standard objection to instrumentalism is that it makes ultimate ends come out arbitrary: your ultimate ends are the things you just happen to want; they are beyond the reach of deliberation and rational control. But we know from experience that this is not what our lives are like.

In fact, many authors sustain that there are categorical – not hypothetical – reasons why an action ought to be done that are independent of desires.

Aristotelians believe that these reasons can be discovered and, consequently, you can say that a choice is rational when the option chosen is a good thing. Human nature determines what is good in connection with the essential characteristics of human beings, and practical reason determines what is good as related to the specifications of these characteristics and contingent traits: that is, what is the most appropriate way of behaving in each particular situation. For Aristotle, desire is necessary to trigger an action; however, desires can differ from goals defined by human nature and practical reason: reasons might be different from desires. The task of practical reason is to discover these essential characteristics in order to determine which actions complete them and how actions are related to a person's contingent traits.

John Searle (2001) emphatically argues for the existence of reasons for actions independent of desires. He calls Hume and Neo-Humean's instrumental rational model "the classical model of rationality" (2001: Chapter 1).[6] Searle thoroughly analyzes its assumptions and criticizes it, while defending freedom, the reality of weakness of will, and the existence of external reasons for action, which are normative reasons outside the agent – independent of his desires – subsequently internalized by him (2001: 114–115).[7] He thus concludes:

> On the Classical Model human rationality is an extension of the chimpanzee rationality [...] The greatest single difference between humans and the rest of the animal kingdom as far as rationality is concerned is our ability to create, recognize, an act on desire-independent reasons for action.
>
> (Searle 2001: 32; see also 124 and Chapter 6).

In these cases, a prior reason underlies the desire, motivating it to perform the corresponding action (cf. 2001: 170).

Another criticism of the instrumentalist conception of practical reason is that it assumes that all ends are commensurable, which is highly debatable.[8] Christine Korsgaard, for example, states: "the limitation of practical reason to an instrumental role does not only prevent reason from determining ends; it even prevents reason from ranking them" (2002: 104). Commensurability of ends means that they can be measured by the same quantitative unit: this is not possible in a direct way. We can compare them qualitatively. Then, indirectly, it is possible to *make* ends commensurable, but this entails a prior exercise of classical practical reason that involves evaluating the comparative relevance of the different ends and, only then, assigning quantitative weights to them.[9] Yet, as Martha Nussbaum notes, the internalized character and plurality of ends and the absence of quantitative measures makes this process weak in precision (2001: 173).

Along these lines, what can be called a "specificationist" criticism supports the need to specify the content of final ends before applying instrumental reason to them: "only when supplemented with the rational specification of ends is instrumental reasoning viable at all" (Millgram 2001: 11). This is a task of classical practical reason. Ends are not given; they are generated in the very process of action. That is, this process is dynamic. David Wiggins (2002: 225) provides a wonderful description in this respect:

> In the non-technical case I shall characteristically have an extremely vague description of something I want – a good life, a satisfying profession, and interesting holiday, an amusing evening – and the problem is not to see what will be causally efficacious in bringing this about but to see what really *qualifies* as an adequate and practically realizable specification of what would satisfy this want. Deliberation is still a *zetesis*, a search, but it is not primarily a search for means. It is a search for the *best specification*. Till the specification is available there is no room for means. When this specification is reached, means-end deliberation can start, but difficulties that turn up in this means-end deliberation may send me back a finite number of times to the problem of a better or more practicable specification of the end, and the whole interest and difficulty of the matter is in the search for adequate specifications, not in the technical means-end sequel or sequels.

Thus, means and ends mutually interact and determine each other.[10] The idea of ends as given implies a truncated view of action that cannot be human. It is actually a fiction. "Acting on such radically truncated judgments would be crazy," Elizabeth Anderson asserts (2005: 8). In the (very common) case of conflict of ends, classical practical reason is also necessary.[11] I concur with Searle, when he elaborates on decision making in the real world (2001: 126–128):

> In a typical case, such as me now trying to allocate my time in writing this book, I have a series of conflicting motivators that bear on the case. I have an obligation to finish this book. But I have other writing obligations that have to be fulfilled before this one [...] I also have teaching and family commitments that absolutely have to be fulfilled [...] Doing philosophy is satisfying, but so are a whole of other things, and I can't do all of them. This is what practical reason is like in real life [...]. The idea that in order to be a rational agent in such a case I would first have to have a well-ordered preference schedule and then make probability estimates as to which courses of action will maximize my expected utility seems absurdly implausible. But in all this apparent intentional chaos, there is in fact an order, and the aim of practical reason is to sharpen and extend that order.

The criticism of the Humean version of practical reason does not abolish instrumental rationality and its normativity.[12] It only shows that practical reason cannot be reduced to instrumental rationality, and that reasoning about ends – classical practical reason – is not only possible but also a necessary complement to instrumental rationality. The normativity of instrumental rationality is not ethical, but the normativity of classical practical rationality is. Searle and others are implicitly (and also explicitly) arguing that this ethical kind of normativity is legitimate and necessary in social science.[13]

Let us turn to the contemporary Kantian view of practical reason. First, it would prove useful to explain Kant's idea of the scope of theoretical reason, since its limited possibilities impact his notion of practical reason. For him, theoretical reason does not penetrate the nature of things. Kant calls the nature or essence of a thing its *noumenon*, that is, "a thing which must be cogitated not as an object of sense, but as a thing in itself (solely through pure understanding)." According to him, "the possibility of such *noumena* is quite incomprehensible and beyond the sphere of phenomena, all is for us a mere void" (*Critique of Pure Reason*, Second Part, Book II, Chapter III, "Of the Ground of the Division of all Objects into Phenomena and Noumena," 1982: 97). We cannot reach the *noumena* with our theoretical reason: we can only know phenomena. As Alfred Whitehead (1929: 60) points out, "Kant drove a wedge between science and the speculative reason" because science is about phenomena, not about unknowable *noumena*. Reason then does not have a "discovery" but rather a "constructivist" role, constructive of the object of knowledge through *a priori* categories and judgments. That leaves a weak ground for science, because it ultimately relies on the very reason that builds it, not on reality.

This removal from reality impacts on Kant's conception of practical reason. Consequently, for him, practical reason is separate or autonomous from theoretical reason. According to Kant, there is not – and cannot be – a theoretical science dealing with the practical world, but only some set of convictions about practical principles. "These postulates," he asserts, "are not theoretical dogmas but suppositions practically necessary" ([1788] 1952: 348).

Hence, in his view, an action should be performed if practical reason defines it as valuable. Agents adopt principles of practical reason as maxims. Kant's categorical imperative, which is the supreme principle of practical reason, constitutes the law of autonomous agents, defined independently of agents' desires and external principles. Agents' freedom consists in this autonomy. As Robert Johnson (2008: 17) explains, "the idea of freedom as autonomy thus goes beyond the merely 'negative' sense of being *free from* causes on our conduct originating outside of ourselves. It contains first and foremost the idea of laws made and laid down by oneself, and, in virtue of that, laws that have decisive authority over oneself." For Cullity and Gaut (1997: 20), this involves relying on foundational claims concerning the nature of practical reason that are unjustified.

Consequently, while for Aristotle an action is good because it is in agreement with what is rationally good to do, for Kant, an action is good because it is chosen by practical reason. In addition, while Aristotle's view concerning the relationship between values and practical reason recognizes that a valuable action is contingent upon its circumstances (for him there are only a few "moral absolutes"), Kant's view is constructivist in the sense that an action is valuable because it is chosen by practical reason and applies universally. That is, in Kant's conception, stress is placed on a constructivist practical reason.

Kant upholds self-determination of ends: no end, outside the agent, can sufficiently determine practical reason, which determines itself. Agents establish their ends through theoretical reason, independently of any indication from nature, because this use of reason cannot know agents' natural ends. Moreover, we have no rational basis to believe in this autonomy of practical reason (cf. Johnson 2008: 18).

The ends of practical reason are nothing but immanent ends of the very action. Actually, practical reason is not distinct from the will. Wallace explains, referring to the Kantian and Neo-Kantian conceptions, that "the realm of the normative, on this approach, is not pictured as a body of truths or facts that are prior to and independent of the will; rather, it is taken to be "constructed" by agents through their own *volitional* activity" (2014, my italics). In his *Critique of Practical Reason*, Kant states that "[t]he objective reality of a pure will, or, what is the same thing, of a pure practical reason, is given in the moral law a priori, as it were, by a fact, for so we may name a determination of the will which is inevitable, although it does not rest on empirical principles" ([1788] 1960, I, Chapter 1, II, 1952: 314).

In a nutshell, according to Kant, the will can set its own ends and laws without any previous knowledge. As a consequence, Kant's theory of human action, in respect to its internal motivation, is ultimately similar to Hume's: the difference is that while for Hume the ends are determined by passions, for Kant they are determined by the will (called by him practical reason). Again, reason has only an instrumental function. Korsgaard points out that Kant contributes a normative status to the instrumental principle, because conformity to the instrumental principle makes us persons.[14]

Hence, while Aristotle's view concerning the relationship between values and practical reason recognizes valuable actions in themselves, Hume reduces practical reason to instrumental reason, whereas Kant's view is constructivist, in the sense that the action is valuable because it has been chosen. These last two theories of action fit very well with individualism – and in fact have served as foundations for political and economic individualist theories – because their rule is not external or heteronomous but internal or autonomous. As a result, given these characteristics of the Humean and Kantian approaches to practical reason, I have adopted the Aristotelian classical approach. This perspective assumes a teleological view of human action: the constellation of ends of a person and the consequences of his/her actions are at the center of the classical conception of practical reason. Practical reason also assumes the existence of freedom to choose ends. An optimal allocation of means to given ends – that is, instrumental reason – calls for a determinate way; on the contrary, people are free to choose their ends. Hence, a social science that reasons practically is a liberal naturalist discipline. I will thus argue the need to analyze the view of practical reason (if any) adopted by the new inverse imperialism movement and other new currents in order to assess whether it contributes or not to the improvement of economic science.

The evolution of economics

The time has come to synthesize and analyze the different positions held by economics from its inception to the present in terms of its understanding of practical reason. A look at 20th century economics will prove useful. When we reflect on the recent evolution of economics, we can discern two simultaneous, related tendencies associated with rationality and, indirectly, with the prevalent materialist/physicalist worldview. Ronald Coase (1978: 207) describes them very accurately:

> The first consists of an enlargement of the scope of economists' interests so far as subject matter is concerned. The second is a narrowing of a professional interest to a more formal, technical, mathematical analysis. This more formal analysis tends to have a greater generality. It may say less, or leave much unsaid, about the economic system, but, because of its generality, [...] economics becomes the study of all purposive human behavior and its scope is, therefore, coterminous with all of the social sciences.

The first tendency noted by Coase – "an enlargement of the scope of economists' interests so far as subject matter is concerned" – involves economic imperialism as it was presented in the previous chapter: the application of economic (instrumental) rationality to the analysis of a wider range of human activities or realities. Gary Becker's (1976 and 1993) economic approach best exemplifies this perspective (see also Lazear 2000). The second tendency – a narrowing of professional interest to a more formal, technical, mathematical analysis – is the result of a modern philosophical stream rooted in Hume's thought and connected with the relations between economics and ethics, sociology and psychology. As I have previously claimed, strictly speaking, the science stemming from this double process is not economic science but a specific way of analyzing different kinds of human actions (cf. Crespo 2013).

Both tendencies can be examined using two notions that prove very adequate to demarcate sciences. Sciences have what philosophers call a *material* object, or a subject-matter, the "about what" the science deals with, and a *formal object*, the specific perspective from which the subject-matter is approached.[15] For example, a human being (a material object) can be studied from different perspectives (a formal object) such as medicine, psychology or sociology; and the same approach (a formal object) can be applied to different subject-matters, as in the different philosophical disciplines. This distinction will help us explore varying concepts of rationality in different economic theories.

In economics, a distinction can be made between what I call "focused" or "ample" material and formal objects. A focused material object of economics consists in what ordinary people consider as "economic": exchange relations, money, etc. French anthropologist Maurice Godelier (1966: 23) upholds that "economic" includes all decisions and actions aimed at the satisfaction of human, material or spiritual needs, measured in material terms. An ample material object expands the concern of economics to include all human reality (economic imperialism).

Today's standard economics tends towards a focused formal object: an analysis of the material object from the specific point of view of a particular form of instrumental rationality. In contrast, an ample formal object considers economic reality from diverse forms of rationality: instrumental and practical; psychological, and sociological perspectives. Analyzed in these terms, the evolution of economics as described by Coase has implied moving from a science with a focused material object and an ample formal object to a science with an ample material object and a focused formal object. Table 2.1 presents examples of representative conceptions of combinations of material/formal objects, thus revealing the underlying notions of rationality assumed throughout the history of economics.

From Aristotle's viewpoint, economic science was a practical science (*praktiké episteme*). For him, "the economic" was the use of what is necessary to reach the "good life," which is a life of virtues that leads to human flourishing (*Politics* I). Aristotle considers it an analogous concept that includes human action, capability, virtue and science (Crespo 2006). It refers to the area of human life related to human material needs (which, for Aristotle, were subjective, albeit not arbitrary). Underlying this concept is a vision of human beings as material, social, free and rational beings.

Others have shared this view. According to Adam Smith ([1776] 1828: 189), political economy is considered "a branch of the science of a statesman or legislator." This explains why he also upheld a notion of economic science as part of moral philosophy, a practical science, assuming practical rationality. Additionally, Alfred Marshall ([1920] 1962: 41) points out:

> Political Economy or Economics is a study of mankind in the ordinary business of life; it examines that part of individual and social action which is most closely connected with the attainment and with the use of the material requisites of wellbeing.
>
> (Marshall [1920] 1962: 1)

Table 2.1 Taxonomy of the concepts of economics

	Focused material object	*Ample material object*
Focused formal object	J. S. Mill, M. Friedman, R. Lucas	L. v. Mises, L. Robbins, G. Becker
Ample formal object	Aristotle, A. Smith, A. Marshall, J. M. Keynes, A. Sen	Inexistent

> Economics is, on the one side, a Science of Wealth; and, on the other hand, the part of the Social Science of man's action in society, which deals with his Efforts to satisfy his Wants, in so far as the efforts and wants are capable of being measured in terms of wealth, or its general representative, *i.e.*, money.

Therefore, Aristotle, Smith and Marshall regard economics as a science with a delimited material object and an ample formal object. In this way, although there is room for enhancement, the domain of economics is roughly depicted: it is still basically composed of human activities dealing with wealth or material resources, and supports an ample notion of rationality which includes practical rationality.

However, as underscored by Henry Phelps Brown (1972: 7), this understanding of economics that confines its field to strictly economic matters, analyzing them from various points of view included in the notion of practical rationality, poses a twofold problem: it makes room for both "rational" and "irrational" behavior (reductively understanding "rationality" as instrumental maximizing rationality), and it is concerned with allocation of means and with decisions about ends as well. It comprises rational, unpredictable, and uncertain behaviors, and subjective decisions related with means or ends, facts or values. This subject is indeed hard to define and to handle.

Consequently, to facilitate knowledge of "the economic," economic science has evolved into a formal science with a more delimited formal object. It has attempted to create a specific, objective, preferably observable subject, because the "positive science" category to which it aspires to belong focuses on this type of subject. To this purpose, it would have to avoid psychological subjectivism, introspection and value judgments.

As argued above, this process by which economic science has evolved is underpinned by a philosophical process of ideas: the modern Humean reduction of practical reason to technical reason. Human rationality is only instrumental rationality. This conception has been broadly adopted not only by economics but by many modern social sciences. Raymond Boudon (2004: 57) explains it quite well:

> In general terms, the equation that assimilates rationality and instrumental rationality is so influent that social sciences' most literature on rationality almost exclusively deals with instrumental rationality. In other words, social sciences tend to admit that the notion of rationality essentially applies to the adequacy of means and ends, actions and objectives, or actions and preferences. At most, they recognize that rationality can also take the form of an exigency of coherence or transitivity of objectives or preferences. But they avoid applying this category to the contents of preferences or objectives.

More specifically, as David Gauthier recognizes, "the maximizing conception of rationality is almost universally accepted and employed in the social sciences"

(1986: 8). This way of thinking, applied to economics, expels normative and ethical considerations from it. As Margaret Archer (2000: 4) adds:

> ... this model of *homo economicus* could not deal with our normativity or our emotionality, both of which are intentional [...] One of the many things with which this model could not cope, is the human capacity to transcend instrumental rationality and to have "ultimate concerns." These are concerns which are not a means to anything beyond them, but are commitments which are constitutive of who we are, and expression of our identities.

Nicholas Rescher (1988: 115) explains in this regard:

> A narrowly construed "economic rationality" based on unevaluated desires and mere preferences as such is rationality in name only; it can be altogether irrational. Rationality is a matter of appropriate alignment all along the line – not just choices with preferences but of preferences with evaluations and of evaluations with values. True rationality demands the pursuit of appropriate ends based on valid human interests, rather than that of unevaluated wants or preferences.

The imperialist wave noted by Boudon and the narrow conception of rationality denounced by Rescher have not only reached into other social sciences but have also dissolved real personal and social identities by attempting to shape them, or "nudge" them, as we will see in Chapter 3. The "grand theory" of modernity is actually and progressively rationalizing the entire world.[16]

Let us undertake a quick review of the history of economic methodology to understand how it applies to this field. Economics started to become a formal science in the 19th century. Nassau Senior was the first economist to argue strongly against consideration of ends and the normative character of economics, maintaining the distinction between positive or neutral analysis and providing recommendations for economic policy in his *Outline of Political Economy* (1836). In 1860, he delivered the presidential address to Section F ("Economic Science and Statistics") of the *British Association for the Advancement of Science* ([1860] 1962: 19–24). As Terence Hutchinson (1962: 9) remarked, "Section F had to assert its scientific respectability and its worthiness to be included alongside the established subjects of natural science." According to Hutchison (1962: 13), Senior sketched a narrow and limited vision of economic science. In other words, under the pressure of natural science requirements, economic science was forced to modify its subject of study in order to conform to this particular notion of science.

And so we arrive at the definition formulated by Robbins (1935: 15) – influenced by Menger, Weber and Mises: "Economics is the science which studies human behavior as a relationship between ends and scarce means which have various applications." That is to say, economics is the science of a specific vision of choice. In this way, economic science became a formal science. It is formal because its subject of study is not a field related to material human needs or to production and distribution. It becomes a science of choice, any choice, to the extent that it requires adaptation of means to certain ends: it is a particular approach to human action. In fact, it was initially concerned with economic matters viewed as efficient distribution of resources, but it has quickly applied its logic to the analysis of other human realities. This is adequately expressed by H. Simon (1978: 1):

> This point of view [the "scarcity" definition of economics] has launched economics into many excursions and incursions into political science and her other sister social sciences, and has generated a certain amount of hubris in the profession with respect to its broader civilizing mission.

Aside from this tendency – the enlargement of the scope of economists' interests – Simon also recognizes the other tendency noted by Coase: economics exports to other social sciences "a very particular and special form" (1978: 2) of rationality. Simon criticizes these tendencies and argues for importing from rather than exporting to other social sciences.

The key to fitting human action into a specific framework is to consider ends or preferences as given. Stable, exogenous preferences (the ends, as considered by economics) prepare the ground for the development of a certain scientific subject. In his *Investigations into the Method of the Social Sciences with Special Reference to Economics* Menger entitled his Appendix VI "The Starting Point and Goal of all Human Activity are Strictly Determined." In this work ([1883] 1985: 217) he claims that "[e]conomy is really nothing else than the way which we travel from the previously indicated starting point of human activity to the previously indicated goal." Strictly speaking, it is a technical path that enables formulation of exact laws whose formal nature does not differ from that of the laws of all other exact sciences and of the exact natural sciences, particularly (cf. [1883] 1985: 217–219). Therefore, economic science considers ends as given. As Robbins (1935: 29) insists, "economics is not concerned at all with any ends, *as such*. It is concerned with ends in so far as they affect the disposition of means. It takes the ends as given in scales of relative valuation." Ethics, normativity and freedom are thus put into brackets. Economics struggles, in the way noted by Dilworth, to be a formal logic without psychological, sociological and moral elements: a "rational choice theory."

Though Robbins (1935: 83) tried to leave psychology aside, he recognized that it was "half of the equation." The very word "utility" carries a psychological resonance. Paul Samuelson (1938: 62; 1948: 243–253) subsequently developed his theory of revealed preference, "dropping the last vestiges of the utility analysis": we come to know preferences by looking at their external manifestations, quantities and prices. However, the very word preference refers to psychology and, later, as I will explain in the following chapter,

Samuelson presented a different version of revealed preference. The relation with psychology remains unclear and I will come back to it in the next chapter.

Finally, John von Neumann and Oskar Morgenstern (1944), as well as Leonard Savage ([1954] 1972), have come up with a completely formal theory of rational choice: the expected utility theory (EUT). An axiomatic theory, it states that if people are rational – in the specific sense they have been defined as such – they will behave as if they were maximizing utility. The order of "well-behaved" (consistent) preferences and probabilities is given and the solution is exact. However, the theory contains very strict assumptions that make it even narrower than those of Robbins. This oversimplification also oversimplifies the problem of uncertainty.

So, there are two wings of economics that exclude ethics and freedom: Samuelson's revealed preference theory and von Neumann, Morgenstern and Savage's axioms. As Nuno Martins (2011: 252) notes:

> There are two dominant approaches in contemporary rational choice theory, which in turn underpin mainstream microeconomic theory. The first starts by defining a set of axioms, from which a preference ordering is obtained. This preference ordering reflects self-interest, and can be represented by a utility function. It is also assumed that actual behavior and "rational" choices will be driven by such preference, which is the "rational" preference.
>
> Contrary to the above mentioned approach that starts from a set of axioms from which a preference ordering that explains choice is obtained, the second approach starts from observed choices and infers an underlying preference ordering that is consistent with those choices. This latter approach serves as a basis for Paul Samuelson's (1947) theory of revealed preference, where an underlying preference ordering is inferred from observed behavior and rational behavior is defined as any type of behavior that is consistent with the revealed preference ordering.
>
> Sen (2002) notes that even though these approaches have opposite starting points, both are committed to the postulates that there exists a single and complete preference ordering that characterizes rational behavior, and that actual behavior mimics rational behavior so defined.

Assuming there is a complete set of preferences represented by a utility function and deriving in a maximizing behavior, it becomes unnecessary to take into account all possible motivations of behavior, which can be reduced into a single one: maximizing utility. This set of preferences suffices to predict resulting behaviors. This way of doing economics fits into the physicalist worldview. We have a determined subject, which sets aside any source of contingency or inexactness (probability provides us an exact expression of what is inexact), and a determined way of dealing with this subject. However, this is not so in real life. Sen criticizes both approaches, as Martins (2011: 252) observes in this passage:

Sen (1982, 2002) criticizes mainstream rational choice theory, and the mainstream microeconomic theory grounded on the latter, for failing to recognize that human behavior cannot be described in terms of a single complete preference ordering only. Sen (2002) notes that human behavior may be driven by motivations other than self-interest, such as social commitment, moral imperatives and conventional rule-following, and argues that not all of these motivations can be described by the same preference ordering. Furthermore, Sen argues that preference orderings need not even be completely specified. Limited information, value conflicts, or the need to act before the judgmental process has been made, may lead to incomplete preference orderings.

The simplification of the rational choice and expected utility theories adopted by current standard economics puts preference contents and motivations in a proverbial black box. Yet, common sense and evidence from experiments suggest that rationality axioms of the rational choice theory are unrealistic in that they are based on the assumption of a hyper-rationalistic individual that does not exist. Thus, it becomes necessary to open this black box in order to examine the roots and contents of preferences, and not only their construction process. However, the danger of domestication, as noted by Davis (2008), still remains.

Conclusion

The aim of this chapter has been to set the frame against which contemporary reverse imperialism approaches – that is, currents importing insights from other sciences – and other developments reviving perspectives with ample formal objects – that is, changes within economics – will be evaluated in the remainder of this book. In the first section, I have shown how scientific empirical observations are influenced by theories and how the latter are subsequently influenced by metaphysical worldviews on the development of sciences. Next, I addressed today's prevalent physicalist worldview, highlighting the fact that this worldview is largely accepted, albeit not without tension.

I then proceeded to argue that physicalism equates with materialism but not with naturalism. To this purpose, I embraced McDowell's (2002) broad notion of naturalism, "liberal naturalism," or in Nagel's words, a non-materialist naturalism, which includes mind, consciousness, meaning and value as fundamental parts of nature non reducible to matter (2012: 20; 44) that thus leaves room for practical reason and free-will in a teleological conception of human action. I have also maintained that this is the frame required in economics as a social science. The third section includes an explanation of the notion of practical rationality, which is central to this book. I have noted its significance in the social sciences and explained my choice of the Aristotelian notion of practical reason over its Humean and Kantian counterparts. Finally, I briefly traced the history of different conceptions of the nature of economics and their underlying metaphysical views up until the beginning of current reverse imperialism.

We have seen how instrumental maximizing rationality of standard economics fits a physicalist and determinist worldview and, conversely, how practical rationality and belief in freedom fits a liberal, naturalist conception of reality. Experiments have shown that instrumental rationality often fails in that agents do not behave according to it. However, we can fall into the temptation to reduce "anomalies" resulting from experiments to modified versions of standard economic rationality; in fact, some of these new approaches in economics probably feel lured into doing so. In the following chapters I will examine whether these approaches escape a physicalist, determinist conception of the human being. Or, to put it in a more positive way, whether these new movements hold a richer conception of human rationality than its predecessors, including practical reason.

Notes

1 However, I am not fully satisfied with the expression "scientific naturalism" because it seems to imply that liberal naturalism is not scientific. This view stems from a reductive conception of science, which is today's stance. Gasser is aware of this: "McDowell pleas for a liberal form of naturalism in which thinking, knowing and feeling are accepted as being part of our way of being animals. Any aims of naturalizing them by integrating them into the realm of causes and natural laws as the proper space of science are rejected because human beings as rational animals find no place in *such a constricted scientific picture* anymore" (2007: 8). I agree with De Caro and Macarthur (2004: 14) when they say "better, scientistic" than "scientific" naturalism.

2 Nagel (2012: 6) argues against both ontological and epistemic materialist naturalism: "It is prima facie highly implausible that life as we know it is the result of a sequence of physical accidents together with the mechanism of natural selection. We are expected to abandon this naïve response, not in favour of a fully worked out physical/chemical explanation but in favour of an alternative that is really a scheme for explanation" (see also Nagel 1998 and 1986: 51–53 about consciousness as an irreducible aspect of reality). Similarly, Mark Bedau (1991: 655) states: "A broader view of nature, perhaps roughly Aristotelian in outlook, could reckon objective standards of value as part of the natural order. According to this broader form of naturalism, which would contrast with supernaturalism and would reject the miraculous in nature, values would be real non-eliminative natural properties, subject to broadly scientific investigation."

3 An introduction to some Aristotelian concepts is advisable to understand Nagel's position. "Nature" comes from "natura", the Latin translation of the Greek "physis." Aristotle, in his first book of the *Metaphysics* (I, 3), reviews Pre-Socratic philosophers' views on the nature of the *physis* and argues that, for them, the origin of all things was material. He then presents his take on a teleological view of nature that includes non-material elements, adding the formal and final cause to the material and efficient cause. The current view of nature as only material is similar to the primitive, pre-Socratic, pre-metaphysic notion of reality. Indeed, Dilworth characterizes the physicalist worldview as materialist and mechanistic: causality is reduced to empirically observable, efficient and material causes (2006: 57ff. and *passim*). However, reality spans beyond matter.

4 On teleology and practical reason in the social sciences see my paper (Crespo 2016).
5 On the complementary between practical and instrumental reason see Alan Gerwith (1983: especially 244).
6 'Classical" in Searle's sense does not correspond to the Aristotelian notion of rationality but to its Humean counterpart.
7 See Bernard Williams's ([1979] 2002) article "Internal and External Reasons" and the discussion surrounding it.
8 See Ruth Chang (1997) for different positions on this debate.
9 See Crespo (2007).
10 See also Kolnai (1962).
11 See Richardson (1997).
12 Rationality is mainly a normative concept. As Nicholas Rescher asserts "the significance of rationality does not, ultimately, lie in its role as a *descriptive* characterization of human proceedings (in how people *do* function) but rather in its *normative* role, as an indication of how people should function in the best interests of their cognitive and practical concerns" (1988: 196, 219–220). Specifically about Rational Choice Theory, which uses instrumental rationality, Daniel Hausman and Michael McPherson state: "The theory of rationality is a normative theory, although not by itself a moral theory. One's preferences can be as rational in the pursuit of evil as in the pursuit of good. If one fails to choose what one prefers, then one is foolish, not necessarily morally culpable. As a normative theory, the theory of rationality says how people should behave, not what people actually do. Behavior that conflicts with the theory may thus show only that people fail to act rationally, rather than revealing any mistake in the theory" (2008: 236). Leonard Savage ([1954] 1972), for example, uses rationality in this normative way. See also Hands (2012).
13 See, e.g., Hilary Putnam (2004); Charles Taylor (1985).
14 C. Korsgaard (1997: 254).
15 Though defined as such – formal and material objects– during Scholasticism, these notions had originated in Aristotle: see, e.g., Ryan Douglas Madison (2011: 400–401). For an explanation of these notions, see Henry van Laer (1956: 43–49).
16 See the sharp and down-to-earth book edited by Archer and Tritter (2001).

References

Ackrill, J. L. (1981). *Aristotle the Philosopher*. Oxford: Clarendon Press.

Agazzi, E. (1988). "Science and Metaphysics: Two Kinds of Knowledge," *Epistemologia* 11: 11–28.

Anderson, E. (2005). "Dewey"s Moral Philosophy," in *Stanford Encyclopedia of Philosophy*, http://plato.Stanford.edu/entries/dewey-moral/, retrieved March 23, 2007.

Archer, M. S. (2000). *Being Human: The Problem of Agency*. Cambridge: Cambridge University Press.

Archer, M. S. and J. Q. Tritter (eds.) (2001). *Rational Choice Theory. Resisting Colonization*. London and New York: Routledge.

Aristotle (1925; 1954). *Nicomachean Ethics*, transl. SirDavidRoss. London and New York:Oxford University Press.

Aristotle (1941). *The Basic Works of Aristotle*, edited and with an Introduction by Richard McKeon. New York:Random House (reprint of the translations prepared under the editorship of W. D. Ross, Oxford University Press).

Aristotle (1984). *The Complete Works of Aristotle*, edited by Jonathan Barnes. Princeton, NJ: Princeton University Press.

Aristotle (1999). *Nicomachean Ethics*, transl. and introduction by Terence Irwin. Indianapolis: Hackett Publishing Company.

Becker, G. (1976). *The Economic Approach to Human Behavior*. Chicago, IL: Chicago University Press.

Becker, G. (1993). "Nobel Lecture: The Economic Way of Looking at Behavior," *Journal of Political Economy* 101/3: 385–409.

Bedau, M. (1991). "Can Biological Teleology be Naturalize?," *The Journal of Philosophy* 88/11: 647–655.

Bogen, J. (2013). "Theory and Observation in Science," *Stanford Encyclopedia of Philosophy*, ed. E. Zalta, http://plato.stanford.edu/entries/science-theory-observation/, retrieved June 28, 2014.

Boudon, R. (2004). "Théorie du choix rationnel, théorie de la rationalité limitée ou individualisme méthodologique: que choisir?," *Journal des Economistes et des Etudes Humaines*. 14/1: 45–62.

Chang, R. (ed.) (1997). *Incommensurability, Incomparability and Practical Reason*. Cambridge, MA: Harvard University Press.

Coase, R. (1978). "Economics and Contiguous Disciplines," *The Journal of Legal Studies* 7/2: 201–211.

Colombo, M., L. Bucher and Y. Inbar (2015). "Explanatory Judgment, Moral Offense and Value-Free Science," *Review of Philosophical Psychology*, doi:10.1007/s13164–13015–0282-z.

Crespo, R. F. (2006). "The Ontology of the 'Economic': An Aristotelian Analysis," *Cambridge Journal of Economics* 30/5: 767–781.

Crespo, R. F. (2007). "'Practical Comparability' and Ends in Economics," *Journal of Economic Methodology* 14/3: 371–393.

Crespo, R. F. (2013). "Two Conceptions of Economics and Maximisation," *Cambridge Journal of Economics* 37/4: 759–774.

Crespo, R. F. (2016). "Causality, Teleology and Explanation in Social Sciences," *CHESS Working Paper No. 2016–2002*, Durham University, February 2016, https://www.dur.ac.uk/resources/chess/CHESS_WP_2016_2.pdf, retrieved October 13, 2016.

Cullity, G. and B. Gaut (eds.) (1997). *Ethics and Practical Reason*. Oxford: Oxford University Press.

Davis, J. B. (2008). "The turn in recent economics and the return of orthodoxy," *Cambridge Journal of Economics* 32: 349–366.

De Caro, M. and Macarthur, D. (2010). "Introduction. Science, Naturalism, and the Problem of Normativity." In M. De Caro and D. Macarthur (eds.), *Naturalism and Normativity*. New York: Columbia University Press.

Dilworth, C. (2006). *The Metaphysics of Science*, second edition. Dordrecht: Springer.

Duhem, P. ([1906, 1954] 1998). "Physical Theory and Experiment." In J. A. Cover and Martin Curd (eds.), *Philosophy of Science: the Central Issues*. New York: W. W. Norton & Co., 1998, pp257–279, from Pierre Duhem, *The Aim and Structure of Physical theory* (transl. P. P. Wiener, Princeton University Press, 1954; original: *La théorie physique. Son object et sa structure*. Paris: Chevalier et Rivière), http://www.ac-nancy-metz.fr/enseign/philo/textesph/duhem_theorie_physique.pdf, retrieved July 3, 2014.

Dupré, J. (2001). *Human Nature and the Limits of Science*. Oxford: Oxford University Press.

Gadamer, H. G. ([1960] 1996). *Truth and Method*, second revised edition. New York: Continuum.

Gasser, G. (2007). "Introduction." In G. Gasser (ed.) *How Successful is Naturalism?*, Publications of the Austrian Ludwig Wittgenstein Society, New Series, Volume 4. Frankfurt, Paris, Ebikon, Lancaster, New Brunswick: Ontos Verlag.

Gauthier, D. (1986). *Morals by Agreement*. Oxford: Clarendon Press.

Gerwith, A. (1983). "Rationality of Reasonableness," *Synthese* 57/2: 225–247.

Godelier, M. (1966). *Rationalité et irrationalité en économie*. Paris: Francois Maspero.

Hampton, J. (1995). "Does Hume Have an Instrumental Conception of Practical Reason?," *Hume Studies* 21/1: 57–74.

Hands, D. W. (2012). "Normative Rational Choice Theory: Past, Present, and Future," *Voprosy Economiki* 10, http://papers.ssrn.com/sol3/papers.cfm?abstract_id=1738671, retrieved July 20, 2016.

Hanson, N. R. (1958). *Patterns of Discovery*. Cambridge: Cambridge University Press.

Hausman, D. M. and M. McPherson (2006). *Economic Analysis, Moral Philosophy and Public Policy*. Cambridge: Cambridge University Press.

Heidelberger, M. (2003). "Theory-Ladenness and Scientific Instruments in Experimentation." In H. Radder (ed.), *The Philosophy of Scientific Experimentation*, Pittsburg: University of Pittsburg Press.

Hume, D. ([1739–1740] 1968). *A Treatise of Human Nature*, ed. L. A. Selby-Bigge. Oxford: Oxford University Press (reprinted).

Hutchison, T. W. (1962). "Introduction." In R. L. Smyth (ed.), *Essays in Economic Method*. London: Gerald Duckworth & Co. Ltd.

Johnson, R. (2008). "Kant: Moral Philosophy," in *Stanford Encyclopedia of Philosophy*, ed. E. Zalta, http://plato.stanford.edu/entries/kant-moral/, retrieved June 28, 2014.

Kant, E. ([1788] 1960). *Critique de la raison pratique*. Paris: PUF. Translation by Thomas Kingsmill Abbott, http://www.philosophy-index.com/kant/critique-practical-reason/i-i-i.php, retrieved September 26, 2016, and University of Chicago Press, Great Books of the Western World, *Kant*, The Critique of Practical Reason, 1952.

Kant, I. ([1787] 1982). *The Critique of Pure Reason*, Chicago and London: Encyclopaedia Britannica.

Kolnai, A. (1962). "Deliberation is of Ends," *Proceedings of the Aristotelian Society* suppl. 36: 91–106.

Korsgaard, C. (1997). "The Normativity of Instrumental Reason" In Cullity and Gaut (eds.), *Ethics and Practical Reason*. Oxford: Oxford University Press.

Korsgaard, C. (2002). "Skepticism about Practical Reason." In E. Millgram (ed.), *Varieties of Practical Reason*. Cambridge, MA: MIT Press.

Ladyman, J. (2002). *Understanding Philosophy of Science*. London: Routledge.

Lazear, E. P. (2000). "Economic Imperialism," *The Quarterly Journal of Economics* 115/1: 99–146.

Madison, R. D. (2011). *First Philosophy: Aristotle's Concept of Metaphysics*, ProQuest, UMI Dissertation Publishing (September 3, 2011).

Marshall, A. ([1920] 1962). *Principles of Economics*. London: MacMillan.

Martins, N. (2011). "Can neuroscience inform economics? Rationality, emotions and preference formation," *Cambridge Journal of Economics* 35/2: 251–267.

McDowell, J. (2002). "Two Sorts of Naturalism." In J. McDowell, *Reason, Value, and Reality*. Cambridge, MA: Harvard University Press.

McDowell, J. (2004). "Naturalism in the Philosophy of Mind." In M. De Caro and D. MacArthur (eds.), *Naturalism in Question*, Cambridge, MA: Harvard University Press.

Menger, C. ([1883] 1985). *Investigations into the Method of the Social Sciences with Special Reference to Economics*, Ed. Louis Schneider, Transl. Francis Cook. Auburn, Alabama: Mises Institute (*Untersuchungen über die Methode der Socialwissenschaften und der Politischen Oekonomie insbesondere*. Leipzig: Ducker & Humblot).

Millgram, E. (1995). "Was Hume a Humean?," *Hume Studies* XXI/1: 75–94.

Millgram, E. (2001). "Practical Reasoning: The Current State of Play." In E. Millgram (ed.) *Varieties of Practical Reason*. Cambridge, MA and London: MIT Press.

Monton, B. and C. Mohler (2012). "Constructive Empiricism," *Stanford Encyclopedia of Philosophy*, ed. E. Zalta, http://plato.stanford.edu/entries/constructive-empiricism/, retrieved June 28, 2014.

Nagel, T. (1986). *The View from Nowhere*. New York and Oxford: Oxford University Press.

Nagel, T. (1998). "Conceiving the Impossible and the Mind-Body Problem," *Philosophy* 73/285: 337–352.

Nagel, T. (2012). *Mind and Cosmos*. Oxford and New York: Oxford University Press.

Nussbaum, M.C. (2001). "The Protagoras: A Science of Practical Reasoning." In E. Millgram (ed.), *Varieties of Practical Reasoning*. Cambridge, MA and London: MIT Press.

Papineau, D. (2015). "Naturalism," *Stanford Encyclopedia of Philosophy*, ed. E. Zalta, http://plato.stanford.edu/entries/naturalism/#RisPhy, retrieved October 13, 2015.

Phelps Brown, E. H. (1972). "The Underdevelopment of Economics," *The Economic Journal* 82/325: 1–10.

Popper, K. R. ([1934] 1959, 2000). *The Logic of Scientific Discovery*. New York: Hutchison; London: Routledge (*Logik der Forschung*, translated by the author).

Putnam, H. (2004). *The Collapse of the Fact/Value Dichotomy and Other Essays*. Cambridge, MA and London: MIT Press.

Quine, W. V. O. (1951). "Two Dogmas of Empiricism," *The Philosophical Review* 60/1: 20–43.

Reiss, J. (2014). "What's Wrong With Our Theories of Evidence?," *Theoria* 80: 283–306.

Rescher, N. (1988). *Rationality. A Philosophical Inquiry into the Nature and the Rationale of Reason*. Oxford: Clarendon Press.

Richardson, H. (1997), *Practical Reasoning about Final Ends*. Cambridge: Cambridge University Press.

Robbins, L. (1935). *Essay on the Nature and Significance of Economic Science*. London: MacMillan, second edition.

Russell, B. (1954). *Human Society in Ethics and Politics*. London: George Allen & Unwin.

Samuelson, P. A. (1938). "A Note on the Pure Theory of Consumer's Behaviour," *Economica* 5/17: 61–71.

Samuelson, P. A. (1948). "Consumption Theory in Terms of Revealed Preference," *Economica* 15/60: 243–253.

Savage, L. J. ([1954] 1972). *The Foundation of Statistics*, New York: Dover.

Schouten, M. and H. L. de Jong (2007). "Mind Matters: the Roots of Reductionism." In Maurice Schouten and Huib Looren de Jong (eds.), *The Matter of the Mind*. Oxford: Blackwell.

Searle, J. R. (2001). *Rationality in Action*. Cambridge, MA and London: MIT Press.

Sellars, W. (1956). "Empiricism and the Philosophy of Mind." In H. Feigl and M. Scriven (eds.), *Minnesota Studies in the Philosophy of Science, Volume I: The Foundations of Science and the Concepts of Psychology and Psychoanalysis*. Minneapolis, MN: University of Minnesota Press.

Sen, A. (1982). *Choice, welfare and Measurement*. Oxford: Oxford University Press.

Sen, A. (2002). *Rationality and Freedom*. Cambridge, MA: Belknap Press, Harvard.

Senior, N. W. ([1860] 1962). "Statistical Science." In R. L. Smyth (editor), *Essays in Economic Method*. London: Gerald Duckworth & Co. Ltd.

Simon, H. A. (1978). "Rationality as Process and as a Product of Thought," *American Economic Review* 68/2: 1–16.

Smith, A. ([1776] 1828). *Inquiry into the Nature and Causes of the Wealth of Nations*, Book IV, Introduction, J. R. McColluch. Edinburgh, Printed for A. Black and W. Tait, 1828.

Stoljar, D. (2015). "Physicalism," *Stanford Encyclopedia of Philosophy*, ed. E. Zalta, online, http://plato.stanford.edu/entries/physicalism/, retrieved January 29, 2015.

Stroud, B. (1996). "The Charm of Naturalism," *Proceedings and Addresses of the American Philosophical Association* 70/2: 43–55.

Sugden, R. (1991). "Rational Choice: A Survey of Contributions from Economics and Philosophy," *The Economic Journal* 101: 751–785.

Taylor, C. (1985). *Philosophy and the Human Sciences. Philosophical Papers 2*, Cambridge: Cambridge University Press.

Van Fraasen, B. (1980). *The Scientific Image*. Oxford: Oxford University Press.

Van Laer, H. (1956). *The Philosophy of Science*. Pittsburgh: Duquesne University and Louvain: Editions E. Nauwelaerts.

Von Neumann, J. and Morgenstern, O. (1944). *Theory of Games and Economic Behavior*. Princeton, NJ: Princeton University Press.

Wallace, R. J. (2014). "Practical Reason," *Stanford Encyclopedia of Philosophy*, ed. E. Zalta, http://plato.stanford.edu/entries/practical-reason/, retrieved March 5, 2016.

Whitehead, A. N. (1929). *The Function of Reason*. Boston, MA: Beacon Press.

Wiggins, D. (2002) *Needs, Values, Truth. Third Edition. Amended*. Oxford and New York: Oxford University Press.

Williams, B. ([1979] 2002). "Internal and External Reasons," in E. Millgram (ed.), *Varieties of Practical Reason*. Cambridge, MA: MIT Press.

3 Economics and psychology

As I have already mentioned, the aim of this book is to appraise the "reverse imperialism" movement and other new economic views from the standpoint of their adoption (or lack thereof) of classical practical rationality and its related escape from a "restrictive or scientific naturalist" notion, which is a materialist or physicalist perspective. I recall that these three expressions, "materialism," "physicalism" and "restrictive or scientific naturalism," are used interchangeably in this book. In this chapter, I will analyze whether economic approaches influenced by psychology escape this generalized mentality since, as I have noted in the introductory chapter, sciences influencing economics can also be materialist conveying this orientation to economics, or they may become "domesticated" by it. Actually, I have already stated that a first group of disciplines, including behavioral, evolutionary and neuroeconomics, are predominantly materialist: they do not take into account classical practical reason and hold a weak conception of freedom. I have also suggested that a tension specially stirred by the idea of freedom still remains in the materialist stance. Is this tension also present in economic approaches influenced by psychology? This is another question that I will answer in this chapter.

The history of the relationship between economics and psychology is not a closed topic. Its "official" history can be described in the following way:

> Throughout the 19th and early 20th century, economics was closely related to psychology and ethics. Freedom was not always the star, but it was present. The roots of the law of decreasing marginal utility lie in psychology, and the view of utility sustained by authors like Hermann H. Gossen, William S. Jevons, Menger and Marshall are also associated with psychology. For Keynes, psychological factors strongly influence behavior. However, it should be noted that the ordinal utility theory, which started with Wilfried Pareto, Eugen Slutsky, and John Hicks and R. G. D. Allen, began to belittle psychology, planting the seeds of a "logical," non-psychological, theory of rational choice. While still maintaining that psychology accounted for "half the equation," Robbins' formulations proved a decisive step, eventually leading to Samuelson's theory of preferences, as

well as to von Neumann and Morgenstern's theory of expected utility (EUT). These key developments paved the way for an explanation of choice in purely formal, supposedly more scientific terms, leaving psychology aside. These theories prevailed from 1945 until nearly the end of the century but, almost simultaneously, empirical evidence of the weaknesses of the theory of rational choice began to appear.

However, D. Wade Hands has shown that this is not strictly right, at least concerning early 20th century consumer theory. Hands provides a new story in line with economists' tension between the requirements of "positive" science and common sense (to believe in volition and freedom), a tension between "restrictive or scientific naturalism" and "liberal naturalism."

Hands (2010 and 2011) concentrates on consumer choice theory. He thus describes its official story: "psychology came into economics during the neo-classical revolution of the 1870s, and remained in for the period of cardinal utility theory, but then was driven out during the ordinal and revealed preference revolutions" (2010: 634). If this is the real story, behavioral economics appears to redeem common sense by reincorporating psychology into economics. However, Hands thoroughly proves that this is not the true story.

The marginal revolution and early neoclassical economics were committed to a hedonistic introspective psychology. Given the 20th century's rise of positivism in science, this position became highly vulnerable and, consequently, economics tried to escape it. Hence, the attempted escape from psychology was a kind of adherence to the early 20th century "politically correct" positivist refusal of mental states and feeling by science. The latter should be substituted by "objective" observable data.

A first step in this process was to replace cardinal utility, reputed as hedonistic, by ordinal utility. However, Hands shows that this escape has been partial. Hands (2011: 391–397) explains how the "integrability condition," a mathematical requisite to represent indifference curves, led Pareto to identify the order of integration with the order of consumption, making the latter "reference-independent" and thus setting aside the subjective elements of choice. However, Hands also provides the passages where Pareto recognized that the assumption of fixed reference-independent preferences created empirical and methodological problems: in fact, the order of consumption matters and, consequently, choice is not independent of references – a "discovery" of current behavioral economics. Hands (2011: 397–404) goes on to present other theorists of the early consumer choice theory who acknowledge reference-dependence: Allen, Nicholas Georgescu-Roegen, Ragnar Frisch, Henry Schultz, and even Morgenstern and Samuelson.

With respect to Slutsky, Hands (2010: 638) emphasizes how after he stated that "if we wish to place economic science upon a solid basis, we must make it completely independent of psychological assumptions" (1915: 27), he then added that "it does not seem opportune to disregard all connections existing between the visible and measurable facts of human conduct and the psychic phenomena by which they seem to be regulated." Hands (2010: 639–640) also highlights an array of passages from Robbins asserting the relevance of introspective psychological elements. For example:

> But even if we restrict the object of Economics to the explanation of such observable things as prices, we shall find that in fact it is impossible to explain them unless we invoke elements of a subjective or psychological nature [...] It is obvious that what people expect to happen in the future is not susceptible of observation by purely behaviorist methods.
>
> (Robbins 1935: 88)

The supposedly final step in the "escape from psychology" is Samuelson's theory of revealed preference. Hands (2001: 67–68; 2010: 401; 2011: 640–641; 2014b) comprehensively analyzes Samuelson's development. In his 1938 article, Samuelson effectively achieved the aim of "dropping off the last vestige of utility analysis" (1938: 62) along behaviorist lines.

Erik Angner and George Loewenstein's article (2012) on behavioral economics accused neoclassical economics of falling into behaviorism, the positivistic psychological theory founded by John B. Watson and more recently led by Burrhus Frederic Skinner. However, this only applies to Samuelson's 1938 article, which has been an isolated behaviorist episode. Samuelson's next writings (1948, 1950) on this topic reintroduce preferences and utility. Hands (2014b: 109–111) proposes a possible interpretation of what he calls the "Das Samuelson Problem": Samuelson's change of mind between the 1938 paper and his later works was not in fact a change of mind, since when his theory was proved to be equivalent to the theory he had criticized and replaced in 1938, and not empirically empty, he went on to endorse it, given that it confirmed his methodological positivist position. This would explain his reluctance to recognize he had changed his mind. Hands concludes that "what had started out as a behaviorist program that rejected the psychological foundations of choice theory, ended up being a means for scientifically bolstering precisely these foundations" (2010: 641).[1]

Considering these previous perspectives, Hands's new story (2010) seems highly reasonable. It is the story of the already mentioned tension between recognizing human volition and freedom in human action and adhering to scientific positivism by escaping these uncertain and scientifically difficult to manage dimensions of action. In Hands's own words (2010: 642):

> The central thesis of my alternative interpretation of the history of consumer choice theory is that economists were never wholly willing to commit to one or the other and always wanted both – volition (and its associated normative implications) and causal science (and the predictive power, explanatory understanding and epistemic distinction it brings) – and this explains the kinds of psychology that were and were not acceptable. If we call the problem of retaining a view of human agency based on free will

and individual choice the volitional problem, and the problem of providing a theory of consumer choice that seemed to be consistent with dominant views about scientific knowledge the scientific problem, then the profession was not willing to accept a solution to one of these problems that did not also offer a solution to the other. The profession was willing to make trade-offs between the quality of the answers provided to these two problems on the margin – depending on context and circumstances – but a corner solution that solved only the volitional problem or only the scientific problem was never acceptable.

Specifically, for example, referring to Samuelson's revealed preference theory, Hands notes that "the observability of the 'revealed' part solved the scientific problem, while the motivational aspect of the 'preference' part solved the scientific problem" (2010: 643).

I also find this tension in Menger. In the previous chapter, I pointed out that Menger entitled an Appendix in one of his books "The Starting Point and Goal of all Human Activity are Strictly Determined." He argues that "[e]conomy is really nothing else than the way which we travel from the previously indicated starting point of human activity to the previously indicated goal" ([1883] 1985: 217), a technical path that enables formulation of exact laws whose formal nature does not differ from that of the laws of all other exact sciences and of the exact natural sciences, particularly (cf. [1883] 1985: 217–219). At the same time, he admits that "volition, error, and other influences can, on the contrary, and actually do, bring it about that human agents take different roads from a strictly set starting point to a just as strictly determined goal of their action" ([1883] 1985: 217). He also recognizes that "*real* human phenomena are not strictly typical [...] and that just for this reason, and also as a result of the freedom of the human will – and we, of course, have no intention of denying this as a practical category – *empirical laws of absolute strictness* are out of question in the realm of the phenomena of human activity" ([1883] 1985: 214, all italics in the original).

Does Menger take into account the nature of practical rationality? So far as he does not venture into the content of preferences and strictly focus on whether preferences are "well behaved" (consistent), it can be said that he does not. However, insofar as he tries to support volition and freedom, we can gather he seems open to considering it. This is the case of Menger. Hands (2011: 401) makes reference to Knight, who argues that tastes can be changed by the act of choice. In my opinion, Knight includes not only psychology but also practical reason. He maintains that given ends are not ends in themselves; ends are redefined in the course of the action itself. In other words, not only are means adapted to their ends, but also, even more often, ends are adapted to their means. He asserted (1956: 128–129):

Economic rationality as a description of deliberative conduct is limited in two further respects, fully as important in principle as the fact that actual results of action diverges in all degrees from the intention of maximizing a given end. First, the end is rarely or never actually given in any strict sense of the word; rather, it is in some degree redefined in the course of the activity directed toward realizing it, and the interest in action centers in this definition and discovery of ends, as well as in their achievement [...] The second limitation to which the notion of given ends is subject [...] is that to the extent to which an end is given, it is not really the end in the sense of finality.

In his article on Slutsky and John Hicks's theory of demand, Knight remarks that "in the discussion of conduct we cannot separate description from teleological interpretation – the 'what' from the 'why' in this sense" (1944: 307). In this case, the presence of practical reason, deliberation and finality is clear.

In sum, recognition of reference-dependence plus volition and freedom by early consumer theorists assumes at least a "bit" of practical rationality.

As of the 1950s, the situation became more obscure: psychology was more acutely disappearing from economics. The general equilibrium theories and the von Neumann and Morgenstern rationality axioms contain little if any psychology. Certainly, developments in economic explanations in the Rational Choice Theory and the Expected Utility Theory prevailing in recent years allow at best for a very basic psychological theory, which departs from actual human psychology. There is no space for practical reason at all.

However, the situation has changed in the last 35 years. Though the mainstream has been reluctant to accept psychological insights into economics, natural and laboratory experiments have been falsifying strict standard economic rationality devoid of psychological factors that actually produce deviations from that rationality. Consequently, at the same time, a more recent interest has arisen in reconsidering psychological factors underlying economic behavior. This flame of interest was lit by behavioral economics representatives and has consolidated as a result of laboratory experiments (and to a lesser extent, natural experiments). However, this particular way of rehabilitating psychology is not new and far from being homogeneous. There are strong predecessors and varying positions. Ying-Fang Kao and Vela Velupillai (2015: 239) distinguish two streams: the "classical," pioneered by Herbert Simon (1955), and the "modern" by Ward Edwards (1954). Davis (2011: 25) called them, respectively, "old" behavioral economics – including Simon and the related contemporary "ecological rationality" program – and "new" behavioral economics, associated with Daniel Kahneman and Amos Tversky. While the latter remains within the framework of optimization under constraints, the former pertains to the field of decision theory. In this chapter, I will analyze three positions which are representative of these streams from the point of view adopted in this book, that is, consideration of practical reason: first, Herbert Simon's bounded rationality proposal; second, the "ecological rationality" or "fast and frugal heuristics" approach (Gerd Gigerenzer and Reinhard Selten) derived from Simon's work; and third, the "new" behavioral economics pioneered by Kahneman and Tversky, along the lines forged by Ward Edwards, which emphasizes systematic biases produced in the representation of expected utility. Finally, I will explore Richard Thaler and Carl Sunstein's libertarian paternalist or "nudge" proposal which directly derives from Modern (or New) Behavioral Economics. Is volition and freedom present in these approaches? Do they use practical reason? Are they physicalist (restrictive naturalist, materialist) stances? These questions will have to be answered.

Herbert Simon and "Bounded Rationality"

Simon's 1947 *Administrative Behavior*[2] book served as a predecessor to his 1955 paper, which laid the foundation for his "bounded rationality" proposal (a label coined in his 1957 book). His familiarity with the theory of business firms led him to believe that there was something wrong with the conventional way in which economics treated decision-making. Thus, in his 1955 paper he recommends a drastic revision of the conventional concept of "economic man," which he characterizes as having an almost complete knowledge of his/her environment, a well-organized, static system of preferences, and a surprising ability to calculate which of the available courses of action allows him/ her to achieve his/her scale of preferences in each situation.

His aim is to "explore possible ways of formulating the process of rational choice in situations where we wish to take explicit account of the "internal" as well as the "external" constraints that define the problem of rationality for the organism" (1955: 101). In this way, he plants the seeds of his proposal to replace maximizing behavior with "satisficing" behavior, and to concentrate on the process (a "procedural" rationality) rather than on the result (a "substantive" rationality), introducing the alternative of "reasonably" setting a dynamically adjustable "aspiration level" which defines a "satisfactory alternative" (1955: 111) that is "good enough." The stress is put in the process because, as Simon argues in his Nobel Lecture, "choice is not determined uniquely by the objective characteristics of the problem situation, but depends also on the particular heuristic process that is used to reach the decision" (1978: 363).There are two parts in play, the organism and the environment: both have to be taken into account (1955: 100). The standard rationality theory applies to situations of certainty and known or knowable probability, but not to uncertain situations in the sense used by Knight or Keynes: "a strong positive case for replacing the classical theory by a model of bounded rationality begins to emerge when we examine situations involving decision making under uncertainty and imperfect competition. These situations the classical theory was never designed to handle, and has never handled satisfactorily" (1978: 349).

Given this criticism of maximizing rationality and the proposal of a different method for decision making – in which the heuristic interaction with the environment is recognized as decisive – it is clear that Simon has enlarged the narrow view of rationality of standard economics. Psychological and sociological dimensions enter now into the game.[3] One might also be tempted to think that Simon is incorporating practical reason in economics. However, it is not the case. Simon's ample rationality is an ample instrumental rationality surpassing the restricted maximizing instrumental rationality, but it is not a rationality of ends. Simon's "reasonableness" is not practical rationality but a "weaker" form of instrumental rationality.

Simon himself is clear in this respect. For him reason is entirely instrumental: "it cannot tell us where to go; at best it can tell us how to get there" (1983: 7); "these are theories of how to decide rather than theories of what to decide" (1978: 350). According to Simon, "reason goes to work only after it has been supplied with a suitable set of inputs" (1983: 6). He maintains that rationality "denotes a style of behavior that is appropriate to the achievement of *given* goals, within the limits imposed by given conditions and constraints" (Simon 1972: 161; Simon 1964: 573, my italics; see also March and Simon 1958: 137). In his chapter IV of *Administrative Behavior* on "Fact and Value in Decision-making" he also explicitly embraces the logical positivist dichotomist position, mentioning Rudolf Carnap and Alfred Ayer ([1947] 1997: 55–56; for a more detailed description of his position, see also 1988: 2–6).[4]

Aside from these quotations, Simon's proposal reveals an absence of practical reason. Wenceslao González (González 1997: 212) notes that "from a philosophical point of view, the underlying notion of 'reason' [in regard to procedural rationality] is clearly deficient, because he conceives of *reason* in purely instrumental terms: 'we see that reason is wholly instrumental. It cannot tell us where to go; at best it can tell us how to get there. It is a gun for hire that can be employed in the service of whatever goals we have, good or bad' (Simon 1983: 7–8)." González adds (1997: 212, footnote 8):

> This instrumental character of human reason is also present in the field where Simon has worked more on goals: political science. In this area, he describes and analyses some problems (conflicting goals, salient goals, focus of attention, group identification ...) and several goals (search of power, pursuit of private interest ...), but he does not offer an examination of the validity or not of those goals. Moreover, he seems to exclude any chance for an evaluative rationality of ends: "rationality can only go to work after final goals are specified; it does not determine them" (Simon 1995: 60).

For Simon, people's goals are auxiliary assumptions, not a part of a theory of rationality (1995: 54). González (1997: 213) points out to resemblances with Hume"s idea of reason that is exclusively linked to means, and asserts that "Simon seems to be unaware of the need of a *rationality of ends* besides the pure instrumental reason with 'given goals' or with a rationality which depends exclusively on the "process" itself that generated it." He also notes that Simon uses this phrase – "given goals" – when he defines "rationality" (Simon 1964: 573 and 1972: 161).

Thomas Hurka (2004: 72) provides another way to express this idea. He observes:

> Whatever its form, a satisficing view can be stated independently of any substantive view about the good. More specifically, it can be stated independently of the choice between subjective and objective views of each person's good. Subjective views identify this good with some subjective state of a person such as pleasure, happiness, or the satisfaction of desires; objective or perfectionist views identify it with states such as knowledge, achievement, and virtue – states that they value independently of how much one wants or enjoys these states. But both views can be combined in the same way with satisficing. Thus, if the good is pleasure, absolute-level satisficing requires agents to ensure that everyone is above some threshold level of pleasure, whereas if the good includes knowledge, the same view requires agents to ensure that everyone has at least some threshold quantity of knowledge [...] Formally, then, satisficing views are independent of views about the good.

That is, satisficing may serve one goal or another, which is always given. Millgram argues that satisficing is "instrumentalist in spirit" (2001: 8–9). Henry S. Richardson (2004) also understands the problem of satisficing: this is clear in his critique of the attempt to estimate what is "good enough" for satisficing, showing this is actually a kind of optimization.[5] Instead, he maintains that the problem – well expressed in the concept of bounded rationality – will only be solved by relating the decision to the ends involved in the action. He thus states (2004: 126):

> What does instead illuminate the everyday context is the idea of a practical commitment, and more specifically that of a final end. The purported cases of satisficing that have been put forward in the literature are better thought of as cases in which people either content themselves with seeing to it that their salient practical commitments are satisfied or else face some conflict among their ends or commitments that they are unable or unwilling to resolve in the time available.

This is a task for practical reason which can be solved in the light of incommensurable ends (see Crespo 2007). Michael Byron (1998) also seems to understand the problem along the same lines when he advances his arguments about satisficing not being more than another form of optimizing instrumental rationality, within the framework of his broader project of rejecting instrumentalism of practical reason (see, e.g., 1998: 67, footnote, and 91). John Conslik (1996: 689–690) mentions the infinite regress problem involved in a second order optimization strategy. Finally, Raymond Boudon sustains that there is a *psychological* tendency, but not a logical implication, to consider instrumental rationality as maximizing rationality (Boudon

2004: 47) and he presents bounded rationality as an example of a form of non-maximizing instrumental rationality (2004: 56). In this regard, he differs from Byron but he nevertheless considers bounded rationality as instrumental.

Has Simon then escaped physicalism? As argued in the previous chapter, the only way of escaping physicalism is introducing the classical concept of practical reason as a rationality of ends in which freedom has a place. Simon might personally have embraced this position, but this is not evident in his bounded rationality proposal. He continuously mentions psychological postulates from cognitive psychology, relies on artificial intelligence, emphasizes computational developments, poses evolutionary arguments, and says he considers the "human organism [...] as a complex information-processing system" (March and Simon 1958: 9).[6] The use of these supporting elements casts doubts about a possible adherence to a practical rationality position. It sounds more like a mechanical, dynamic and interactive adaptation process than a conscious, free one. Agents do not maximize taking into account all relevant information, which is impossible for the human mind; thus, we have bounded rationality. However, this alternative does not seem to open the doors to a free-decision process, but to a computer-like process. People seem to react rather unconsciously through a heuristic process following rules of thumb. As Kao and Vela Velupillai state, "Classical Behavioral Economics was underpinned, always and at any and every level of theoretical and applied analysis, by a model of computation. Invariably, although not always explicitly, it was Turing's model of computation" (2015: 256); "agents and institutions and all other kinds of decision-making entities, in CBE [classical behavior economics], are information processing systems which in their ideal form are Turing machines" (Kao and Velupillai 2015: 259). They additionally believe that Allen Newell and Simon (1972) actually applied the Turing model (1954) (Kao and Velupillai 2015: 257). Simon considers the possible presence of "components of conscious intention, as in much human learning and problem solving" (1990: 2) but represents them with a model that combines "human and computer psychology" (1990: 3). The predominant elements in his models of human behavior are drawn from evolutionary biology and computer science. He tries to design a computer program capable of solving human problems, explaining them and predicting behavior. His 1971 paper written together with Newell proves prophetic:

> All of this is a prospect for the future. We cannot claim to see in today"s literature any firm bridges between the components of the central nervous system as it is described by neurophysiologists and the components of the information-processing system we have been discussing here. But bridges there must be, and we need not pause in expanding and improving our knowledge at the information-processing level while we wait for them to be built.[7]

> (Simon and Newell 1971: 158)

He also calls this heuristic process "means-ends analysis" (1971: 152). Therefore, in Simon, regardless of appearances to the contrary and given his considera- tion of the psychological limitations of human nature, the tension between scientificity and volition; instrumental and practical reason; restrictive and liberal naturalism seems to be inclined towards the first element of these pairs. Simon is thus part of and contributes to what Hands calls the "naturalistic turn" in economics (cf. Hands 2001: 152–154).[8]

The "ecological rationality" or "frugal heuristics" approach

Simon's theory was naturally followed by the "ecological rationality" or "frugal heuristics" approach (Gigerenzer and Selten). For Simon, agents deliberately use "selective heuristics and means-ends analysis to explore a small number of promising alternatives" (1976: 136). This line of thought was developed by Gigerenzer and his group. Gigerenzer founded and currently heads the Center for Adaptive Behavior and Cognition (ABC Group) at the Max Planck Institute in Berlin. The webpage of the Center informs:

> Our research addresses a key question: How do humans and other animals make decisions under uncertainty, that is, when time and information are limited and the future is unknown? In an uncertain world, humans often rely on simple cognitive strategies (heuristics) when making decisions. To investigate heuristics, we developed three key concepts: bounded rationality, ecological rationality, and social rationality. On the basis of these concepts, we design models of cognitive processes and environments in which these processes are successful. Using experiments, computer simulations, and mathematical analyses, we then test the models to determine when and why heuristics perform well. The best test of our research is to apply it in the real world, for instance, to train decision-makers in medicine, law, and business.[9]

How do ABC group researchers understand bounded, ecological and social rationality? The idea behind bounded rationality is strictly Simon's: "people often make decisions without knowing everything about their current situation or about what will happen in the future. Under these circum- stances fully rational behavior and weighing all pros and cons is impossible and often unhelpful" (Simon 1976). Bounded rational people use simple rules of thumb (heuristics), fast-and-frugal, that may work in uncertain situations since they ignore irrelevant information. As for ecological rationality, "it studies humans in real-world domains and explores which heuristics are promising in which environment" (ibid.). Finally, "models of social rationality explore heuristics that are not only fast and frugal but also morally acceptable and justifiable, thereby leading to consensus. Social norms as well as emotions play an important role and are hence a special focus of the research in this area" (ibid.). The ABC group report refers to it as "social and evolutionary rationality"[10] to stress its interactive and adaptive characteristics.

Some additional considerations can be derived from the previous definitions. First, "fast and frugal heuristics" are not a means to surpass cognitive biases produced by human mind limitations, but, as noted by Davis (2013: 5), "rational and efficient means of making choices in the form of cognitive tools adapted to the occasion of choice." This characteristic can be divided into two further characteristics highlighted by Gigerenzer (2004: 390): bounded rationality is not optimization under constraints and it is not the recognition of cognitive illusions and anomalies. Concerning the first "not," Gigerenzer remarks that optimization is computationally intractable in most natural situations, and also impossible when the problem is unfamiliar and the time scarce in situations where in principle it is possible to optimize. Another important point made by Gigerenzer is that optimization does not imply an optimal outcome; in other words, bounded rationality often makes better predictions than optimization.[11] The second "not" points against the third position that I will discuss later in this chapter: the perspective initiated by Kahneman and Tversky that detects "anomalies" in people's judgments, decisions and behavior. For Gigerenzer, bounded rationality is not the study of errors: "unlike the cognitive illusions program, it [the fast and frugal heuristic program] directly analyzes the decision process rather than try to demonstrate violations of the assumptions underlying 'as-if' models" (2004: 402). He explains that this would mean, using the analogy proposed by Simon (1990: 7), paying attention to only one blade of a pair of scissors, the mind, neglecting the environment (physical and social) (2004: 397). Gigerenzer speaks of "reasonableness" to express the ample concept of rationality which includes judgments and choices that would appear as irrational or anomalies to other approaches. In his view, "the reasonableness of bounded rationality derives from ecological rationality, not from coherence or an internal consistency of choices. A strategy is ecologically rational to the degree that it is adapted to the information in an environment, whether the environment is physical or social" (2001: 48). These reflections lead us to the next consideration.

Second, the use of ecological and social rationalities means that this approach takes into account people's representation of their environment (a key point of Simon's proposal), including society. Individuals in this perspective, as also Davis (2013: 6) notes, are not purely subjective. For Gigerenzer, when the environment includes other human agents, bounded rationality strategies employ social norms, social imitation, and social emotions (2001: 48). Gigerenzer does not exclude rational deliberation and moral rules from moral behavior – "behavior in morally significant situations" – (2010: 528–529), but he greatly downsizes their impact on actual people's behavior. He states that he does not pretend to build a moral theory but only "a descriptive theory with prescriptive consequences, such as how to design environments that help people to reach their own goals" (2010: 530).[12] He proposes four heuristics underlying moral behavior: "do what the majority of your peers do," "to distribute a resource, divide it equally," "tit-for-tat" in personal relations, and "if there is a default, do nothing about it."

Third, the process is dynamic, with feedback effects coming from the environment including other people. Social rationality is also evolutionary. As Till Grüne-Yanoff states, it is close to evolutionary psychology (2007: 552 and 556). For the ABC group, biological evolution has equipped the human being with the adaptive toolbox of fast and frugal heuristics.

The last question concerns the position of this program with respect to practical reason and naturalism. Gigerenzer often speaks of "reasonableness," a term that has sometimes been used to express "practical rationality." He includes not only psychological but also social factors in human choice and decision, and he considers the possibility of a sort of reflection or feed-back, making the process dynamic. However, as Hands (2014a: 404–408) points out, ecological rationality is included under the umbrella of instrumental rationality: the ecological rationality position considers that Rational Choice Theory is only a form of instrumental rationality, and that ecological rationality is another form of it. In fact, Gigerenzer and Thomas Sturm assert that the ecological dimension is a "supplement" (2012: 245), but that it "is broadly defined in terms of success, and thus involves looking for means suited to certain goals" (2012: 255), that is, instrumental rationality. Hands concludes that despite rhetoric to the contrary, it "is not a radical alternative to the dominant theory" (2014a: 408).

Accordingly, my view is that this program leaves very little space for freedom and for a rationality of ends. Gigerenzer states this explicitly (2010: 528). Its relation to evolutionary theories, its use of a toolbox with heuristics designed by computer simulations and mathematical analyses leave almost no room for practical reason. Actually, its relation with the environment and heuristic strategies seem to replace it. As Werner Callebaut argues (2007: 78), "I think that this movement is part of a wider wave of 'naturalization'." As a result, and in accordance with Simon, I conclude that the first elements of the scientificity versus volition, instrumental versus practical reason, and restrictive versus liberal naturalism pairs, eventually predominate.[13]

Modern behavioral economics (MBE)

Kao and Velupillai (2015: 241) trace MBE back to Ward Edwards. They agree that Edwards's work can be labelled a "neoclassical theory of behavioral economics" because it follows Savage's subjective expected utility theory (SEUT), which revises von Neumann and Morgenstern's objective probability theory. The unfolding history that led to MBE is widely known. In 1952 Savage was completing a book proposing a theory of rational behavior under uncertainty taking into account ideas of Frank Ramsey, Bruno de Finetti, von Neumann and Morgenstern. He attended a seminar in Paris organized by Maurice Allais. On this occasion, Allais verified his famous paradox by causing Savage to make an "irrational" decision. This spurred Savage to write in his *Foundations of Statistics* (1954) that his SEUT was normative, not empirical. Edwards took this idea from Savage and established an "Engineering Psychology Laboratory" at the University of Michigan in 1958 to empirically investigate decision-making under uncertainty. One of Edwards's students was Tversky who then joined psychologist Kahneman to work on this field. Kahneman and Tversky became the modern pioneers of MBE with their founding paper "Prospect Theory: An Analysis of Decision under Risk" (*Econometrica*, 1979). After this first article, they continued working together, achieving a decidedly influential scientific production. In 1984, Eric Wanner made a significant contribution to this field by starting a research program aimed at applying cognitive psychology to finance. This program was sponsored by the Sloan Foundation and, subsequently, by the Russell Sage Foundation. Other key scholars in the field include Richard Thaler, George Lowenstein, Mathew Rabin, Paul Slovic, Sarah Lichtenstein, and Colin Camerer.[14]

In their 1979 article, Kahneman and Tversky present experimental choice situations that violate EUT axioms, thus proving it does not constitute a satisfactory descriptive theory.[15] Formerly, they had presented their Prospect Theory (PT), which distinguishes two phases: the first stage involves individual "edits," during which the agent performs a preliminary analysis of the possible prospects of choice, ordering them according to various heuristics; in the second phase, the agent evaluates the edited prospects, relative to a "reference point." PT introduces people's habitual psychological biases as causes of violations of EUT axioms. Individuals react to changes in relation to a reference point, rather than in relation to absolute magnitudes. This kind of behavior stems more from intuition than from conscious rational arguments (Kahneman 2003b: 1469). In Kahneman's words, "prospect theory (Kahneman and Tversky, 1979) was offered as a descriptive model of risky choice in which the carriers of utility are not states of wealth, but gains and losses relative to a neutral reference point" (2003a: 164). This model entails abandoning the standard assumption of reference-independence (as was called in Tversky and Kahneman 1991): the idea that choice is independent of irrelevant alternatives. The perception of probabilities and the subjective valuation of utility differ from their objective values. This is why the "experienced utility" differs from the "decision utility": "Our analysis begins with a distinction between two senses of the term utility. Decision utility [EUT's concept of utility] has also been called "wantability"; it is inferred from choices and used to explain choices. In contrast, experienced utility refers to the hedonic experience associated with an outcome" (Kahneman and Thaler 2006: 21–22).

In another significant paper, Tversky and Kahneman (1986) introduce the "framing effect" notion. According to this idea, preferences are influenced by the framing of a decision problem. This violates the axiom of invariance or extensionality. This axiom postulates that varying presentations of the same problem should not affect the decision made by the agent, or in other words, that preference is independent from the formulation of options.[16]

One important difference between this approach and the ecological rationality approach is that the former holds that "anomalies" discovered by MBE are not anomalies but a kind of behavior. This is a frequent criticism of MBE directed by Gigerenzer and his group (e.g., Gigerenzer 2010: 532–534; 2001: *passim*). Werner Güth, in his paper on the "ultimatum game," shares this point of view: "we prefer the natural psychological categories of human decision making over their artificial analogues resulting when they are represented in the typical neoclassical framework of utility maximization based on subjective beliefs" (1993: 17). In effect, as Kahneman makes clear, "the rational-agent model was our starting point and the main source of our null hypothesis" (2003: 1449). For MBE, anomalies are such in relation to RCT and SEUT. Hence, the theory can be viewed as a supplement to mainstream theory. As noted by Esther-Mirjam Sent, MBE "strengthens mainstream economics by taking rationality as the yardstick as opposed to ones to develop an alternative squarely based on bounded rationality" (2004: 747).

In Rabin's words, "this research program is not only built on the premise that mainstream economic *methods* are great, but also that most mainstream economic *assumptions* are great. It does not abandon the correct insights of neoclassical economics, but supplements these insights to be had from realistic new assumptions" (2002: 658–659). According to Rabin, it is a natural continuation of mainstream economics. The anomalies discovered by empirical experiments "are used as inspiration to create alternative theories that generalize existing models" (Camerer and Loewenstein 2004: 7). Consequently, the aim of the MBE research project is to formulate a general theory that includes the current simplified RCT and EUT models. Kao and Velupillai (2015: 246) adequately describe it:

> The anomalies and puzzles that were discovered and discussed are departures with respect to the neoclassical normative benchmark for judging rational behavior, which is expected utility maximization. These evidences or anomalies are in turn used to formulate more realistic utility functions and, further, these modified utility functions are incorporated into the existing models. In some sense, modern behavioral economists modified fractured pieces in the foundations of neoclassical theories, but still they worked within its basic premises (preferences, utility, equilibrium and maximization). Thus, MBE preserves the doctrine of utility maximization and does not go beyond it or discard it. Though behavioral models do consider more realistic psychological or social effects, economic agents are still assumed to be optimizing agents whatever the objective functions may be. In other words, MBE is still within the ambit of neoclassical theories or it is in some sense only an extension of traditional theory by replacing and repairing the aspects which proved to be contradictory.

Accordingly, though modified by the psychological perception, MBE continues using models with utility functions. Kahneman recognizes that these models cannot be very different from standard economics models: "The constraint of tractability can be satisfied with somewhat more complex models, but the number of parameters that can be added is small. One consequence is that the models of behavioral economics cannot stray too far from the original set of assumptions" (Kahneman 2003a: 166). In fact, the logic is the same; the only difference is that new MBE models maximize prospective utility (see, e.g., Benartzi and Thaler 1995: 79ff.). The anomalous conduct is a case of maximization of experienced or prospective utility. The omniscient maximizer agent is replaced by a limited knower maximizer agent. Hence, MBE agents are rational in the neoclassical sense of the term rational. Davis indicates that the only difference between Kahneman-Tversky's proposal and EUT is that subjectivity is contextualized, though it continues working with a utility function (Davis 2011: 33). Ana Santos also argues that the strategy of this approach allows economists to retain the economic principle (utility maximization) solely assuming that individuals' preferences are different (2011: 711). Jean Hampton (1994: 196) considers behavioral economics as a form of EUT. For Michiru Nagatsu (2015: 443) MBE's adoption of mainstream economic modeling tools is one important reason why MBE has been greatly successful.[17]

Regardless of MBE's neoclassical character, does the change in the utility concept mean an introduction of practical reason? All depends on the character of the psychology that modifies decision utility, transforming it into experienced utility. I agree with Davis when he states that "the psychology that underlies behavioral economics is its most naturalistic branch" (2011: 14). He adds that "they [Kahneman and Tversky] have a very naturalistic understanding of human beings, so that their biological constitution always broadly explains their psychological behavior" (2011: 37). He bases this interpretation on Kahneman's education and antecedents – for example, his research into the psychophysics of vision perception depicted in his autobiography (2002). His scientific naturalism is clear, for example, in his 246-page book *Attention and Effort*, a cognitive psychology analysis of attention, with plenty of laws and mechanistic considerations. Indeed, his notion of "objective happiness" (see Kahneman 2000) is both hedonistic and naturalist. Objective happiness is a temporal integral of moment-based happiness reports. However, as Anna Alexandrova notes, "assessing happiness moment by moment leaves no place for both cognitive and moral ex post evaluation of our own inner states" (2005: 307), which is a role of practical reason.[18]

In addition, in an article on neuroeconomics, though insisting that psychological and neural correlates are still doubtful, Kahneman exposes his belief in the future usefulness of neurosciences (2009: 525). In Chapter 5 in this book, where I address neuroeconomics, I will show how this approach, based on materialist neurosciences, leaves no room for practical reason and freedom. Moreover, Kahneman's description of behavior seems to indicate that most people could not act in other ways: system 1 – intuition – seems to be rather innate and it is not usually successfully corrected by system 2 – the rational process. He repeats in his Nobel Lecture: "Intuitive thoughts seem to come

spontaneously to mind, without conscious search or computation, and without effort. Casual observation and systematic research indicate that most
thoughts and actions are normally intuitive in this sense" (2003b: 1450).

I started this chapter asking whether or not economic movements influenced
by psychology eventually domesticate it, thus enlarging economics' imperialism
over other social sciences. On the one hand, as mentioned, cognitive psychology
is increasingly becoming restrictive naturalistic and, on the other hand, we are
effectively witnessing a domestication process. As Hands asserts, Kahneman-
Tversky's "view of what a rational agent ought to do is essentially the same as
the traditional Rational Choice Theory-based view" (2014a: 398). MBE
imports elements from psychology but, then, it domesticates them, as Davis
(2008: 363) sustains, framing them in terms of economics' concerns and originating a new more sophisticated imperialism: economics plus psychology
imperialism under the leadership of economics (Davis 2013).[19] This is the
topic of the next section.

Libertarian paternalism

In the introduction to this chapter, I committed myself to analyze the libertarian
paternalist or "nudge" proposal, which derives from Modern (or New) Behavioral Economics and which is highly relevant due to its practical effects on
social and economic policies of many countries. In 2003, Thaler and Sunstein
published "Libertarian Paternalism" (2003a), an article presented at the
Annual Meeting of the American Economic Society. Soon after, they published
"Libertarian Paternalism Is Not an Oxymoron" (2003b), a paper addressed to
lawyers. These articles rapidly triggered plenty of comments and criticism.
The main assumption in their papers stems from MBE: people often unin-
tentionally make wrong choices (i.e., against their best interest). Without
coercing them, they argue, we may arrange things in order that people make
the right choice: "if no coercion is involved, we think that some types of
paternalism should be acceptable to even the most ardent libertarian. We call
such actions *libertarian paternalism*" (2003a: 175). This passage taken from
the second article clearly explains their proposal:

> The idea of libertarian paternalism might seem to be an oxymoron, but it
> is both possible and desirable for private and public institutions to influ-
> ence behavior while also respecting freedom of choice. Often people's
> preferences are unclear and ill-formed, and their choices will inevitably be
> influenced by default rules, framing effects, and starting points. In these
> circumstances, a form of paternalism cannot be avoided. Equipped with
> an understanding of behavioral findings of bounded rationality and
> bounded self-control, libertarian paternalists should attempt to steer
> people's choices in welfare-promoting directions without eliminating
> freedom of choice.
>
> (Thaler and Sunstein 2003b: 1159)

In 2008 they published *Nudge: Improving Decisions about Health, Wealth and Happiness*, in which they extensively develop their program. It was and still is a best-seller, profusely commented upon and criticized. A "sensible planner" designs choice architecture to make people "better off" and decide in the way they would have chosen had they not been subject to any bias (2008: 5). The "objective" way for the planner to define the best choices is to apply a cost-benefit analysis, and when this is not possible, to use some indirect methods to ascertain what is better for people.

"Nudging" has both critics and defenders. Besides, there are different precisions that originate different combinations of situations – more paternalistic or more libertarian – and differences between nudge and libertarian paternalism. As in any field where philosophers become involved, it quickly becomes sophisticated (sometimes too much).[20] I will mention only a few criticisms and defenses. Hausman and Welch (2010) argue that paternalist policies may threaten liberty. In the same thread of thought, José Edwards (2016) even suggests that nudge shares the controlling *ethos* of Watson and Skinner's behaviorism. Sugden (2009) seriously doubts and warns about the possibility of respecting the presumed will of *nudgees* when liberated from their biases. He also makes a point, related to the previous point, which he shares with others: "Thaler and Sunstein seem to be assuming that inside every Human there is an Econ – that, deep down, each of us has coherent preferences, of the kind that economic theory has traditionally assumed" (2009: 370). If RCT or EUT is considered as "the" rational model, as in MBE, it is right. But this cannot be taken for granted. Gilles Saint-Paul is also against the utilitarian model behind the cost-benefit tool for defining the content of people's presumed goals: "there is no outside system of values" (2001: 91). Or the values are utilitarian. Adrien Barton and Grüne-Yanoff note that though Sunstein (2014) claims that libertarian paternalism is not a form of ends paternalism but of means paternalism, it actually judges people's preferences which are their ends (2015: 346). By nudging, Davis holds (2013 and forthcoming) that RCT becomes not only normative but performative. He argues (forthcoming: 3):

> Contrary to the view that these programs [mechanism design and nudge theory] are a departure from rational choice theory, I take them to be intrinsic to the evolution of neoclassicism from a science claiming rational choice is descriptive of the world to a performative science intent on securing the practice of rational choice behavior in the world.

Thomas C. Leonard appropriately expresses a paradox about behavioral economics and nudging: "The irony is that behavioral economics, having attacked *Homo Economicus* as an empirically false description of human choice, now proposes, in the name of paternalism, to enshrine the very fellow as the image of what people should want to be" (2008: 359).

On the other hand, Gigerenzer (2010: 542) defends nudging on the grounds that "changing environments may be more efficient than changing minds, and creating environments that facilitate moral virtue is as important as improving moral values." However, he distinguishes nudging from libertarian paternalism, defending the former and criticizing the latter for its adherence to a narrow view of rationality (RCT and EUT), its consequent disapproval of other forms of rationality, its skepticism about educating people, and for omitting mentioning the responsibility of firms that invest great budgets to nudge people into unhealthy behavior. He proposes to invest in teaching people to become "risk savvy" (2015).

When discussing the differences between the Aristotelian and the Humean and Kantian views of practical reason in the previous chapter, I explained that from the Aristotelian point of view, practical reason must succeed in discovering what is good for people to aim at and to do, thus originating a theory of the good. First, practical reason should discover the content of a list of basic human goods. Second, it has to deliberate about specific ways to realize alternative means to achieve those goods. Then, we have to discriminate between decisions that should be imposed for "political reasons" by a "genuine paternalism," not using welfare-based criteria (see Guala and Mittone 2015), and decisions that can fall under the umbrella of nudging. Concerning the latter kind of decisions, from this viewpoint, nudging can be considered legitimate provided that:

** It clearly leaves room for alternative decisions.
** It adequately defines the target of "better off" decisions.

In Chapter 6 of my book on Aristotle's economic thought (Crespo 2014), I draw from his ethical and political writings a list of goods: good health, good nutrition, work, freedom, political participation, provision of justice, education, fostering intermediate organizations that promote family, education, friendship, child and elder care, job creation, sports, arts, religion, charity and, specially, virtues of all kinds.[21] Aristotle provides rational arguments for all these objectives, regarding which most people generally agree. The argument about incommensurability of ends previously considered also applies to using cost-benefit analysis to decide actions concerning this kind of objectives: it is not a matter of instrumental rationality, but of practical reason. Practical reason must prudently harmonize the attainment of heterogeneous ends.

For Aristotle, political authorities must safeguard a fair and non-abusive harmonization of ends. However, one might ask whether a program intended for a small, homogeneous Greek *polis* can be applied to our more complex modern world. Aristotle also considers the difficulties resulting from the size of the city, and he is also aware that his ideal city and its ideal authorities did not even exist in his own time. However, we should not forget that Aristotle's proposal is ethical: it addresses what ought to be done, a normative ideal, a paradigm. In fact, I think that we, as citizens of different states, aspire to more than a mere liberal alliance. In this context, I also defend a different type of nudging. It is a way of helping people who are not able to soundly analyze at all time all circumstances surrounding their decisions, uninformed people, or poor people facing difficult trade-off decisions (see Reiss 2013: 296–297). However, I do not defend the "neoclassical" method for ascertaining the content of welfare and means towards it advocated by libertarian paternalists. This vision would render society unlivable.

Conclusion

The aim of this chapter was to analyze whether the reinsertion of psychological insights into new economic streams leads to a consideration of "classical practical rationality" and if it concomitantly involves an escape from today's prevalent physicalist and deterministic metaphysical worldview. The chapter has firstly considered the early 20th-century consumer theory, exposing a tension between its defense of freedom and the exactness demanded by its contemporary view of science. However, I have concluded that early consumer theorists' recognition of reference-dependence plus volition and freedom presumes at least a "bit" of practical rationality and a step to overcoming the physicalist perspective.

Next, I examined Herbert Simon's thinking. Has he escaped physicalism and introduced the classical concept of practical reason as a rationality of ends in which freedom has a place? The conclusion was that, notwithstanding his consideration of the psychological limitations of human nature, in the tension between scientificity and volition, and instrumental and practical reason the first elements of the pairs seem to prevail, and that it can be assumed that Simon is predominantly scientific naturalist.

Concerning Gigerenzer's program, though he also includes social factors in human choice and decision, the resulting balance leaves very limited place for freedom and practical reason. My conclusion was that, once again, in the tension between scientificity and volition, instrumental and practical reason, and restrictive and liberal naturalism, the first elements of the pairs seem to predominate.

I have argued that it is clear that MBE does not consider practical reason and that, despite appearances to the contrary, it is a physicalist approach. Güth and Kliemt (2013) show that behavioral and experimental economics are still rooted in behaviorism, and they advocate for abandoning "immunizing strategies" to shield the coherence of preferences by invoking aversions, and/or incorporation considerations of human internal motivations in economics.[22]

This process of incorporating psychological elements into economics with a physicalist spirit and without considering practical reason paves the way for a dangerous movement like libertarian paternalism which tries to shape human life turning people into standard economic maximizing beings: "given that people are not *econs* but *humans*, let us transform them in *econs.*"

One last question to answer is whether the approach changes considered here come from outside or from within economics. Psychology was traditionally mixed with economics before the 20h century. However, leaving aside the early 20th century's consumer theory, this new introduction of psychological elements into economics stems more from the influence of psychology as a discipline than from the restoration of old psychological elements of economics.

The next chapter will deal with evolutionary economics. The use of the term "evolution" may suggest a non-deterministic conception of human behavior. However, its possible link to or the influence of biological evolution might indicate the contrary (i.e., a physicalist position). Chapter 4 will attempt to shed light on this issue.

Notes

1 See also S. B. Lewin (1996: 1295) and José Edwards (2016, *passim*).
2 On the origin and diffusion of the expression 'bounded rationality' see Klaes and Sent (2005) and Grüne-Yanoff (2007).
3 He asserts, for example, that "under the rubric of problem representation, it is a central research interest of cognitive psychology" (1978: 353) and that "It [satisficing] had its roots in the empirically based psychological theories, due to Lewin and others, of aspiration levels" (1978: 356).
4 Nieuwenburg (2007) shows how Simon's conception of rationality fits with Bernard Williams's (1982: 101ff.) "sub-Humean" model.
5 This notion is largely supported; for example, by Byron (1998) and Dreier (2004).
6 See Hands (2001: 151–154).
7 Hands (2001: 153) highlights the relevant influence of Simon on the development of cognitive science, which is one form of naturalizing the explanation of knowledge (of naturalized epistemology).
8 On account of the increasing and spreading influence of neurosciences on the explanation of human thinking and behavior, cognitive science is becoming more and more naturalistic: see Thagard (2004) for a recent review.
9 See https://www.mpib-berlin.mpg.de/en/research/adaptive-behavior-and-cognition, retrieved February 26, 2016.
10 See https://www.mpib-berlin.mpg.de/sites/default/files/media/pdf/21/abc_research_report_social_and_evolutionary_rationality_0.pdf, retrieved February 26, 2016.
11 This was already anticipated by Simon in his 1955 article (1955: 104).
12 However, it actually constitutes a (very basic) moral theory.
13 Cognitive and evolutionary psychologies, though not as extremely scientific naturalist as behaviorist psychology, are also scientific naturalist developments of psychology. Evolutionary psychology is the intersection between the cognitive revolution and evolutionary biology. John Tooby and Leda Cosmides, founders of evolutionary psychology, propose a program that involves developing a new social science based on it. They state: "Because mental phenomena are the expression of complex functional organization in biological systems, and complex organic functionality is the downstream consequence of natural selection, then it must be the case that the sciences of the mind and brain are adaptationist sciences, and psychological mechanisms are computational adaptations" (2005: 10). They also argue: "Like cognitive scientists, when evolutionary psychologists refer to the mind, they mean the set of information processing devices, embodied in neural tissue, which is responsible for all conscious and nonconscious mental activity, that generates all behavior, and that regulates the body. Like other psychologists, evolutionary psychologists test hypotheses about the design of these computational devices using methods from, for example, cognitive psychology, social psychology,

developmental psychology, experimental economics, cognitive neuroscience, genetics, physiological psychology, and cross-cultural field work" (2005: 13). The self-criticism of the evolutionary psychologist Jerry Coyne is telling: "[t]he problem is that evolutionary psychology suffers from the scientific equivalent of megalomania. Most of its adherents are convinced that virtually every human action or feeling, including depression, homosexuality, religion, and consciousness, was put directly into our brains by natural selection. In this view, evolution becomes the key – the only key – that can unlock our humanity" (2000: 27). Jack Vromen stresses the close and constraining link between evolutionary psychology and biological evolution and mentions Gigerenzer and his ABC group as an example of application of it (2004: 228). For a recent review of evolutionary psychology, see Downes (2014).

14 For the history of modern behavioral economics, see Floris Heukelom (2011 and 2014).
15 I do not intend to enumerate and describe all these violations or anomalies.
16 I strongly recommend reading Kahneman's autobiography (2002): it is a charming narration of his life, his relation with Tversky, and his intellectual development.
17 However, as Alexandre Truc (2016: 27) maintains, "the new behavioral economics cannot be analyzed as a homogeneous field when we try to examine its relationship to mainstream." He believes that some approaches are strategically or sociologically mainstream but intellectually heterodox.
18 Infante, Lecouteux and Sugden (2016) have criticized behavioral economics for considering that context-dependent choices are mistakes and need to be "purified" by rational reflection, as well as Hausman's (2012) presumed agreement on this need for "purification." In his response, Hausman (2016: 30–31) has expressed his differences with behavioral economics. The way in which he formulates choice theory, asking "what do I have most reason to do?" (2012: 5), seems to refer to classical practical reason. However, the requirements he imposes on preferences – transitivity, completeness and context-independence – pertain to the logic of instrumental reason.
19 In addition, Kahneman's poor conception of happiness, fundamentally hedonist and physiologically measurable, is consistent with this domestication (see Kahneman 2000).
20 See Barton and Grüne-Yanoff (2015) for a classification.
21 On the relation of this list with Nussbaum's proposal of a list of goods (e.g., 2003) see Chapter 7 of this book and Crespo (2013: 56–62).
22 My thanks to Andrea Klonschinski for letting me know about this paper and for sending it to me.

References

Alexandrova, A. (2005). "Subjective Well-Being and Kahneman's 'Objective Happiness,' *Journal of Happiness Studies* 6/3: 301–324.

Angner, E. and G. Loewenstein (2012). "Behavioral Economics." In U. Mäki (ed.) *Philosophy of Economics*, Handbook of the *Philos Sci*, 13, North Holland: Elsevier.

Barton, A. and T. Grüne-Yanoff (2015). "From Libertarian Paternalism to Nudging– and Beyond," *Review of Philosophy and Psychology* 6/3: 341–359.

Benartzi, Sh. and R. Thaler (1995). "Myopic Loss Aversion and the Equity Premium Puzzle," *Quarterly Journal of Economics* 10/1: 73–92.

Boudon, R. (2004). "Théorie du choix rationnel, théorie de la rationalité limitée ou individualisme méthodologique: que choisir?," *Journal des Economistes et des Etudes Humaines* 14/1: 45–62.

Byron, M. (1998). "Satisficing and Optimality," *Ethics* 109: 67–93.

Callebaut, W. (2007). "Herbert Simon's Silent Revolution," *Biological Theory* 2/1: 76–86.

Camerer, C. F. and G. Loewenstein (2004). "Behavioral Economics: Past, Present, Future." In C. F. Camerer, G. Loewenstein and M. Rabin (eds.), *Advances in Behavioral Economics*, New York: Russell Sage Foundation; and Princeton and Oxford: Princeton University Press.

Coyne, J. A. (2000). "The fairy tales of evolutionary psychology. Review of 'A Natural History of Rape: Biological Bases of Sexual Coercion,' by Randy Thornhill and Craig T. Palmer, MIT Press, 2000," *The New Republic*, March, 4, 2000: 27–34.

Conslik, J. (1996). "Why Bounded Rationality?," *Journal of Economic Literature* XXXIV: 669–700.

Crespo, R. F. (2007). "'Practical Comparability' and Ends in Economics," *Journal of Economic Methodology* 14/3: 371–393.

Crespo, R. F. (2013). *Theoretical and Practical Reason in Economics. Capacities and Capabilities.* Dordrecht: Springer.

Crespo, R. F. (2014). *A Re-assessment of Aristotle's Economic Thought.* London: Routledge.

Davis, J. B. (2008). "Recent Economics and the Return of Orthodoxy," *Cambridge Journal of Economics* 32: 349–366.

Davis, J. B. (2011). *Individuals and Identity in Economics*, Cambridge and New York: Cambridge University Press.

Davis, J. B. (2013). "Economics Imperialism under the Impact of Psychology: The Case of Behavioral Development Economics," in *Oeconomia*, 3/1, https://oeconom ia.revues.org/638, retrieved February 29, 2016.

Davis, J. B. (forthcoming). "Economics imperialism versus multidisciplinarity," *History of Economic Ideas.*

Downes, S. M. (2014). "Evolutionary Psychology," *Stanford Encyclopedia of Philosophy*, http://plato.stanford.edu/entries/evolutionary-psychology/, retrieved April 12, 2016.

Dreier, J. (2004). "Why Ethical Satisficing Makes Sense," in M. Byron (ed.) *Satisficing and Maximizing. Moral Theorists on Practical Reason.* Cambridge: Cambridge University Press.

Edwards, J. (2016). "Behaviorism and control in the history of economics and psychology," *History of Political Economy* 48 Supplement 1: 170–197.

Edwards, W. (1954). "The Theory of Decision Making," *Psychological Bulletin* 51: 380–417.

Gigerenzer, G. (2001). "The Adaptive Toolbox," in G. Gigerenzer and R. Selten (eds.), *Bounded Rationality. The Adaptive Toolbox.* Cambridge, MA: MIT Press.

Gigerenzer, G. (2004). "Striking a Blow of Sanity in Theories of Rationality." In B. Augier and J. G. March (eds.), *Models of a Man. Essays in Memory to Herbert A. Simon.* Cambridge, MA: MIT Press.

Gigerenzer, G. (2010). "Moral Satisficing: Rethinking Moral Behavior as Bounded Rationality," *Topics in Cognitive Science* 2: 528–554.

Gigerenzer, G. (2015). "On the Supposed Evidence for Libertarian Paternalism," *Review of Philosophy and Psychology* 6/3: 361–383.

Gigerenzer, G. and T. Sturm (2012). "How (far) can rationality be naturalized?," *Synthese* 187: 243–268.

González, W. J. (1997). "Rationality in Economics and Scientific Predictions: A Critical Reconstruction of Bounded Rationality and its Role in Economic Predictions," *Poznan Studies in the Philosophy of the Sciences and the Humanities* 61: 205–232.

Grüne-Yanoff, T. (2007). "Bounded Rationality," *Philosophy Compass* 2/3: 534–563.

Guala, F. and L. Mittone (2015). "A Political justification of Nudging," *Review of Philosophy and Psychology* 6/3: 385–395.

Güth, W. (1993). "On Ultimatum Bargaining Experiments. A Personal Review," *Center for Economic Research Discussion Paper* 9317, https://pure.uvt.nl/portal/files/1152142/WG5621690.pdf, retrieved January 26, 2016.

Güth, W. and H. Kliemt (2013). "Behaviorism, optimization and policy advice," Radein Workshop, 2013.

Hampton, J. (1994). "The Failure of Expected-Utility Theory as a Theory of Reason," *Economics and Philosophy* 10: 195–242.

Hands, D. W. (2001). *Reflection without Rules: Economic Methodology and Contemporary Science Theory.* Cambridge and New York: Cambridge University Press.

Hands, D. W. (2010). "Economics, Psychology and the History of Consumer Choice Theory," *Cambridge Journal of Economics* 34/4: 633–648.

Hands, D. W. (2011). "Back to the Ordinalist Revolution: Behavioral Economic Concerns in Early Modern Consumer Choice Theory," *Metroeconomica* 62/2: 386–410.

Hands, D. W. (2014a). "Normative ecological rationality: normative rationality in the fast-and-frugal-heuristics research program," *Journal of Economic Methodology* 21/4: 396–410.

Hands, D. W. (2014b). "Paul Samuelson and Revealed Preference Theory," *History of Political Economy* 46/1: 85–116.

Hausman, D. (2012). *Preference, Value, Choice, and Welfare.* New York: Cambridge University Press.

Hausman, D. (2016). "On the Econ within," *Journal of Economic Methodology* 23/1: 26–32.

Hausman, D. and B. Welch (2010). "Debate: To nudge or not to nudge," *Journal of Political Philosophy* 18/1: 123–136.

Heukelom, F. (2011). "Behavioral economics." In J. B. Davis and D. W. Hands (eds.), *The Elgar Companion to Recent Economic Methodology.* Cheltenham and Northampton: Edward Elgar.

Heukelom, F. (2014). *Behavioral Economics: A History.* Cambridge: Cambridge University Press.

Hurka, T. (2004). "Satisficing and Substantive Values." In M. Byron (ed.) *Satisficing and Maximizing. Moral Theorists on Practical Reason.* Cambridge: Cambridge University Press.

Infante, G., G. Lecouteux and R. Sugden (2016). "Preference purification and the inner rational agent: A critique of conventional wisdom of behavioural welfare economics," *Journal of Economic Methodology* 23/1: 1–25.

Kahneman, D. (1973). *Attention and Effort.* Englewood Cliffs, NJ: Prentice-Hall.

Kahneman, D. (2000). "Experienced Utility and Objective Happiness: A Moment-Based Approach." In D. Kahneman and A. Tversky (eds.), *Choices, Values and Frames.* New York: Cambridge University Press and the Russell Sage Foundation.

Kahneman, D. (2002). "Daniel Kahneman. Biographical," http://www.nobelprize.org/nobel_prizes/economic-sciences/laureates/2002/kahneman-bio.html, retrieved February 28, 2016.

Kahneman, D. (2003a). "A Psychological Perspective on Economics," *American Economic Review* 93/2: 162–168.

Kahneman, D. (2003b). "Maps of Bounded Rationality: Psychology for Behavioral Economics," *American Economic Review* 93/5: 1449–1475.

Kahneman, D. (2009). "Remarks on Neuroeconomics." In Glimcher, P. W., C. Camerer, E. Fehr and R. Poldrack, *Neuroeconomics: Decision Making and the Brain*. Amsterdam: Elsevier.

Kahneman, D. and J. Riis (2005). "Living, and thinking about it: two perspectives on life." In N. Baylis, F.A. Huppert, and B. Keverne (eds.), *The Science of Well-Being*. Oxford: Oxford University Press.

Kahneman, D. and R. H. Thaler (2006). "Anomalies: Utility Maximization and Experienced Utility," *The Journal of Economic Perspectives* 20/1: 221–234

Kahneman, D. and A. Tversky (1979). "Prospect Theory: An Analysis of Decision under Risk," *Econometrica* 47: 313–327.

Kao, Y.-F. and K. V. Velupillai (2015). "Behavioral Economics: Classical and Modern," *The European Journal of the History of Economic Thought* 22/2: 236–271.

Klaes, M. and E.-M. Sent (2005). "A Conceptual History of Bounded Rationality," *History of Political Economy*. 37/1: 27–59.

Knight, F. H. (1944). "Realism and Relevance in the Theory of Demand," *The Journal of Political Economy* 52/4: 289–318.

Knight, F. H. (1956). *On the History and Method of Economics*. Chicago, IL: University of Chicago Press.

Leonard, T. C. (2008). "Review of Richard Thaler and Cass Sunstein, Nudge: Improving Decisions about Health, Wealth and Happiness," *Constitutional Political Economy* 19/4: 356–360.

Lewin, S. B. (1996). "Economics and Psychology: Lessons for Our Own Day from the Early Twentieth Century," *Journal of Economic Literature* 34/3: 1293–1323.

March, J. G. and H. Simon (1958). *Organizations*. New York, London, Sydney: John Wiley and Sons.

Menger, C. ([1883] 1985). *Investigations into the Method of the Social Sciences with Special Reference to Economics*, (ed.) L. Schneider, transl. F. Cook. Auburn, AL: Mises Institute (*Untersuchungen über die Methode der Socialwissenschaften und der Politischen Oekonomie insbesondere*. Leipzig: Ducker & Humblot).

Millgram, E. (2001). "Practical Reasoning: The Current State of Play." In E. Millgram (ed.) *Varieties of Practical Reason*. Cambridge, MA and London: MIT Press.

Nagatsu, M. (2015). "Behavioral Economics, History of." In J. D. Wright (ed. in chief) *International Encyclopedia of the Social & Behavioral Sciences*, second edition. Amsterdam: Elsevier.

Newell, A. and H. A. Simon (1972). *Human Problem Solving*. Englewood Cliffs, NJ: Prentice-Hall.

Nieuwenburg, P. (2007). "Practical reasoning and action: Simon's *Administrative Behavior* in context." In G. Morcöl (ed.) *Handbook of Decision Making*. London: Taylor & Francis.

Nussbaum, M. C. (2003). "Capabilities as fundamental entitlements: Sen and social justice," *Feminist Economics* 9/2–3: 33–59.

Rabin, M. (2002). "A perspective on psychology and economics," *European Economic Review* 46: 657–685.

Reiss, J. (2013). *Philosophy of Economics. A Contemporary Introduction*. London and New York: Routledge.

Richardson, H. S. (2004). "Satisficing. Not Good Enough." In M. Byron (ed.) *Satisficing and Maximizing. Moral Theorists on Practical Reason*. Cambridge: Cambridge University Press.

Robbins, L. (1935). *Essay on the Nature and Significance of Economic Science.* London: MacMillan, second edition.

Saint-Paul, G. (2001). *The Tyranny of Utility: Behavioral Social Science and the Rise of Paternalism.* Princeton, NJ: Princeton University Press.

Samuelson, P. A. (1938). "A note on the pure theory of consumer's behavior," *Economica* 5: 61–71.

Samuelson, P. A. (1948). "Consumption theory in terms of revealed preference," *Economica* 15: 243–253.

Samuelson, P. A. (1950). "The problem of integrability in utility theory," *Economica,* 17: 355–385.

Santos, A. C. (2011). "Behavioral and experimental economics: Are they really transforming economics?," *Cambridge Journal of Economics* 35: 705–728.

Savage, L. J. (1954). *The Foundations of Statistics.* New York: John Wiley & Sons.

Sent, E.-M. (2004). "Behavioral Economics: How Psychology Made Its (Limited) Way Back Into Economics," *History of Political Economy* 34/4: 735–760.

Simon, H. A. ([1947] 1997). *Administrative Behavior: A Study of Decision-Making in Administrative Organizations,* fourth edition. New York: The Free Press.

Simon, H. A. (1955). "A Behavioral Model of Rational Choice," *Quarterly Journal of Economics* 69/1: 99–128.

Simon, H. A. (1957). *Models of Man.* New York: John Wiley & Sons.

Simon, H. A. (1964). "Rationality." In J. Gould and W. L. Kolb (eds.), *A Dictionary of Social Sciences.* Glencoe, IL: Free Press. Reprinted in: H. Simon, (1982), *Models of Bounded Rationality, vol. 2: Behavioral Economics and Business Organization.* Cambridge, MA: MIT Press.

Simon, H. A. (1972). "Theories of Bounded Rationality." In C. B. McGuire and R. Radner (eds.), *Decision and Organization.* Amsterdam: North-Holland.

Simon, H. A. (1976). "From Substantive to Procedural Rationality." In S. J. Latsis (ed.) *Method and Appraisal in Economics.* Cambridge: Cambridge University Press.

Simon, H. A. (1978). "Rational Decision Making in Business Organizations," Nobel Memorial Lecture, http://www.nobelprize.org/nobel_prizes/economic-sciences/laureates/1978/simon-lecture.pdf, retrieved January 29, 2016. Reprinted in the *American Economic Review* 69/4 (1979): 493–513.

Simon, H. A. (1983). *Reason in Human Affairs.* Stanford, CA: Stanford University Press.

Simon, H. A. (1988). "Freedom and Discipline," *Religious Human* 22/1: 2–6.

Simon, H. A. (1990). "Invariants of Human Behavior," *Annual Review of Psychology* 41: 1–19.

Simon, H. A. (1995). "Rationality in Political Behavior," *Political Psychology* 16: 45–63.

Simon, H. A. and A. Newell (1971). "Human Problem Solving: The State of the Theory in 1970," *American Psychologist* 26/2: 145–159.

Simon, H. A. and A. Newell (1972). *Human Problem Solving.* Englewood Cliffs, NJ: Prentice-Hall.

Slutsky, E. E. (1915). "Sulla teoria del bilancio del consonatore," *Giornale degli Economisti,* 51: 1–26, translated in Stigler, G. J. and Boulding, K. E. (eds) (1952). *Readings in Price Theory.* Homewood, IL: Richard D. Irwin, pp27–56.

Sugden, R. (2009). "On Nudging: A Review of Nudge: Improving Decisions About Health, Wealth and Happiness by Richard H. Thaler and Cass R. Sunstein", *International Journal of the Economics of Business* 16/3: 365–373.

Sunstein, C. (2014). *Why Nudge? The Politics of Libertarian Paternalism*. New York: Palgrave MacMillan.

Thagard, P. (2004). "Cognitive Science," *Stanford Encyclopedia of Philosophy*, http://plato.stanford.edu/entries/cognitive-science/, retrieved April 12, 2016.

Thaler, R. H. and C. R. Sunstein (2003a). "Libertarian Paternalism," *American Economic Review* 93/2: 175–179.

Thaler, R. H. and C. R. Sunstein (2003b). "Libertarian Paternalism Is Not an Oxymoron," *The University of Chicago Law Review* 70/4: 1159–1202.

Thaler, R. H. and C. R. Sunstein (2008). *Nudge: Improving Decisions about Health, Wealth and Happiness*. New Haven, CT: Yale University Press.

Tooby, J. and L. Cosmides (2005). "Conceptual foundations of evolutionary psychology." In D. M. Buss (ed.), *The Handbook of Evolutionary Psychology*. Hoboken (NJ): John Wiley & Sons.

Truc, A. (2016). "Is there a 'new mainstream' behavioral economics?," Paper presented at the III International Conference in Economic Philosophy, Aix-en-Provence, June 15, 2016, http://www.sciences-sociales.univ-paris8.fr/IMG/pdf/is_there_a_new_mainstream_behavioral_economics_-_led.pdf, retrieved July 4, 2016.

Turing, A. M. (1954). "Solvable and Unsolvable Problems." In A.W. Haslett (eds.), *Science News*, 31, London: Penguin Books.

Tversky, A. and D. Kahneman (1986). "Rational Choice and the Framing of Decisions," *Journal of Business* 59/4: S251–S278.

Tversky, A. and D. Kahneman (1991). "Loss Aversion in Riskless Choice: A Reference-Dependent Model," *Quarterly Journal of Economics* 106/4: 1039–1061.

Vromen, J. (2004). "Conjectural revisionary economic ontology: Outline of an ambitious research agenda for evolutionary economics," *Journal of Economic Methodology* 11/2: 213–247.

Williams, B. H. (1982). "Internal and External Reasons." In B. H. Williams, *Moral Luck. Philosophical Papers 1973–1980*. Cambridge: Cambridge University Press.

4   Evolutionary economics

The time has come to consider economic evolutionary theories from the point of view of whether or not they adopt practical reason and, consequently, whether or not they reject physicalism. Let me remind you that the argument set forth in this book is that economics needs to take this step in order to enrich its consideration of economic behavior drivers. This book aims to ascertain whether reverse imperialism and other new approaches, which are prone to make this move, actually do it or not.

Concerning evolutionary perspectives in recent economics, D. Wade Hands (2001: 384) states:

> The body of literature that could reasonably be classified as "evolutionary economics" is both enormous and extremely diverse. The field overlaps with both institutionalism (going back to at least Veblen 1919) and Austrian economics (particularly Hayek and Schumpeter), and it has a number of contemporary strains that are fairly close to mainstream economics both in emphasis and theoretical tools.

We can also point out to the Scottish Enlightenment (Bernard de Mandeville, David Hume, Adam Smith), Robert Malthus, Karl Marx and Alfred Marshall as antecedents of an evolutionary conception of economics. However, the seminal work and starting point of modern evolutionary economics is Richard Nelson and Sidney Winter"s 1982 book *An Evolutionary Theory of Economic Change.*[1]

Within more recent evolutionary economists, Jack Vromen (2004b) distinguishes three major groups. First, the "conservatives" who believe that taking into account the evolutionary aspects of economic processes does not imply discarding standard economics, which can accommodate those evolutionary aspects (he mentions Armen Alchian, Milton Friedman and Gary Becker as examples of this group). Second, there are the "revisionists," who argue that changes in the standard economic theory are necessary if we are to seriously consider evolution, although amending the constrained maximization principle is not included in those changes. The third group comprises the evolutionary game theory, Gigerenzer and the ABC group (analyzed in the previous chapter), and Nelson and Winter's work.[2] This last group calls for drastic changes in standard economic theory. At the same time, as Hodgson notes (2011: 299), there is not yet an integrated theory of evolutionary economics – and it seems there will never be one.[3]

I will not address all of these different perspectives in this chapter. Rather, I will concentrate on those aspects of modern evolutionary economics related to the aim of this book. These aspects have to do with a tension within evolutionary economics noted by Nelson (2005: 10) himself:

> Economic evolution, human cultural evolution more generally, clearly differs from biological evolution in that the human and organizational actors are purposeful, they often make conscious efforts to find better ways of doing things, and their efforts to innovate are far from completely blind.

In effect, as Muñoz, Encinar and Cañibano maintain, "one important challenge to evolutionary economics consists in tackling the paradoxical relationship between purposeful human action and the 'blindness' of evolutionary processes" (2011: 193). This paradox is aligned with the tensions that run throughout this book: free will versus determinism; restricted or scientific versus liberal naturalism. However, I believe this is an unnecessary tension within human conscious evolutionary processes, given that these processes are not actually blind. This tension seems to arise from linking the idea of cultural or social evolution with a materialist Darwinian or Neo-Darwinian conception; and, as Hodgson notes, "there is nothing in the etymology or usage of the term 'evolution' that necessarily connotes Darwinism" (2011: 300).

What is the usefulness of trying to relate economic evolution to Darwinian theories? This chapter will conclude that it might have a heuristic use, but that sometimes this heuristics will be misleading. As Vromen argues, "it seems that any attempt to find out whether or not economic evolution is Darwinian, properly understood, does not enhance our understanding of economic evolution, but rather presupposes an understanding of it" (2004a: 224).

Schumpeter ([1912] 2002: 95) states that "development, as far as I can see, has neither formal nor material connections with the biological development of any organic body." He (Schumpeter 1934 and 1942) does not mention Darwin and proposes a very rich theory of economic evolution (Hodgson 1999: 129). Nelson and Winter rarely quote Darwin or Darwinians when presenting their ideas on economic evolution. The only reference to Darwin in their 1982 book is about the influence of Malthus on him (1982: 9; see Hodgson 1994: 62ff.). In fact, rather than Darwinian, they describe their theory as Lamarckian, because it allows for the possibility of inheriting acquired characteristics. Though their theory has an evolutionary flavor, they assert that they "make no effort to base our theory on a view of human nature as the product of biological evolution" (1982: 11). They frequently cite Schumpeter's work (1934), where, as mentioned, there is no reference to

Darwin (also in their previous 1974 article). In their 2002 article, yet again they refer to Schumpeter (1942), where Darwin is also absent.[4]

Nelson contends that the rationality of actors in evolutionary economics is Simon's bounded rationality plus the capacity for innovation (2007a: 2). He also recognizes the strong influence of Schumpeter's theory of innovation on his work with Winter, which reveals a close connection between innovation and uncertainty in Knight's sense (2007a: 5). He claims that "economic actors often are not in a position to 'maximize' in any meaningful sense of that term, generally because the situation is in flux, and the best action highly uncertain, in the sense of Frank Knight and Joseph Schumpeter" (2007a: 22). Nelson and Winter advance the concept of "routine" as the unit of analysis of an evolutionary theory of economic processes. In their 1982 book, they apply this idea to the behavior and structure of firms and to innovation processes. Firms act through changeable routines rather than maximizing. According to Vromen (2008: 3), evolutionary economics is characterized by two features: first, its level of analysis, where key players are not individual persons but firms or other organizations and, second, its focus on firm-specific capabilities and routines, not on firm"s internal organization, as in many recent theories of the firm.

Evolutionary economics, when applied to specific economic topics, has developed freely without close links to biology and Darwinism; at most, it has used some metaphors with biological resonances. Economists devoted to this stream of thought merely describe the observed processes of economic growth and the dynamics of firms and innovation, and they are not particularly interested in establishing relations with Darwin and Neo-Darwinian theories (see Nelson 2007b: 75).[5] In fact, some of the classical authors mentioned above wrote their works in an evolutionary spirit well before Darwin (see Hayek 1988: 24ff.).[6] The movement actually unfolded in the opposite direction: early concepts of evolution during the Scottish Enlightenment influenced Darwinian ideas. Darwin himself recognized the influence of Malthus, and believed that his selection mechanism could also apply to the human realm.[7] Influenced by Darwin, Veblen also considered this possibility. Over the last 50 years, many social scientists have developed evolutionary explanations for the dynamics of science and technology, the evolution of firms and innovation, etc., without reference to Darwin's ideas, though in some cases showing some similarities (see Nelson 2007b: 78–85 for a review of these developments).

However, during the last years of the last century, a parallel approach relating social evolution with Darwinism has been developed. In his famous book *The Selfish Gene*, Richard Dawkins holds that there is an analogue of a gene, a replicator in the human culture realm, which he labels "meme." The overall concept is not totally new, it actually refers to the old idea about propagation in the human realm not depending on biological heredity, although in Dawkins's theory, it is produced by imitation (see [1976] 2006: Chapter 11). Dawkins coined the expression "Universal Darwinism" in 1983. In his view, Darwin's theory of natural selection is the only theory that performs the task that any theory of evolution should perform, that is, to explain the evolution of organized, living adaptive complexity, an evolution that cannot come about just for coincidence ([1983] 2010: 360, 362). He writes that "Darwin's theory of evolution by natural selection is more than a local theory to account for the existence and form of life on Earth. It is probably the only theory that can adequately account for the phenomena that we associate with life" ([1983] 2010: 360) – including, human culture and society.

Dawkins's ideas are part of an extended wave of applications of the Darwinian and neo-Darwinian evolution theories, which constitute the specific way in which the present materialist *ethos* explains biological and social processes. It is an essential dimension of current metaphysics implicit in natural and social sciences. An example in the human field is sociobiology. Within this theory, we can mention renamed scholars as Daniel Dennett, Michael Ghiselin, Richard C. Lewontin, Robert L. Trivers, and Edward O. Wilson. For his part, in 1975, Wilson published a book with a suggestive title: *Sociobiology: The New Synthesis.*[8] Nonetheless, in the field of evolutionary economics, different scholars have taken different positions concerning the biologicist wave. In this chapter I will examine Richard Nelson, Geoffrey Hodgson and Ulrich Witt's evolutionary approaches.

However, before doing this, I want to lodge a caveat. The perspective adopted in this chapter – analyzing evolutionary economists' thought from the point of view of their adherence or not to universal Darwinism – will address the central issue of this book as it applies to this recent school in economics: whether evolutionary economics escapes materialism and considers practical reason. I think it has been an unnecessary mistake to involve economics in a struggle – Darwinism or not – alien to it. Indeed, we can perfectly develop a theory of economic dynamics or evolution without any reference to Darwin, as has often been the case. In addition, I believe that, sometimes implicit in this involvement, lies the discussion regarding the position adopted for or against classical liberal views about state intervention in market economies: Darwin's selection theory fits very well with the classical liberal conception. A clear commitment to this position, for example, is found in Viktor Vanberg (2004). Advocates of the Darwinian position do not generally accept the action of final causes in the biological and social fields, and they consequently fit very well with classical liberal ideas about the possibility of invisible hand processes and explanations (i.e., the existence of automatic, not designed, market coordination). This position assumes that evolutionary selection always means progress, an assumption that is not scientifically valid (see Hodgson 1993: 223–228). Referring to Dawkins's position, Mary Midgley notes its connection with Herbert Spencer's ideas and questions the notion that they give "the explicit scientific blessing of evolutionary theory to the wilder excesses of free-enterprise capitalism" (1983: 366). Indeed, Darwinism can also fit with institutionalism, because the evolutionary process can also develop at the level of habits and institutions (see Hodgson 1993: 228–237).

Richard Nelson on "Universal Darwinism"

Universal Darwinism has acquired a relevant strength in the world of ideas. And though Nelson is against fully applying it to economics, the growing interest in this approach led him to take it into consideration. In a 1995 review article published in the *Journal of Economic Literature* he asserts (1995: 51):

> The recent work on formal evolutionary economic theories has had several distinct, if connected, sources. One is the influence of developments in evolutionary theory in biology, and sociobiology, and the attempts to extend these lines of analysis to explain the evolution of human patterns of cooperation, coordination, and social behavior more generally.

He immediately states his view from the beginning of the article (Nelson 1995: 51):

> My review will describe these developments. However, I will argue that the ideas developed to date in evolutionary sociobiology are not adequate to deal with the questions of most interest to economists concerned with long run economic change, for example the evolution of technologies and institutions.[9]

Nelson (2006 and 2007b) specifically deals with the matter of "Universal Darwinism." He first notes that, as already mentioned, "evolutionary theorizing about cultural, social, and economic phenomena has a long tradition, going back well before Darwin" (2007b: 73). He secondly argues that "the evolutionary processes involved in these areas differ in essential ways from those we now know are operative in the evolution of biological species" (2007b: 73). In conclusion, then, a universal Darwinism should include these differences inasmuch as it claims to be truly "universal." Nelson holds that (2007b: 74):

> virtually all the scholars associated with the writings on Universal Darwinism tend to start with contemporary biological evolutionary theory, and from that base try to develop generalizations intended to enable a Universal Darwinism to encompass processes of cultural change (and perhaps some other "evolutionary processes") as well as biological change.

He then distinguishes two orientations within Universal Darwinism: one associated with Dawkins and Dennett, which emphasizes applicability of biological analogies to human culture and society, and the other, which extends the content of evolutionary theory beyond biological analogies in order to rightly encompass the human realm. Nelson favors the latter stream.

He sustains: "In my view, a Universal Darwinism is acceptable, welcome, if the character of evolutionary process associated with that conception is broad and general enough to square with the details of what is going on in both arenas [biology and social science]" (2007b: 85). Thus, he proposes four characteristics of cultural evolution that a "universal" theory should adopt: to recognize the key role of human purpose and reason; the almost complete absence of survival or reproduction criteria in this field; the collective character of human phenomena; and the different ways [from biological evolution] in which individuals and societies relate to culture and its dynamics.

These characteristics are highly relevant from the point of view of this book, particularly the stress on human purpose. However, Nelson rejects planning, and this seems contradictory with the recognition of purpose and intelligence. He states, for example, that "the clear fact that scientists, and technologists, carefully consider what they do does not mean that progress in science and technology can be understood as the result of a coherent plan" (2007b: 87). He prefers the idea of a kind of invisible hand explanation, where there are indeed individual intentions, but they coordinate themselves without a previously designed common plan. Sure, there is a lot of spontaneous evolution in human affairs, but this does not necessarily mean we should always discard planning. Sometimes we certainly need it: we can have not only spontaneous order but also spontaneous disorder if we do not have coordinated plans.

I conclude that Nelson's position suffers from the typical tensions that are the object of this book. He wants to acknowledge human intentionality – and, implicitly, freedom – but he does not want to accept planned elements, which would entail intentionality. Practical reason is present, but in a limited way. It is worth mentioning that Witt (2008: 555, 559), in his typology of evolutionary economics approaches, considers Nelson and Winter neo-Schumpeterian evolutionary economics position as a non-monistic ontological stance (and consequently, non-naturalistic) using biological evolutionary metaphors as heuristic tools, – a position closer to a liberal stance than to restrictive naturalism.

Geoffrey Hodgson on "Universal Darwinism"

Hodgson has developed his ideas about evolutionary economics in relation to the old institutional economics associated with Veblen. Veblen's institutionalist approach was also evolutionary. Hodgson has written extensively about these two streams of economic thought: institutionalism and evolutionary economics.

Hodgson categorically declares that "an adequate evolutionary economics must be Darwinian" inasmuch as "Darwinism includes a broad theoretical framework for the analysis of the evolution of all open, complex systems, including socio-economic systems" (2002: 259) and it is firmly committed to causal explanations. However, he also recognizes that Darwinism is not enough: we need complementary explanations in economics. For him, "Universal Darwinism" is at a "higher" level of abstraction than the biological evolution theory: "Darwinian evolution," he argues, "shares common grounds with economics at a much higher level of abstraction [than the level of biological analogies], as a result of the fact that both biology and the social sciences address complex, open, evolving systems" (2002: 273). He believes that the main Darwinian principles, variation, inheritance and selection, apply to any evolving system (2002: 272–274; 2011: 309–311), but with different specific mechanisms acting in each field with different consequences. For example, replication of habits, routines and institutions is more inexact in human processes than in biological replication; human processes do not rely on inheritance because they can be learnt; the environment changes faster in the human world than in the biological realm (Hodgson 2001: 274; 2011: 310). This is why Hodgson, in his later writings, recommends replacing the term "Universal Darwinism" by "Generalized Darwinism" (for example, Hodgson, 2011: 311; Aldrich et al 2008; Mokyr 2005: 203; Metcalfe 2005: 399).[10,11]

Hodgson contends Darwin"s ideas constitute a threat to intentional action. He argues that, as a theory committed to causal explanations, Darwinism must also find a cause for intentional action. In his opinion (2002: 268):

> This causal explanation has to show how intentions are formed in the psyche and also how the capacity to form intentions itself gradually evolved [...] However, the fact that intentions are somehow determined does not mean that human agency is any less substantial or real [...] In principle, all outcomes have to be explained in an interlinked causal process. There is no teleology or goal in nature.

He asserts that this constitutes an "ontological commitment to the existence of causes." In a later article (2004), Hodgson considers teleology and the final cause, and quotes Aristotle, but he states that "any such cause is irrelevant unless it also involves such movements of matter and transfers of energy or momentum, including at the neurological level" (2004: 177). This reduction of final cause to efficient and material causes is frequent today.[12]

At this point, let me interrupt this exposition to suggest that if the existence of causes is a reason for adopting Darwinism, most philosophers in the history of philosophy should be Darwinian, from the time of the Pre-Socratics to the present: this is not an exclusive characteristic of Darwinism. In addition, acknowledging the existence of causes does not discard the existence of final causes. On the contrary, efficient causes – the kind of causes about which Hodgson is speaking – only act if they are triggered by final causes in the human realm.[13] In the human realm, that is, it is clear that we need a purpose, an aim, a reason or motive to act, an objective or goal, and then we select the means to achieve it. This is not a "mystical or religious explanation of events," as Hodgson declares (2002: 274).[14] Here Hodgson seems to endorse the modern refusal to recognize teleology.

However, at present, teleology is coming back into science.[15] Concerning the role of teleology, it is interesting – and also relevant for the next chapter on neuroeconomics – to quote UCLA neuroscientist Joaquin Fuster (2015: 5):

Teleology is anathema in any scientific discourse, if nothing else because it blatantly defies the logic of causality. Yet in the discourse about prefrontal physiology goal, like purpose, is of the essence. All cognitive functions of the lateral prefrontal cortex are determined, we might say "caused," by goals. If there is a unique and characteristic feature of that part of the brain, it is its ability to structure the present in order to serve the future, in this manner inverting the temporal direction of causality.

That is, there is a teleological cause acting at the neurological level as a goal or purpose. Teleology, then, is not something "mystical"; it is an inner capacity of nature, a *dynamis* (see, for example, Nancy Cartwright 1999: Chapter 4). This, as I have already mentioned, does not imply that everything in this world is the result of design: individuals may coordinate themselves quite spontaneously in many social processes. However, this does not reject the existence of and sometimes the need for a common aim, and an arranged design. To the contrary, Hodgson assumes that all evolutionary economics rejects design (2011: 304). He only marks a distinction between those who think that the interaction of individuals in the market is enough to gain coordination and those who think that institutional intervention is also necessary to achieve coordination (Hodgson 2011).

Hodgson objects to the "revulsion" against determinism provoked by Darwin's theory. He offers three definitions of determinism, and assigns to Darwinism "the notion that every event has a cause." However, this is not determinism, but the principle of causality. Hodgson takes Mario Bunge's "principle of determinacy" – "everything is determined in accordance with laws by something else" (1959: 26) as an equivalent of the principle of causality, as the Darwinian notion of determinism (2002: 274). But they are not the same.[16]

Elizabeth Anscombe may prove useful at this point. In "Causality and Determination" (Anscombe [1971] 1993), she advances two main theses. The first is that she "refuse[s] to identify causation as such with necessitation" ([1971] 1993: 88). "Causality," she explains, although warning that this may sound obvious "consists in the derivativeness of an effect from its cause" ([1971] 1993: 91–92). And she reasons: "it's not difficult to show it prima-facie wrong to associate the notion of cause with necessity or universality [...]. For it being much easier to trace effects back to causes with certainty than to predict effects from causes, we often know a cause without knowing whether there is an exceptionless generalization of the kind envisaged, or whether there is a necessity" ([1971] 1993: 91). Her second thesis involves an argument against determinism and for indeterminism; she also establishes a classification of the latter. She distinguishes between being determined in the sense of pre-determined and determinate. What has happened is determined once it happens, and this is obvious (this is the sense in which Aristotle states that past and present are necessary). Anscombe is concerned with pre-determination. Here, another distinction arises: there are non-necessitating causes, "one that can fail of its effect without the intervention of anything to frustrate it" and necessitating causes, that can only be frustrated by interference. Anscombe's definition of indeterminism is the thesis that not all physical effects are necessitated by their causes. This does not mean, however, that indeterminate effects have no causes ([1971] 1993: 101). That is, all events have causes, but not all "is determined in accordance with laws."[17] In my opinion, this typology of causality could help Hodgson defend his version that determinism is compatible with novelty and free-will (2002: 273–276).

In a nutshell, Hodgson holds that *Generalized Darwinian* is insufficient but not wrong (2011: 313). He denies final causes or teleology but defends novelty and free-will. Now, there certainly seems to be a tension in Hodgson's thought: a tension between trying to hold human intentionality and at the same time denying it. This is a tension between practical reason and free will and determinism, between liberal naturalism and scientific naturalism.

Ulrich Witt, evolution and Darwinism

Witt has headed the Evolutionary Economics Group at the Max Planck Institute of Economics, Jena, ever since he founded it in 1995. Witt is at odds with, in the first place, direct application of biological evolution to economic behavior because it applies only to genetically determined behaviors and because Darwinian theory does not comprise intra-generational evolution by learning. Second, he also disapproves of the use of Darwinian concepts as heuristic devices because he believes they can be misleading (2008: 551). Third, he objects to Dawkins's Universal Darwinism. In Witt's view, generic features of evolution as considered by Universal Darwinism – variation, selection and retention/replication – are domain specific and do not apply to cultural and social evolution (2008: 551). Witt labels his proposal the "continuity hypothesis" – CH (2004: 127–129). According to this theory, the generic feature for evolution is self-transformation over time of a system under consideration (2004: 130). It is endogenous and governed by regularities. Self-transformation can be split into two processes: the emergence and the dissemination of novelty.

Natural evolution, Witt notes, preceded other forms of evolution. He expounds: "it has therefore shaped the ground, and still defines the constraints, for man-made or cultural evolution. In this sense, there is, thus, also a historical ontological continuity, notwithstanding that the mechanisms and regularities of cultural evolution differ from those of natural evolution" (2004: 131). In spite of this original influence of biological evolution, human cultural behavior processes evolve in ways that need to be explained by other theories. At the same time, for Witt, natural evolutionary characteristics of human beings are the basis on which other forms of evolution are built. Vromen (2008: 7) describes Witt's CH in the following way:

> psychological features of human beings are outcomes of antecedent processes of biological evolution that are of special importance to ongoing processes of economic evolution. In particular, ancient processes of

biological evolution produced both the basic, innate wants and primitive, non-cognitive forms of learning (such as conditioning) that still constrain and influence the behavior of present-day human beings. On the basis of their basic wants, for example, people also learn new acquired wants through conditioning (or associative learning).

From Witt's perspective, there is a close connection between biological and cultural characteristics of human beings: all evolutionary phenomena share "one and the same ontological basis" (2004: 129). In 2007, he criticizes non-naturalist positions on evolutionary economics and argues for CH's ontologically monistic and naturalistic condition. He emphasizes that "once a monistic ontology is accepted, the postulate of an ontological continuity between evolution in nature and cultural and economic evolution is trivial" (2007: 21). "Ontological monism" means that "both change in the economy and change in nature belong to connected spheres of reality and are therefore potentially inter-dependent processes" (2008: 550). They are connected to a naturalistic sub-stratum (2008: 550). Though Witt criticizes Hodgson's Generalized Darwinism (e.g., 2007: 6; Levit et al 2011) for its application of Darwinian heuristic concepts, as Vromen (2008) shows, both positions are compatible and share, as also Witt (2007: 6) recognizes, a non-reductionist monist ontology (2007: 7).

It is my belief that philosophical considerations about ontology and Darwinism – the continuity hypothesis – "contaminate" Witt's conception of evolutionary economics. In his work, for example, in his paper about "economic policy making in evolutionary perspective" (2003), he includes the relevance of agents' inventive learning, experience and even normative concerns. However, Witt's CH leaves no room to practical reason because CH is explicitly declared to be a monistic naturalist conception of economic evolution. Tensions between human free agency, intentionality, and a narrow naturalism are yet again present.

Conclusion: evolutionary economics and practical reason

Is it possible that an evolutionary economic theory include consideration of practical reason? We have not found it yet, at least distinctly, in the authors analyzed. However, as I see it, this is not only possible but desirable in that it would produce a richer and more realistic evolutionary theory. Nevertheless, this theory should employ a conception of evolution which, in addition to recognizing biological evolutionary influences and using biological evolutionary heuristic metaphors, leaves room for consideration of humans' free creative capacities, not determined, but only conditioned by biological causes.[18] Moreover, in my view, this consideration should be the distinctive feature of a true theory of economic evolution.

As Hodgson states, "important additional features that have to be brought into the picture at some stage are human intentionality, the capacity of humans for mental analysis and prefiguration, the nature of human sociality and cooperation, social institutions, and the development of different types and technologies of information transmission" (2011: 312). But if we recognize the task of practical reason, these features cannot be conceived, as Hodgson seems to do, as the product of biological evolution. Evolutionary economics should return to Schumpeter's conception of creative capacities of innovation, detach itself from its Darwinian ties and turn to them in a limited way, when they prove adequate and depending on the topic to be explained (see Witt 2013: 14).

What alternative strategies could we take up in order to adopt practical rationality in a liberal naturalistic version of evolutionary economics? Brian Loasby (2002), who quotes Knight and Shackle on uncertainty and the role of imagination, notes that uncertainty justifies an evolutionary approach to the growth of academic, technological and everyday knowledge, but an approach that goes beyond the biological model (2002: 1230). According to him, "evolutionary economics has important differences from the biological model, which may however provide a useful complement to it" (Loasby 2002: 1227): "a reliable baseline" (2002: 1230). Muñoz et al's (2011) article "On the role of intentionality in evolutionary economic change" opens a door to practical rationality. They want to show the essential relevance of intentionality in explaining economic evolution. They base their proposal on the non-naturalistic side of Witt, and on Schumpeter, and they also positively mention Searle's theory of action. They apply the idea of an "action plan" to insert human intentionality into economic evolution. They explain:

> [U]sing the action plan approach, we introduce the role of purposeful action or intentionality. Intentionality becomes apparent in agents' action plans, plans that interact (at the meso-level) and are evaluated by agents in terms of performance. Depending on performance, action plans are revised, renewed, or simply abandoned. Renewed variety fuels emergent orders and intentionality thus shapes emergent orders. If we are right, evolutionary processes are not (at least not totally) blind.
>
> (Muñoz et al 2011: 194)

Muñoz and Encinar also argue that intentionality is at "the origin of emergent properties as innovation within economic complex systems" (2014: 317). Hodgson had considered the Aristotelian final cause as a possible source of "genuine novelty," and he ascribes this position to James Buchanan, Knight, Loasby and Shackle (Hodgson 1999: 147). However, he discards it on the grounds that, in the first place, an "uncaused cause" like the final cause is disturbing for modern science and, second, the recognition of final causes makes evolution of humans from animals problematic (1999: 147).[19] Instead of rejecting final causes, it would be reasonable to assume that there is something wrong with modern science and that the evolutionary theory presents an inexplicable leap from animals to human. Though it may sound heretical, we are not mere evolved animals.

I hold that these kinds of approaches, apart from scientific naturalistic conditionings, enrich evolutionary economics because they make room for the most human driver of evolution – the creative capacity of individuals as human free agents.

The conclusion of this chapter confirms the presumption I advanced in the Introduction to this book: that a first group of schools of thought, including behavioral, evolutionary and neuroeconomics (to be discussed in the next chapter) are predominantly materialist, they do not take into account classical practical reason and adopt a weak concept of freedom. However, in this approach influenced by evolutionary theories, as well as in those influenced by psychology, a tension remains. In the case of evolutionary economic movements, the notions of novelty and free will push in the contrary direction of scientific naturalism of evolutionary psychology and biology. While the New Behavioral Economics seems to recognize a certain economic domestication of psychological inputs (that also have a physicalist proclivity), evolutionary economics seems to display a relaxation of scientific naturalism in favor of recognition of human freedom and creativity.

The last issue to examine about evolutionary economics is whether the changes incorporated in it stem from outside or from within economics. I think that the approaches that are closest to Darwinian evolutionary theories are more subservient to them than the ones drawing away from these theories.

Notes

1 For a complete summary of the history of evolutionary thinking in economics from 1880 to 1980, see Geoffrey Hodgson (1999: Chapter 5; and 2005).
2 However, Vromen (2015: 88–89) points at the ambivalence concerning the neo-classical theory of Nelson and Winter. Hodgson (1997: 14–19; and 1999: 131–136) proposes another taxonomy on the basis of four criteria: ontological (whether or not substantial emphasis is given to evolutionary processes), methodological (whether reductionist or not), temporal (sustaining gradual or disruptive processes), and metaphorical (use or not of biological metaphors).
3 This is also his conclusion in a recently bibliometric study with Lamberg (Hodgson and Lambert, 2015: 12–13). See also Silva and Teixeira's bibliometric study (2009).
4 Ulrich Witt (2013: 4) states, "The Neo-Schumpeterians' lack of interest in a naturalistic interpretation of evolutionary economics also shows up in the complete inattention to prominent pleas for blending the evolutionary perspective on the economy with a (naturalistic) ecological one such as in Georgescu-Roegen (1971) and Boulding (1978)."
5 One exception may be Armen Alchian (1950) who, though not mentioning Darwin, states that his "suggested approach embodies the principles of biological evolution and natural selection by interpreting the economic system as an adaptive mechanism which chooses among exploratory actions generated by adaptive pursuits of 'success' or 'profits'"(1950: 211).
6 Hayek upholds that cultural evolution is not Darwinian and that Darwin got his basic ideas on evolution from the former evolutionary account (1988: 23–24).

7 Struggle for existence happens for the reason explained by "the doctrine of Malthus applied with manifold force to the whole animal and vegetable kingdoms" ([1873] no date: 57; and see also 1871: 132–134). On the relation between Malthus and Darwin, see, e.g., Dopfer (2005: 13–14) and Gilson (2009: 88–94).

8 For a critical assessment of sociobiology, see Sahlins (1977), Philip Kitcher (1987) and Peter Koslowski (1996: Part II).

9 Another scholar holding similar ideas is, for example, Vromen (2015: 86): "it is not biological evolution that is directly relevant for economics, but cultural evolution and related things"; see also Camerer and Loewenstein (2004: 40). On the contrary, Arthur J. Robson (2001 and 2002), for example, directly applies biological evolution to explain economic behavior. A related position is "Genoeconomics," which studies the relation between the genetic constitution of individuals and their economic behavior. See Daniel J. Benjamin et al (2012), for a recent review of this field.

10 For a vivid description of Hodgson's position about Darwinism and economics, see his interview (2010: 80–85).

11 Koppl et al (2015) suggest an application of generalized Darwinism as supporting an unpredictable, creative economic evolution.

12 Veblen, to whom Hodgson repeatedly refers, holds that although it is not a matter of evolutionary economics, "economic action is teleological" (1898b: 391). However, in the context of his conception of human behavior, he also reduces final cause to efficient cause (see Hodgson 1998: 423, note 2). I will develop Veblen's thought in Chapter 7, which deals with institutional economics.

13 It could be discussed whether final causes are present in the following passage of the conclusion of Darwin's *Origin of Species*: "Authors of the highest eminence seem to be fully satisfied with the view that each species has been independently created. To my mind it accords better with what we know of the laws impressed on matter by the Creator, that the production and extinction of the past and present inhabitants of the world should have been due to secondary causes, like those determining the birth and death of the individual" ([1873] no date: 473). On the difficult topic of Darwin, evolution and teleology, see Gilson (2009: Chapter 3).

14 There is a tendency in many modern thinkers to mix up teleological explanations with mystical or supernatural accounts, thus putting them outside science (see, e.g., Don Ross 2014: 12, note 6) and also to consider that Aristotle's teleological view of nature is anthropocentric. As the German scholar Eduard G. Zeller has explained, "the most important feature of the Aristotelian teleology is the fact that it is neither anthropocentric, nor it is due to the actions of a creator existing outside the world or even of a mere arranger of the world, but is always thought of as immanent in nature." At the same time, this does not necessarily discard the existence of a creator (1931: 48).

15 On old and new forms of teleology, see the bibliography cited in my 2016 paper (Crespo 2016).

16 Vromen (2001) supports compatibility between evolutionary theory and agency (and, consequently, the deliberate creation of novelty) by adopting Ernst Mayr's (1961: 1503) distinction between ultimate (external evolutionary) and proximate (internal agency) causes. However, Vromen asserts that the former are causes of the latter. Vromen's (2004a) argument to sustain that "even if genetic determinism were true, behavior can be the outcome of flexible and deliberate choice" (2004a: 231), is that "physicalism or materialism do not exclude the appreciation of emerging properties at higher levels of organization [...] Thus, genuine agency and intentionality are not ruled out. What is ruled out are conceptions of agency and intentionality that presuppose that there is a mysterious free-floating ghost in the machine" (2004a: 232–233). This emergentist account is also present in Hayek (see Lewis 2016). In the next chapter, I will explore the emergency theory.

17 I find that Hodgson's 1988 (cf. pp10–12 and Chapter 5) thinking seems more open
    to intentionality.
18 Hodgson (2011: 305) criticizes George Shackle's conception of human action, a
    conception, I think, that would contribute to an evolutionary economic theory.
19 Hodgson (2002: 276) criticizes Ludwig Lachmann and Shackle's notion of human
    intentionality as an "uncaused cause". I will not try to ascertain here the meaning
    of Shackle's expression but I actually find Anscombe's explanation of causality
    clearer than the former's.

References

Alchian, A. (1950). "Uncertainty, Evolution, and Economic Theory," *Journal of Political Economy* 58/3: 211–221.

Aldrich, H. E., G. M. Hodgson, D. L. Hull, T. Knudsen, J. Mokyr, and V. J. Vanberg (2008). "In Defence of Generalized Darwinism," *Journal of Evolutionary Economics* 18: 577–596.

Anscombe, G. E. M. ([1971] 1993). "Causality and Determination," reprinted in E. Sosa and M. Tooley (eds.), *Causation*. Oxford: Oxford University Press.

Benjamin, D. J., D. Cesarini, C. F. Chabris, E. L. Glaeser, D. I. Laibson et al (2012). "The Promises and Pitfalls of Genoeconomics," *Annual Review of Economics* 4: 627–662, http://www.annualreviews.org/doi/abs/10.1146/annurev-economics-080511-110939, retrieved May 14, 2016.

Boulding, K. E. (1978). *Ecodynamics: A New Theory of Societal Evolution*. Beverly Hills, CA: Sage Publications.

Bunge, M. A. (1959). *Causality*. Cambridge, MA: Harvard University Press.

Camerer, C. F. and G. Loewenstein (2004). "Behavioral Economics: Past, Present, Future." In C. F. Camerer, G. Loewenstein and M. Rabin (eds.), *Advances in Behavioral Economics*. New York: Russell Sage Foundation and Princeton and Oxford: Princeton University Press.

Cartwright, N. C. (1999). *The Dappled World. A Study of the Boundaries of Science*. Cambridge: Cambridge University Press.

Crespo, R. F. (2016). "Causality, Teleology and Explanation in Social Sciences," *CHESS Working Paper No. 2016–2002*, Durham University, February 2016, https://www.dur.ac.uk/resources/chess/CHESS_WP_2016_2.pdf.

Darwin, C. (1871). *The Descent of Man, and Selection in Relation to Sex*, London: John Murray, http://darwin-online.org.uk/content/frameset?pageseq=1&itemID=F937.1&viewtype=text, retrieved April 27, 2016.

Darwin, C. ([1873] no date). *The Origin of Species*, reprinted from the sixth London edition. New York: Hurst & Co.

Dawkins, R. ([1976] 2006). *The Selfish Gene*, 30 Anniversary Edition. Oxford: Oxford University Press.

Dawkins, R. (1983). "Universal Darwinism." In D. S. Bendall (ed.), *Evolution from Molecules to Man*. Cambridge: Cambridge University Press. Reprinted in M. A. Bedau and C. E. Cleland (eds.) (2010). *The Nature of Life: Classical and Contemporary Perspectives from Philosophy and Science*. Cambridge: Cambridge University Press.

Dopfer, K. (2005). "Evolutionary Economics: A Theoretical Framework." In K. Dopfer (ed.), *The Evolutionary Foundation of Economics*. Cambridge: Cambridge University Press.

Fuster, J. M. (2015). *The Prefrontal Cortex*, 5th edition. London and Oxford: Academic Press (Elsevier).

Georgescu-Roegen, N. (1971). *The Entropy Law and the Economic Process*. Cambridge, MA: Harvard University Press.

Gilson, E. (2009). *From Aristotle to Darwin and Back Again*. San Francisco, CA: Ignatius Press.

Hayek, F. A. von (1988). *The Fatal Conceit: The Errors of Socialism. The Collected Works of Friedrich August Hayek, Vol. I*, ed. by W.W. Bartley, III. London: Routledge.

Hodgson, G. M. (1988). *Economics and Institutions. A Manifesto for a Modern Institutional Economics*. Cambridge: Polity Press.

Hodgson, G. M. (1993). "Evolution and Institutional Change." In U. Maki, B. Gustafsson and C. Knudsen (eds.), *Rationality, Institutions and "Economic Methodology*. London: Routledge.

Hodgson, G. M. (1994). *Economics and Evolution. Bringing Life Back into Economics*. Cambridge: Polity Press.

Hodgson, G. M. (1997). "Economics and Evolution and the Evolution of Economics." In J. Reijnders (ed.), *Economics and Evolution*Cheltenham: Edward Elgar.

Hodgson, G. M. (1998). "Thorstein Veblen's Evolutionary Economics," *Cambridge Journal of Economics* 22: 415–431.

Hodgson, G. M. (1999). *Evolution and Institutions. On Evolutionary Economics and the Evolution of Economics*. Cheltenham: Edward Elgar.

Hodgson, G. M. (2002). "Darwin in Economics: from Analogy to Ontology," *Journal of Evolutionary Economics* 12: 259–281.

Hodgson, G.M. (2004). "Darwinism, causality and the social sciences," *Journal of Economic Methodology* 11/2: 175–194.

Hodgson, G. M. (2005). "Decomposition and growth: biological metaphors in economics from the 1880s to the 1980s." In K. Dopfer (ed.), *The Evolutionary Foundation of Economics*. Cambridge: Cambridge University Press.

Hodgson, G. M. (2010). "Making economics more relevant: An interview with Geoffrey Hodgson," *Erasmus Journal for Philosophy and Economics* 3/2: 72–94, http://ejpe. org/pdf/3-2-int.pdf, retrieved April 12, 2016.

Hodgson, G. M. (2011). "A Philosophical Perspective on Contemporary Evolutionary Economics." In J. B. Davis and D. W. Hands (eds.), *The Elgar Companion to Recent Economic Methodology*. Cheltenham: Edward Elgar.

Hodgson, G. M. and J.-A. Lambert (2015). "The Past and Future of Evolutionary Economics: Some Reflections Based on New Bibliometric Evidence," mimeo.

Kitcher, P. (1987). "Précis of Vaulting Ambition: Sociobiology and the Quest for Human Nature," *Behavioral and Brain Sciences* 10/1: 61–71.

Koppl, R., S. Kauffman, T. Felin and G. Longo (2015). "Economics for a creative world," *Journal of Institutional Economics* 11/1: 1–31.

Koslowski, P. (1996). *Ethics of Capitalism. A Critique of Sociobiology: Two Essays with a Comment by James M. Buchanan*. Heidelberg, New York: Springer Verlag.

Levit, G. S., U. Hossfeld and U. Witt (2011). "Can Darwinism be 'generalized' and of what use would this be?," *Journal of Evolutionary Economics* 21: 545–562.

Lewis, P. (2016). "The Emergence of 'Emergence' in the Work of F.A. Hayek: A Historical Analysis," *History of Political Economy* 48/1: 111–150.

Loasby, B. J. (2002). "The evolution of knowledge: beyond the biological model," *Research Policy* 31/8–9: 1227–1239.

Mayr, E. (1961), "Cause and Effect in Biology," *Science* 134/3489: 1501–1506.

Metcalfe, J. S. (2005). "Evolutionary concepts and evolutionary economics." In K. Dopfer (ed.), *The Evolutionary Foundation of Economics*. Cambridge: Cambridge University Press.

Midgley, M. (1983). "Selfish Genes and Social Darwinism," *Philosophy* 58/225: 365–377.

Mokyr, J. (2005). "Is there a theory of economic history?" In K. Dopfer (ed.), *The Evolutionary Foundation of Economics*. Cambridge: Cambridge University Press.

Muñoz, F.-F., M.-I. Encinar and C. Cañibano (2011). "On the role of intentionality in evolutionary economic change," *Structural Change and Economic Dynamics* 22/3: 193–203. Reprinted in Dopfer, K. & Potts, J. (eds.) *The New Evolutionary Economics*. Cheltenham: Edward Elgar, Vol. I, Evolutionary Microeconomics, Part I: The Agent, 2014, Chapter 3.

Muñoz, F.-F. and M.-I. Encinar (2014). "Intentionality and the emergence of complexity: an analytical approach," *Journal of Evolutionary Economics* 4/2: 317–334.

Nelson, R. R. (1995). "Recent Evolutionary Theorizing About Economic Change," *Journal of Economic Literature* XXXIII: 48–90.

Nelson, R. R. (2005). "Where Are We Now on an Evolutionary Theory of Economic Growth, and Where Should We Be Going?" (Presidential Lecture, Schumpeter Society, December 7, 2004), Center on Capitalism and Society, The Earth Institute at Columbia University, *CCS Working Paper No. 3 February 2005*, http://capitalism.columbia.edu/files/ccs/workingpage/2015/ccswp3_nelson.pdf. Retrieved March 24, 2016.

Nelson, R. R. (2006). "Evolutionary social science and universal Darwinism," *Journal of Evolutionary Economics* 16: 491–510.

Nelson, R. R., (2007a). "Economic Development from the Perspective of Evolutionary Economic Theory," *GLOBELICS QTa Working Paper Series No. 2007–2002*, http://dcsh.xoc.uam.mx/eii/globelicswp/wpg0702.pdf. Retrieved March 24, 2016.

Nelson, R. R. (2007b). "Universal Darwinism and evolutionary social science," *Biology and Philosophy* 22: 73–94.

Nelson, R. R. and S. Winter (1974). "Neoclassical versus Evolutionary Theories of Economic Growth: Critique and Prospectus," *Economic Journal* 84: 886–905.

Nelson, R. R. and S. Winter (1982). *An Evolutionary Theory of Economic Change*, Cambridge, MA: Harvard University Press.

Nelson, R. R. and S. Winter (2002). "Evolutionary Theorizing in Economics," *Journal of Economic Perspectives* 16/2: 23–46.

Robson, A. J. (2001). "The Biological Basis of Economic Behavior," *Journal of Economic Literature* 39: 11–33.

Robson, A. J. (2002). "Evolution and Human Nature," *Journal of Economic Perspectives* 16/2: 89–106.

Ross, D. (2014). *Philosophy of Economics*. Houndmills: Palgrave MacMillan.

Sahlins, M. (1977). *The Use and Abuse of Biology. An Anthropological Critique of Sociobiology*. Ann Arbor, MI: University of Michigan Press.

Schumpeter, J. A. ([1912] 2002). "The Economy as a Whole. Seventh Chapter of The Theory of Economic Development," translated by U. Backhaus, *Industry and Innovation* 9/1–2: 93–145.

Schumpeter, J. A. (1934). *The Theory of Economic Development*. Cambridge, MA: Harvard University Press.

Schumpeter, J. A. (1942). *Capitalism, Socialism, and Democracy*. New York: Harper and Row.

Silva, S. T. and A. A. C. Teixeira (2009). "On the divergence of evolutionary research paths in the past 50 years: a comprehensive bibliometric account," *Journal of Evolutionary Economics* 19: 605–642.

Vanberg, V. J. (2004). "Human Intentionality and Design in Cultural Evolution," *Papers on Economics and Evolution # 0402*, Evolutionary Economics Group, MPI Jena.

Veblen, T. (1898). "Why is Economics not an Evolutionary Science?," *The Quarterly Journal of Economics* 12/4: 373–397.

Vromen, J. (2001). "The Human Agent in Evolutionary Economics." In J. Laurent and J. Nightingale (eds.) *Darwinism and evolutionary economics.* Cheltenham: Edward Elgar.

Vromen, J. (2004a). "Conjectural revisionary economic ontology: Outline of an ambitious research agenda for evolutionary economics," *Journal of Economic Methodology* 11/2: 213–247.

Vromen, J. J. (2004b). "Taking evolution seriously: what difference has it make for economics?." In J. B. Davis, A. Marciano and J. Runde (eds.), *The Elgar Companion to Economics and Philosophy.* Cheltenham: Edward Elgar.

Vromen, J. J. (2008). "Ontological issues in evolutionary economics: The debate between generalized darwinism and the continuity hypothesis,"*Papers on Economics and Evolution #0805*, Max Planck Institute of Economics, Jena, http://www.jackvromen. nl/papers/ontological-issues-in-evolutionary-economics-2008.pdf, retrieved April 14, 2016.

Vromen, J. J. (2015). "Learning from the right neighbour: An interview with Jack Vromen," *Erasmus Journal for Philosophy and Economics*, 8/1: 82–97, http://ejpe. org/pdf/8-1-int.pdf. Retrieved March 24, 2016.

Wilson, E. O. (1975). *Sociobiology. The New Synthesis.* Cambridge, MA: Harvard University Press.

Witt, U. (2003). "Economic policy making in evolutionary perspective," *Journal of Evolutionary Economics* 13: 77–94.

Witt, U. (2004). "On the proper interpretation of 'evolution' in economics and its implications for production theory," *Journal of Economic Methodology* 11/2: 125–146.

Witt, U. (2007). "Heuristic Twists and Ontological Creeds – A Road Map for Evolutionary Economics," *Papers on Economics and Evolution # 0701*, Max Planck Institute of Economics, Jena, http://www.fep.up.pt/conferencias/eaepe2007/Papers% 20and%20abstracts_CD/witt_heuristics.pdf, retrieved April 14, 2016.

Witt, U. (2008). "What is specific about evolutionary economics?," *Journal of Evolutionary Economics* 18: 547–575.

Witt, U. (2013). "The Future of Evolutionary Economics: Why Modalities Matter," *Papers on Economics and Evolution # 1309*, Max Planck Institute of Economics, Jena, https://papers.econ.mpg.de/evo/discussionpapers/2013-09.pdf, retrieved April 14, 2016.

Zeller, E. ([1931] 2001). *Outlines of the History of Greek Philosophy.* Abingdon: Routledge.

5   Neuroeconomics

The purpose of this chapter is to establish whether the tension permeating this book – for or against physicalism – is also present in this new field. A "natural" first reaction would be to conclude that, given that neuroeconomics is based on current neuroscience, which provides materialist explanations for all human phenomena, the former should be clearly materialist. However, on the one hand, neuroeconomics has been naturally developed as an extension of behavioral economics, which is not necessarily materialist. On the other hand, results of a recent survey on the philosophical views of contemporary, mainly Anglo-Saxon professional philosophers (David Bourget and David Chalmers 2014) are really surprising, and justify assessing this approach in the context of this book. While I believe that we are witnessing an increasing predominance of materialist reductionist positions in the philosophy of neuroscience, this survey shows that this position is far from unanimous. For example, only 12.2 percent of philosophers surveyed deny free-will and only 16.9 percent hold a biological view of personal identity, while 56.5 percent uphold a physicalist position about the mind. From this last figure, it follows that 43.5 percent maintains a non-physicalist position. What does this mean? They may have a dualist view and argue that the mind is not physical, thus considering that human beings are composed of matter and something like a spiritual stuff. Another, more likely possibility, is that they are "non-reductive" physicalists about the mind.

Determining the different positions in the philosophy of neuroscience constitutes a fundamental step to figure out whether the determinism-freedom tension is present in neuroeconomics. Accordingly, the first section in this chapter will briefly review these stances in order to identify which perspective would be the most persuasive for the philosophers interviewed. Section 2 will concentrate specifically on neuroeconomics and will expose yet again a tension between physicalism and a defense of intentionality and free-will.

The metaphysics of neuroscience

According to the survey mentioned above, there are physicalist and non-physicalist positions within the philosophy of neuroscience. Dilworth (2006: 265) notes:

The fundamental problem for modern science with regard to the spirit is evident already in early Greek atomism, with its lacking categories for the self and psychic states. This problem remains in modern science, both as a paradox with respect to the nature of its own activities, as well as a major lacuna with respect to what it is capable of explaining. [...] [T]he spiritual element generally acknowledged to exist in human activities cries for explanation. Science, limited as it is to physicalist categories, cannot handle either of these issues.

Indeed, this limitation introduces a tension into the philosophy of neuroscience. Though a materialistic reductionism seems to prevail, not all authors share this stance. Morality, responsibility, complex or high reasoning, conscience, affective relations are evident realities pointing to something beyond matter. Many reductionists cannot accept that everything can be explained by biological interactions. David Chalmers (1996) speaks about an explanatory gap, or "the hard problem of consciousness," while John Bickle et al (2010: 11) wonder, "Why should that particular brain experience give rise to conscious experience?" The introspective aspect of individual sensory experiences also raises doubts. In the first place, I will present the physicalist and dualist views and, second, other non-physicalist positions.

Types of physicalism and dualism

William Jaworski (2016: Chapter 11) has thoroughly analyzed different definitions of physicalism applied to the nature of the mind. He establishes two criteria for an adequate definition: first, it must involve the thesis that everything is physical and, second, it must include all existent varieties of physicalism – eliminativist, reductivist and non-reductivist.[1] After reviewing numerous definitional issues, he defines physicalism as the thesis that "everything can be exhaustively described and explained by the most empirically adequate theories in current or future physics" (2016: 224).

First, there is eliminative physicalism, which denies the existence of mental states.[2] William Ramsey (2013) explains:

Modern versions of eliminative materialism claim that our common-sense understanding of psychological states and processes is deeply mistaken and that some or all of our ordinary notions of mental states will have no home, at any level of analysis, in a sophisticated and accurate account of the mind. In other words, it is the view that certain common-sense mental states, such as beliefs and desires, do not exist.

This position is really extreme. One of its strongest defenders, Paul Churchland, states:

Eliminative materialism is the thesis that our common sense conception of psychological phenomena constitutes a radically false theory, a theory so fundamentally defective that both the principles and the ontology of that theory will eventually be displaced, rather than smoothly reduced, by completed neuroscience.

(Churchland 1981: 67)

Second, there is reductive materialism, also called type physicalism or identity theory, which "holds that states and processes of the mind are identical to states and processes of the brain" (J. J. C. Smart 2007: 1).[3] Tim Crane (1995) describes how identity theorists explain mental causation of physical events by considering the mental identical to the physical: "it is because physicalists want to maintain the causal efficacy of the mental that they identify mental phenomena with phenomena in the brain" (1995: 7). For them, ultimately, all "psychical phenomena" can be physically explained.

Crane is surprised – he uses the term "notable" – by the fact that few physicalists accept the identity theory: they consider it far too strong to be plausible. Thus, they tend to adhere to a third alternative: non-reductive physicalism. It is worth noting that, in the philosophy of mind, "reduction" is understood as an epistemological concept: the mental can be described or explained (or not) in physical terms, independently of its ontologically physical character (which is not questioned by non-reductive physicalists). A well-known and much discussed non-reductionist position is the "multiple realizability" of mental states thesis. It was originally proposed by Hilary Putnam (1975) and it has several versions; one particularly well-known is the "special sciences" argument developed by Jerry Fodor (1974). In Fodor's opinion, there are other taxonomies, apart from the physical taxonomy, which apply to the same thing (1974: 114). As Jaworski (2016: Chapter 11) explains, the lack of systematic correlations between taxonomies impedes physics from taking over the description and explanation performed by special sciences (like psychology).

"Supervenience" is a concept related with the previous theses. Brian McLaughlin and Karen Bennett (2011) explain: "Non-reductive physicalists think that mental properties supervene with metaphysical necessity upon physical properties." The idea of supervenience is that if some properties of type A supervene on properties of type B, two things that are exactly alike in their B properties cannot have different A properties. Donald Davidson (1980: 214) states:

[M]ental characteristics are in some sense dependent, or supervenient, on physical characteristics. Such supervenience might be taken to mean that there cannot be two events alike in all physical respects but differing in some mental respect, or that an object cannot alter in some mental respect without altering in some physical respect.

Jaworski (2012: 166) speaks about a "lower-determination thesis" – a necessitation relation of supervenience plus explanation: "if F-things determine G-things, then necessarily F-twins must be G-twins, and something's F-properties explain its G-properties." James Madden (2013: 122) explains supervenience in the following way: "There can be no variation in the psychological without a variation in the physical, even though it does not entail a strict reducibility of psychological states to physical states." Supervenience has generated a profuse literature, with a plethora of distinctions and discussions (for a review, see McLaughlin and Bennett 2011).

Out of 46 percent of philosophers who oppose physicalism, some may hold non-reductive physicalist positions. However, this possibly implies a mis-understanding of non-reductive physicalism, because, as already explained, this is an epistemological, not an ontological thesis. Non-reduction does not imply the existence of any reality outside the physical.

A different position, more fitting for non-physicalists, is emergentism. The very description of emergentism by Timothy O'Connor and Hong Yu Wong (2012) entails its non-reducible character: "emergent entities (properties or substances) 'arise' out of more fundamental entities and yet are 'novel' or 'irreducible' with respect to them (For example, it is sometimes said that consciousness is an emergent property of the brain)." Emergentism has its roots in British philosophers: one kind of emergentism, epistemological or weak emergence, descends from Samuel Alexander, and the other, ontological or strong emergence, from John Stuart Mill and C. D. Broad.

Ontological emergentism holds that what emerges are non-physical prop-erties. For epistemological emergentism, instead, what emerges are no more than macroscopic patterns running through microscopic interactions (see O'Connor and Wong 2012). For ontological emergentists, emergent laws have not only same-level effects but also effects in lower levels; this is called "downward causation." This seems to be a dualist position: if mental prop-erties really cause physical phenomena, we are asserting that there are two kinds of entities involved.

Dualism is more emphasized – a substance dualism – in William Hasker's (1999) conception of the mind as an emergent non-composite substance. In his view, what emerge are substances, not properties. Daniel Stoljar (2009: 12) also notes emergentism's dualism. My desire to break a window (a mental entity) causes my arm to move and throw a brick against it (a physical entity).

In a nutshell, there are two main alternatives in current philosophy of mind: eliminative or reductive materialism and a dualism of physical and mental realities. Of the 43.5 percent of philosophers who are not physicalists, some may favor this second option. However, I suppose that a large number of them may also reject substance dualism: Gilbert Ryle's criticism of Descartes dualism, "the dogma [or the myth] of the ghost in the machine" ([1949] 2009, *passim*) in reference to mind is widely accepted. Since Ryle, dualism is "philo-sophically incorrect." However, Ryle's description of Descartes's dualism is simplistically exaggerated and, also, Descartes's dualism thus described has been considered as the only possible dualism, discarding any other more sensible forms of it.[4] Additionally, emergentism does not adequately explain the relation between the physical and the psychical and it is empirically dis-confirmed. Therefore, as Jaworski (2011: 69) remarks, in the end, physicalism "remains the most popular mind-body theory today."

Looking for alternative explanations for non-physicalist positions

I have suggested that, rather than dualists, the 43.5 percent of non- physicalists in the survey are non-reductive physicalists or emergentists. From an "exis-tential" point of view, this is a sensible attitude. The idea that we are only a bundle of chemical neural interactions in the brain is contra-intuitive and repelling. Owen Flanagan and David Barack claim that we are currently living a third wave of existentialism, namely "neuroexistentialism" (2010), a time of terrible anguish stemming from the advances of neuroscience which threaten our last hopes for the existence of human spiritual realities. Neu-roscience claims that we are only material stuff. We do not have immortal souls, we are not free, we are not in control of our decisions, and we are completely dependent on chemical neural interactions. It follows that we are not responsible for our actions. God is absent. And, as Dostoyevsky posits in *The Brothers Karamazov*, "if there is no God, then everything is permitted" – a distressing scenario, certainly. Flanagan and Barack explain: "for most ordinary folk and many members of the non-scientific academy, the ideas that humans are animals and thus the mind is the brain, and in addition, being revealed as such, is destabilizing and disenchanting, quite possibly nauseating, a source of dread, fear and trembling, sickness unto to death even" (2010: 579). The solution they allude to relies on living a sort of pagan Aristotelian ethics or to be deceived by false positive illusions: "far-fetched stories about the grounding of human life, or consoling stories about our fates, noble lies" (2010: 588). Philosophers naturally seek more moderate positions. Hence, non-reductive forms of physicalism arise. However, they are as paradoxical as "I want but I do not want" strategies that remind me of the Catullus's epigram: "Odi et amo, quare id faciam fortasse requiris. Nescio, sed fieri sentio et excrucior."[5] Non-reductive physicalists ultimately either reject non-reductivism in an ontological sense or they fall into dualism. Some positions are closer to a materialist monist option and others to the dualist alternative. The first alternative – reduction to reductive materialism – is argued by many, such as Jaegwon Kim (1989, referring to Putnam, Fodor and Donald Davidson's theses), or Tim Crane (1995) referring to mental causation.[6]

Additionally, philosophers of neuroscience have a tendency to attribute properties or activities either to the mind or to our physical bodies. Neither reductive physicalism nor dualism considers the possibility that an "I" – something surpassing but including mind and body – desires and thinks. In this sense, Maxwell Bennett and Peter Hacker (2003: Part I, Chapter 3) argue that neuroscientists are plagued by a "mereological fallacy," attributing psychological acts to the brain or the mind as part of a human being. This idea is drawn from Aristotle (*On the Soul* 408b 12–15). Anthony Kenny

(1971) referred to this mistake as "the homunculus fallacy," while Ludwig Wittgenstein noted that "only of a living human being can one say it has sensations; it sees, is blind; hears, is deaf; is conscious or unconscious" (*Philosophical Investigations*, & 281, [1958] 1986: 97c). A human being is an organic whole not reducible to the sum of its parts. Additionally, resorting to similar arguments, voices have also been raised against materialist reductionism in psychiatry and psychology. William Wimsatt (e.g., 2006) speaks about "functional localization fallacies" – that is, attributing a property of the whole to one of its parts.

I have suggested that ontological emergentism is a more fitting option for non-physicalists. This perspective tends to recognize the unity of the whole by downward or top-down causation. In contrast, epistemological or weak emergentism only recognizes bottom-up causation. As David C. Witherington asserts, "By embracing downward cause as ontologically real and irreducible, ontological emergence endows the emergent organization of a system – its structure, form, pattern – with causal significance" (2011: 71). He conceives top-down causation of the system as an Aristotelian formal and final cause (2011: 75):

> downward cause, via formal and final cause, offers explanation at the level of systems as wholes, capturing causality in the system qua system. The system as a whole cannot be fully understood through decomposition into temporally sequenced part-to-part relationships. It must also be simultaneously understood as a totality, in its own terms, by means of its organization and invariant ordering across the particularities of specific time and context.

This specific kind of emergentism seems close to offering a satisfactory solution. Recognition of formal and final causes is, in fact, a key step in such a self-organizational conception. These are not backward causes but intrinsic causes that are always present defining a direction, and guiding and choosing specific efficient bottom-up causes to achieve the pursued end. In his study of Aristotle's concept of teleology in nature, David Bostock indicates that the material is provided "in a relatively unstructured state, and it is the end or goal that then determines what precise structure it takes on" (2006: 57). Similar positions are held by an extended literature on neurophenomenology, "autopoiesis," the "enactive approach," "organizational teleology," and top-down causation, stressing the teleological and self-organizational character of living organisms.[7]

At this point, I will take up the idea of a formal/final cause of the unique acting "I." This idea is embodied in the Aristotelian hylomorphic conception of natural beings, a liberal naturalist position.[8] I believe this could prove a valid frame for the "non-physicalists" interviewed by Bourget and Chalmers. In addition, as Christopher Shields argues, "his [Aristotle's] hylomorphic rejection of reductive materialism does not recommend dualism" (2014: 332). This is a metaphysical position. Metaphysical entities are not necessarily supernatural entities. They are natural entities, like essences or causes, which are not directly known by the senses or instruments but by the mind, indirectly via the senses. A metaphysical, hylomorphic vision of the natural world captures the so-called formal cause (the essence or nature), the final cause of each natural entity, which is the soul (*psyché* for Aristotle) in the case of the human person, and also the efficient cause.[9] Fred Miller (1999) shows the incompatibility of non-reductionist materialism, emergentism and supervenience with the Aristotelian position. He points out that "Aristotle's philosophy of soul has a deep and recalcitrant top-down character, putting at odds with any currently popular counterpart in the philosophy of mind" (1999: 333). While avoiding a dualistic view of the human being, Aristotle's hylomorphic conception of the soul as the form of the body allows for two compatible non-reductionist explanations (*On the Soul* 403a 39–403b 2):

> the natural philosopher [the scientist] and the logician [philosopher, psychologist] will in every case offer different definitions, e.g., in answer to the question what is anger. The latter will call it a craving for retaliation, or something of the sort; the former will describe it as a surging of the blood and heat around the heart. The one is describing the matter, the other the form or formula of the essence.

As Vittorio Mathieu explains, "the physiological basis and the corresponding mental event are the same thing, in two different modes of existence" (Mathieu 1992: 115). Nonetheless, to make these explanations compatible, physicalism must be replaced by a liberal naturalist – not materialist – view. This may sound terribly naïve to our narrow contemporary scientific ears.[10] Though tensions remain in this field, the balance is clearly tipped in favor of an epistemological and ontological reduction of the mind to the physical brain, according to the underlying physicalist worldview. Yet, the situation is not hopeless: in the introduction to their book on reductionism, Maurice Schouten and Huib Looren de Jong (2007: 21), after saying that the most reductionist position on the book is John Bickle's, conclude:

> most of other authors, however, will acknowledge that to a more or lesser degree higher-level explanations are indispensable, but not autonomous; and that psychology and neuroscience are and should be connected and perhaps integrated, but not unified along physicalist lines.

In fact, as Grant S. Shields (2014) argues, based on neurological experiments, neuroscience does not prove that we cannot consciously cause or control our actions. Alfred Mele (2014) has philosophically argued that Benjamin Libet's famous experiments do not reject the existence of free-will (see also John Searle 2001, Chapter 9, specifically p. 290 about Libet's experiments).[11] In short, though a physicalist reductionism seems to predominate in the field of the philosophy of neuroscience, there still remains a tension in it. This tension has not yet been adequately solved by non reductivists or dualists. I have hinted that top-down conceptions as ontological emergentism and Aristotelian hylo-morphism may prove satisfactory ways out of this tension. With these positions in mind, let us then pass on to neuroeconomics.

The metaphysics of neuroeconomics

In his article "The Metaphysics of Neuroeconomics," Michiru Nagatsu maintains that "metaphysics is an indispensable part of scientific practice that provides scientists with worldviews and directions in research" (2010: 198). However, the first step is to clarify what it is that constitutes neuroeconomics. Neuroeconomics is not a well-defined and homogeneous research field. Roberto Fumagalli (2010: 121–22) lists five different definitions for it, while Caterina Marchionni and Jack Vromen (2010) narrow them down to two,[12] noting (2010: 104; 2012: 2):

> One might easily get the impression that neuroeconomics involves a one-way transfer of data and insights from neuroscience to economics and that if neuroeconomics is to make a lasting contribution, it should be to the field of economics. But this is not at all obvious. As most of the essays collected in this Special Issue recognize, there are at least two rather different strands within neuroeconomics: *Behavioural Economics in the Scanner* (BES) and *Neurocellular Economics* (NE) (Ross 2008; see also Vromen 2007). Whereas BES takes existing neuroscience to task to better understand economic behaviour, NE takes existing ("standard") economic theory to task to better understand neural activity in the brain. Whereas BES argues for radical, if not revolutionary changes in economic theory, NE argues for radical, if not revolutionary changes in neuroscience.
>
> As several authors in this special issue observe, some leading proponents of neuroeconomics expect that neuroscientists have more to gain from introducing standard economic theory in the study of neural activity than economists can gain by trying to accommodate neuroscientific data and insights in the study of traditional economic phenomena.

In addition, Colin Camerer et al. (2005: 10) make a distinction between neu-roeconomics as an "incremental" approach (adding variables to standard economics) and as a "radical" approach that might deeply change economics. The former kind of neuroeconomics tries to analyze economics using neu-roscience experiments because, as mentioned, the rationality of both rational choice theory and expected utility theory – the basis for standard economics – has been challenged and often refuted by behavioral economics.

The second – according to Marchionni and Vromen's classification (2010) – type of neuroeconomics, *Neurocellular Economics*, advocated by Don Ross (2005 and 2008), assumes that the brain's internal logic is the neoclassical economic logic. Ross states that "the first high-profile publication in neuroeconomics, Paul Glimcher (2003), is the basic methodological statement of NE [Neurocellular Economics]" (2008, p. 474). In effect, for Glimcher, "neuroeconomics will play a critical role in explaining how the brains of humans and other animals actually solve the maximization problems these two other disciplines [behavioural ecologist and neurobiology] have identified" (2003: 321).[13] For Ross, as summarized by John Davis, "individuals are collections of optimizing sub-personal neural agents who interact in coordination games internal to the individual" (Davis 2011: 127). His conception is based on evolutionary theory and is supplemented by the postulation of interactions between individuals that sculpt and re-sculpt them due to shared language. Though Ross makes a good case for his thesis, I will not delve into this topic here, because it concerns the status of neuroscience rather than economics.

The first type of neuroeconomics, then, as Glenn Harrison and Ross (2010: 187) describe it:

> consists in repeating protocols that putatively demonstrate human "irrationality" under neuroimaging, and trying to show how "anomalies" in rational choice have origins and explanations in framing effects that result from the computational processing architecture of the brain.

These neuroeconomists recommend replacing the traditional economic notion of utility – the mathematical representation of consistent preferences questioned by actual experiments of behavioural theory – with a "neural" notion of utility, a "true," "objective" representation of utility, measured in terms of the activation of particular areas of the brain.[14] In other words, the intention to overcome the oversimplified analysis of standard economics with a refined search into the causes and neural content of preferences, far from doing away with the materialistic representation of utilities, deepens the materialist approach. It thus skips the realm of free conscious decisions – rational or not – to move straight into their supposedly materialistic causes. Neuroeconomics opens the black box only to find neural mechanisms. As Mario Graziano (2013: 32) explains, in neuroeconomics "[t]he utility of a choice is not determined by formal preference relationships, but rather it is the result of a complex [neural] mechanism." He adds (2013: 40), "the *Homo Economicus* is replaced by the *Homo neurobiologicus*, whose behaviour derives for a neurobiological development able to generate sentiments, beliefs, actions and the capacity to make decisions." This cooperation between economics and neuroscience may seem sensible. As John Dupré (2001: 3) explains: "It would be nice for economists to have an access to an independent theory that helped to explain why people have the particular endogenously generated tastes they do, and here there is a natural alliance between economics and the parts of biology just mentioned."

Notwithstanding this, many economists frown upon neuroeconomics. Its most severe critics, Faruk Gul and Wofgang Pesendorfer (2008), point to the definition of economics: while neuroeconomics pays attention to the choice process involved in opening the brain's black box, for Gul and Pesendorfer, economics deals with rational choices under specific conditions. Relevant data are revealed by observable external information, not by information about the brain's internal interactions. According to these authors, neuroeconomics addresses other concerns and has nothing to do with economics.[15]

It thus seems that there are different ontological conceptions about the mind behind these different perspectives. Nagatsu concludes (2010: 203), "In this paper, I have attempted to identify a genuine, metaphysical disagreement between the advocates and critics of neuroeconomics. The disagreement arises when scientists take different stances on the same object of investigation." Similarly, Robert McMaster (2011: 119) finds divergent ontological positions regarding the structure of the brain in a number of neuroeconomic research studies.

However, regardless of their different ontological views, they all imply materialist notions of the brain. Debates between economists and neuroeconomists and also within the neuroeconomic field are largely methodological. When they move beyond this dimension onto the metaphysical realm, they do not question their physicalist perspective. For example, Kurt Dopfer (2005: 23–24) suggests that the model of *Homo sapiens* – that should replace the *Homo oeconomicus* – includes neural, cognitive and psychological aspects, but then actually reduces the last two aspects to just the first, the neural.

Consequently, neuroeconomics seems plagued by paradox. Its goal is to open the black box of preferences – a worthy endeavor as part of efforts to learn more about choice causes and its processes as well as the ends of economic agents. Neuroeconomics intends to replace economics' typical "as if" or *ceteris paribus* assumptions with realistic "as is" observations. However, this intention leads neuroeconomics to eliminate human intentionality and freedom: there is ultimately nothing but neural interactions. Knowing them, we will be able to predict human responses in different economic (in a broad sense) scenarios, because "neural activity causally determines economic choices" (Fehr and Ragel 2001: 3).

Nonetheless, several voices have risen in opposition. For example, basing his claims on specific neuroeconomic experiments, Alessandro Antonietti (2010) concludes that neuro-mental correspondences only achieve a heuristic purpose, at most providing conjectures, "which must be verified by psychologists in the context of mental (and not neural) phenomena and which must be explained in psychological (and not neurobiological) terms"(2010: 217). Jaakko Kuorikoski and Petri Ylikoski (2010) also point to the priority of psychology, relying on a theory of explanation in which higher-level explanations cannot be reduced to lower-level ones. They emphasize that "neuroeconomic data are explanatory and relevant only when they inform a causal and explanatory account of the psychology of human decision-making" (2010: 227). Similarly, Roberta Muramatsu (2009: 283) argues that "[a] careful look at some experiments lead us to suggest that they identify some interesting statistical associations (correlations) between variables (parameters) but there is no room for an indisputable move to a 'causation talk'." Harrison (2008) also assigns a priority role to psychology. Franz Dietrich and Christian List (2016) uphold – based on a broad naturalist position like the one endorsed in this book – that mental states are real and that economics should not explain behavior in terms of brain neural processes. Thus, it seems it would be more sensible to note a correlation between neural activities and psychological movements while prioritizing psychology. This does sound like a more prudent approach, which is naturalist but not physicalist – that is, a liberal naturalist approach.

An additional key problem remains unsolved. Economics not only has a descriptive, predictive or explicative role: it also serves a normative purpose – what should an economic agent or an economic policy look for? Typically, the answer is maximizing individual or social utility, but, what is the definition of true utility, a hedonic utility? Or should more refined aspects of happiness be included, transforming happiness into more than a descriptive, normative concept? In recent research, economics' normative role is increasingly being taken into account and developed. For example, Amartya Sen's capability approach focuses on capabilities, opportunities or freedoms that people should have. How are capabilities related to utility? Happiness economics also pursues a different sort of normative goal. Moreover, which concept of happiness should we adopt? Crespo and Belén Mesurado (2015) argue for a human "flourishing" notion of happiness, which is a very refined construct that includes social impact of individual actions. What are the neural counterparts of the components found in flourishing? It seems that physicalism's closure does not apply to these kinds of elements. As Nuno Martins notes, "[t]he relevant conception of reality in neural analysis is that of an open system" (2011: 255). Not everything is deterministic – not even inside the brain.

In brief, I do not deny the relation between neural interactions and behavior, nor do I underestimate neuroeconomic experiments' contributions. However, apart from actions clearly determined by the brain, other behaviors are only conditioned by it, and there is room for intentionality and free decisions. Neuroeconomics will contribute to economics under the condition that it recognizes this most human characteristic of the human person which is the root of uncertainty but also of creativity.

Conclusion

Modern philosophy has leaned towards reductionism, reducing spirit to matter, human rationality to instrumental rationality, classical formal and final causes to material and efficient causes, freedom to determinism. This set of reductions has shaped a physicalist, materialistic metaphysics that pervades modern science and curtails its explanatory capability. Tensions in neuroscience and in social sciences point to the limited scope of this metaphysical worldview. Neuroeconomics addresses these tensions but tries to solve them in a materialist fashion. This reveals the need for a broader metaphysical perspective in science. The materialist approach in neuroscience and neuroeconomics is a recent development. Barely 50 years ago, German pathologist Franz Büchner (1957: 205), faced with the reality of the close link between mind and body, stated:

> The human body is expression of the human soul and represents not only the manifestations of our conscience but also the whole no conscious sphere. Thus, we face the question whether the soul is not the dominant principle of human existence, if it is not essentially the creator of our body and if the latter is not a creature of our soul. In another stage of these reflections we arrived to think that what is truly real in our human being is our soul and that our body behaves only as symbol of our soul.

Whether or not this assertion is true, it is worth noting that, looking at the same reality, this interpretation opposes that of neuroscientists and neuroeconomists. We perceive a relation, but causality is a metaphysical reality that is not captured by our senses but by our mind. True metaphysics is required to secure proper knowledge. Hopefully, the future will bring new and better explanations and practices, with a broader naturalism as a more humane option. A metaphysically-sensible approach would be integrative rather than reductive, underscoring psychology and mind (see Craver and Alexandrova 2008). At present, as noted in the previous sections, a tension still remains between physicalism and the recognition of human freedom, both in the philosophy of neuroscience and in neuroeconomics. However, the balance is tipped in favor of the former: neuroeconomics is an almost completely "restrictive or scientific" naturalist approach. In this regard, neuroeconomics takes a step beyond behavioural and evolutionary economics towards physicalism. In addition, it is clear that this view pertains plainly to a "reverse imperialism" approach, as there are no precedents within economics of a consideration of neurosciences. In the next chapter I will tackle happiness economics, a concept that may or may not fit with neuroeconomics, depending on the notion of happiness endorsed by it.

Notes

1 There is a massive amount of literature on these topics. I am well aware that this chapter will offer a simplified exposition.
2 For a longer description and criticism, see Hands (2001: 165–170).
3 Strictly speaking it also includes behaviourism, but this current is outdated.
4 On contemporary forms of dualism, see Howard Robinson (2011).
5 Carmen 85, "I hate and I love. Why do I do it, perchance you might ask? I don't know, but I feel it happening to me and I'm burning up."
6 For example, he concludes: "The lesson of the mental causation debate is that there is no well-motivated physicalist position which is not an identity theory" (1995: 1).
7 See, for example, Varela and Thompson (1991), Thompson (2004), Di Paolo (2005), Mossio et al (2009), Auletta et al (2008).

8   According to the *Encyclopaedia Britannica*: "Hylomorphism, (from Greek *hylē*, 'matter'; *morphē*, 'form'), in philosophy, metaphysical view according to which every natural body consists of two intrinsic principles, one potential, namely, primary matter, and one actual, namely, substantial form. It was the central doctrine of Aristotle's philosophy of nature" (https://www.britannica.com/topic/hylomorphism, retrieved September 15, 2016). See also Jaworski (2016).

9   In my forthcoming paper, I develop the hylomorphic account.

10 Robert Pasnau (2012: 492) asserts: "It is hard to see how we, today, could accept the existence of anything like a substantial form [...] Our physics and biology have developed in ways that do not tolerate any such central organizing principle".

11 Searle criticizes the compatibilist position sustaining that free-will and determinism are compatible (2001: 278), though his position about the mind-body problem is fluctuating.

12 And also Harrison and Ross (2010), and Glimcher et al (2009: 7).

13 Geerat J. Vermeij poses a similar thesis: a parallelism between economic and all natural processes. He states: "the fundamental processes operating in economic systems – competition, cooperation, selection, adaptation, and the feedback between living things and their environment – apply to all such systems, from those as small as a cell to human societies and to the biosphere as a whole" (2004: 3).

14 Fumagalli (2013) raises doubts about the accuracy of these measurements. This is a generalized criticism of neuroeconomics.

15 See also David Levine (2011) for a similar argument.

References

Antonietti, A. (2008). "Do neurobiological data help us to understand economic decisions better?," *Journal of Economic Methodology* 17/2: 207–218.

Aristotle (1957). *On the Soul*, trans. W. S. Hett, Loeb Classical. Cambridge, MA: Harvard University Press.

Aristotle (1995). *The Complete Works of Aristotle. The Revised Oxford Translation*, J. Barnes (ed.). Princeton, NJ: Princeton University Press, 6th printing with corrections.

Auletta, G., Ellis, G. F. R. and L. Jaeger (2008). "Top-down causation by information control: from a philosophical problem to a scientific research programme," *Journal of the Royal Society Interface* 5: 1159–1172.

Bennett, M. and P. Hacker (2003). *Philosophical Foundations of Neuroscience*. Oxford: Blackwell.

Bickle, J., Mandik, P., Landreth, A. (2010). "The philosophy of neuroscience", *Stanford Encyclopedia of Philosophy*, ed. E. Zalta, online, http://plato.stanford.edu/entries/neuroscience/, retrieved June 30, 2014.

Bostock, D. (2006). *Space, Time, Matter and Form. Essays on Aristotle's Physics*. Oxford: Clarendon Press.

Bourget, D. and D. J. Chalmers (2014). "What do Philosophers Believe?," *Philosophical Studies* 170: 465–500.

Büchner, F. ([1957] 1969). *Cuerpo y espíritu en la medicina actual*. Madrid: Rialp (*Vom geistegen Standort der modernen Medizin*, Freiburg: Hans Ferdinand Schulz Verlag).

Camerer, C., G. Loewenstein and D. Prelec (2005). "How Neuroeconomics Can Inform Economics," *Journal of Economic Literature* 43/1: 9–64.

Chalmers, D. (1996). *The Conscious Mind*. Oxford: Oxford University Press.

Churchland, P. M. (1981). "Eliminative Materialism and the Propositional Attitudes," *The Journal of Philosophy*, 78/2: 67–90, http://www.sfu.ca/~kathleea/docs/Eliminative%20materialism.pdf, retrieved January 29, 2015.

Crane, T. (1995). "The Mental Causation Debate," *Proceedings of the Aristotelian Society Supplementary* LXIX: 211–236, http://www.timcrane.com/uploads/2/5/2/4/25243881/the_mental_causation_debate.pdf, retrieved May 12, 2016.

Craver, C. F. and A. Alexandrova, (2008). "No Revolution Necessary: Neural Mechanisms for Economics," *Economics and Philosophy* 29: 381–406.

Crespo, R. F. (forthcoming). "Aristotelian hylomorphism: A framework for non-physicalist philosophers about philosophy of mind," in P.A. Gargiulo and H. L. Mesones (eds.), *Psychiatry and Neuroscience Update: Bridging the Divide. Update 2016.* Dordrecht: Springer.

Crespo, R. F. and B. Mesurado (2015). "Happiness Economics, Eudaimonia and Positive Psychology: From Happiness Economics to Flourishing Economics," *Journal of Happiness Studies,* 16/4: 931–946. doi:10.1007/s10902–10014–9541–9544.

Davidson, D. (1980). "Mental Events." In D. Davidson (ed.) *Essays on Actions and Events.* Oxford: Clarendon Press.

Di Paolo, E. A. (2005). "Autopoiesis, adaptability, teleology, agency," *Phenomenology and the Cognitive Sciences* 4: 429–452.

Dilworth, C. (2006). *The Metaphysics of Science,* 2nd edition. Dordrecht: Springer.

Dietrich, F. and C. List (2016). "Mentalism versus Behaviourism in Economics: A Philosophy-of-Science Perspective," *Economics and Philosophy* 31/2: 249–281.

Dopfer, K. (2005). "Evolutionary Economics: A Theoretical Framework." In K. Dopfer (ed.), *The Evolutionary Foundation of Economics.* Cambridge: Cambridge University Press.

Dupré, J. (2001). *Human Nature and the Limits of Science.* Oxford: Oxford University Press.

Fehr, E. and A. Rangel (2011). "Neuroeconomic Foundations of Economic Choice – Recent Advances," *Journal of Economic Perspectives* 25/4: 3–30.

Feser, E. (2006). *Philosophy of Mind.* London: Oneworld Publications.

Flanagan, O. and D. Barack (2010). "Neuroexistentialism," *EurAmerica* 40/3: 573–590.

Fodor, J. A. (1974). "Special Sciences: Or, the Disunity of Science as a Working Hypothesis," *Synthese* 28/2: 97–115.

Fumagalli, R. (2010). "The disunity of neuroeconomics: a methodological appraisal," *Journal of Economic Methodology* 17/2: 119–131.

Fumagalli, R. (2013). "The Futile Search for True Utility," *Economics and Philosophy* 29: 325–347.

Glimcher, P. (2003). *Decisions, Uncertainty and the Brain.* Cambridge, MA: MIT Press.

Glimcher, P. W., C. Camerer, E. Fehr and R. Poldrack (2009). *Neuroeconomics: Decision Making and the Brain.* Amsterdam: Elsevier.

Graziano, M. (2013). *Epistemology of Decision.* Dordrecht: Springer.

Gul, F. and W. Pesendorfer (2008). "The Case for Mindless Economics." In A. Caplin and A. Schotter (eds.) *The Foundations of Positive and Normative Economics.* Oxford: Oxford University Press.

Hands, D. W. (2001). *Reflection without Rules: Economic Methodology and Contemporary Science Theory.* Cambridge and New York: Cambridge University Press.

Harrison, G. W. (2008). "Neuroeconomics: A Critical Consideration," *Economics and Philosophy* 24: 303–344.

Harrison, G. W. and D. Ross, 2010. "The methodologies of neuroeconomics," *Journal of Economic Methodology* 17/2: 185–196.

Hasker, W. (1999). *The Emergent Self.* Ithaca, NY: Cornell University Press.

Jaworski, W. (2011). *Philosophy of Mind. A Comprehensive Introduction*. Malden and Oxford: Willey-Blackwell.

Jaworski, W. (2012). "Powers, Structures, and Minds." In R. Groff and J. Greco (eds.), *Powers and Capacities in Philosophy: The New Aristotelianism*. New York: Routledge.

Jaworski, W. (2016). *Structure and the Metaphysics of Mind: How Hylomorphism Solves the Mind-Body Problem*. Oxford: Oxford University Press.

Kenny, A. (1971). "The homunculus fallacy." In M. Grene (ed.), *Interpretations of life and mind: Essays around the problem of reduction*. London: Routledge.

Kim, J. (1989). "The Myth of Nonreductive Materialism," *Proceedings and Addresses of the American Philosophical Association* 63/3: 31–47.

Kuorikoski, J. and P. Ylikoski, (2010). "Explanatory relevance across disciplinary boundaries: the case of neuroeconomics," *Journal of Economic Methodology* 17/2: 219–228.

Levine, D. K. (2011). "Neuroeconomics?" *International Review of Economics* 58: 287–305.

Löffler, W. (2007). "What Naturalists Always Knew about Freedom: A Case Study in Narrative Sources of 'Scientific Facts'." In G. Gasser (ed.), *How Successful is Naturalism?*, Publications of the Austrian Ludwig Wittgenstein Society. New Series. Volume 4, Frankfurt, Paris, Ebikon, Lancaster, New Brunswick: Ontos Verlag.

Madden, J. D. (2013). *Mind, Matter and Nature*. Washington, DC: CUA Press.

Marchionni, C. and J. Vromen (2010). "Neuroeconomics: Hype or Hope?," *Journal of Economic Methodology* 17/2: 103–106.

Martins, N. (2011). "Can neuroscience inform economics? Rationality, emotions and preference formation," *Cambridge Journal of Economics* 35/2: 251–267.

Mathieu, V. (1992). "What Kind of Unity?." In G. del Re (ed.), *Brain Research and the Mind-Body Problem: Epistemological and Metaphysical Issues*. Vatican City: Pontificia Academiae Scientiarum Scripta Varia, 79.

McLaughlin, B. and K. Bennett (2011). "Supervenience," *Stanford Encyclopedia of Philosophy*, http://plato.stanford.edu/entries/supervenience/, retrieved January 29, 2015.

McMaster, R. (2011). "Neuroeconomics: A Skeptical View," *Real-World Economics Review* 58: 113–125.

Mele, A. (2014). *Free: Why Science Hasn't Disproved Free Will*. Oxford and New York: Oxford University Press.

Miller, F. D., Jr. (1999). "Aristotle's Philosophy of Soul," *The Review of Metaphysics* 53/2: 309–337.

Mossio, M., C. Saborido and Á. Moreno (2009). "An organizational account of biological functions," *British Journal for the Philosophy of Science* 60/4: 813–841.

Muramatsu, R. (2009). "The Possibilities of Neuroeconomics: An Account through the Lens of Economic Methodology." In G. Marqués (ed.) *Racionalidad, Economía e Interdisciplinariedad*. Buenos Aires: CIECE (FCE-UBA).

Nagatsu, M. (2010). "Function and mechanism. The metaphysics of neuroeconomics," *Journal of Economic Methodology* 17/2: 197–205.

O'Connor, T. and H. Yu Wong (2012). "Emergent properties," *Stanford Encyclopedia of Philosophy*, http://plato.stanford.edu/entries/properties-emergent/, retrieved January 30, 2015.

Pasnau, R. (2012). "Mind and Hylomorphism." In J. Marenbon (ed.), *The Oxford Handbook of Medieval Philosophy*. Oxford: Oxford University Press.

Putnam, H. (1975). "The Nature of Mental States," in *Mind, Language and Reality: Philosophical Papers*, vol. II. Cambridge: Cambridge University Press.

Ramsey, W. (2013). "Eliminative materialism," *Stanford Encyclopedia of Philosophy*, http://plato.stanford.edu/entries/materialism-eliminative/, retrieved January 29, 2015.

Robb, D. and J. Heil (2013). "Mental Causation," *Stanford Encyclopedia of Philosophy*, http://plato.stanford.edu/entries/mental-causation/, retrieved January 30, 2015.

Robinson, H. (2011). "Dualism," *Stanford Encyclopedia of Philosophy*, http://plato.stanford.edu/entries/dualism/, retrieved March 4, 2015.

Ross, D. (2005). *Economic Theory and Cognitive Science: Microexplanation*. Cambridge, MA: MIT Press.

Ross, D. (2008). "Two styles of neuroeconomics," *Economics and Philosophy* 24/3: 473–483.

Ryle, G. ([1949] 2009). *The Concept of the Mind*. Abingdon: Routledge (60th anniversary edition).

Schouten, M. and H. Looren de Jong (2007). "Mind Matters: the Roots of Reductionism." In M. Schouten and H. Looren de Jong (eds.), *The Matter of the Mind*. Oxford: Blackwell.

Searle, J. R. (2001). *Rationality in Action*. Cambridge, MA, and London: MIT Press.

Shields, C. (2014). *Aristotle*, 2nd edition. Abingdon: Routledge.

Shields, G. S. (2014). "Neuroscience and Conscious Causation: Has Neuroscience Shown that We Cannot Control Our Actions?," *Review of Philosophical Psychology* 5: 565–582.

Smart, J. J. C. (2007). "The Mind/Brain Identity Theory," *Stanford Encyclopedia of Philosophy*, http://plato.stanford.edu/entries/mind-identity/#Typ, retrieved January 29, 2015.

Stoljar, D. (2015). "Physicalism," *Stanford Encyclopedia of Philosophy*, http://plato.stanford.edu/entries/physicalism/, retrieved January 29, 2015.

Thompson, E. (2004). "Life and mind: From autopoiesis to neurophenomenology. A tribute to Francisco Varela," *Phenomenology and the Cognitive Sciences* 3: 381–398.

Varela, F. and E. Thompson (1991). *The Embodied Mind*. Cambridge, MA: MIT Press.

Vermeij, G. J. (2004). *Nature. An Economic History*. Princeton and Oxford: Princeton University Press.

Wimsatt, W. (2006). "Reductionism and its heuristics: Making methodological reductionism honest," *Synthese* 151: 445–475.

Witherington, D. C., (2011). "Taking Emergence Seriously: The Centrality of Circular Causality for Dynamic Systems Approaches to Development," *Human Development* 54: 66–92

Wittgenstein, L. ([1958] 1986). *Philosophical Investigations*. Oxford: Blackwell.

6 Happiness economics

Happiness economics, one of the new and growing branches of the reverse imperialist wave, incorporates elements from social psychology and ethics into economics. However, given that classical political economy addressed the concerns of happiness and ethics, as Sen (1987) noted in his take on the ethical-related tradition of economics, happiness economics features a mixture of insights coming from outside economics and other old elements coming from within. Whether the approach is naturalistic, scientific or liberal and if it takes practical reason into consideration will depend on the concept of happiness that is involved. However, the mere fact that it explicitly deals with an end – as is happiness – opens the door to the idea of practical reason, provided that its conception of happiness is not materialistic. This makes this approach somehow different from the other currents considered previously.

In this chapter I will first present a brief history of happiness in economics (section 1). Then, I will consider the different conceptions of happiness in current happiness economics (section 2). One of the concepts of happiness that has been recently promoted in the psychological literature that I will emphasize is the idea of "flourishing." In section 3, I will describe this notion and explain how the classical Aristotelian *eudaimonia* or "flourishing" fits the liberal naturalistic economic position. I will also relate this notion with the ideas of "calling" and "flow," two concepts developed by the recent branch of knowledge called "positive psychology," and will show how these three notions are linked to one another. In a paper I wrote in collaboration with a colleague, we proposed replacing the notion of "happiness" by that of "flourishing" in the economics of happiness (Crespo and Mesurado, 2015). In a subsequent paper we built an instrument to measure flourishing, applied it and related it to other instruments, we measured calling and flow in the same sample, and found positive correlations between the three variables (Mesurado et al 2016). This way of conceptualizing and measuring happiness emphasizes practical reason. Section 4 will deal with these measurement topics.

Happiness and economics

Since its inception, economics has been meant to contribute to people's happiness. For Aristotle, this discipline was about how to use things in order to have a "good life" – the Greek philosopher's notion of happiness (see Crespo 2006). Adam Smith viewed happiness as tranquility and enjoyment (cf. [1759] 1976, III.3.30: 149), with commercial society providing the freedom and security that promoted them and that prevented misery (see, e.g., Rasmussen 2011: 96). Thomas Robert Malthus noted that Smith mixed the causes of the wealth of nations and the causes of happiness of the lower orders of society (cf. [1798] 1914, II: 126). The "Greatest Happiness Principle" is repeatedly mentioned in Jeremy Bentham's *Economic Writings* as the aim of political economy (1954: see term in index, p569), a view also shared by John Stuart Mill. More recently, many studies of "civil happiness" – viewed as the wealth of nations by Neapolitan economists, notably Antonio Genovesi – have also linked economics and happiness (see, e. g., Sabetti 2012 and Chapter 9 of this book). Clearly, however, the notions of happiness used by these authors are quite different,[1] while they all consider happiness as something positive different from wealth. The same can be said of the notions of happiness used by Alfred Marshall, Cecil Pigou and Henry Wicksteed (see Bruni and Zamagni 2016: 74–76; and Steedman 2011: 23–34).

David Hume, a philosopher and friend of Smith, wrote a number of essays on economics. In one of these essays ([1752] 1970: 21–22), he emphatically argued that economic growth enhanced happiness. Economists have consistently shared this belief, which is why a 1974 article by Richard Easterlin came as a shock to many of them. The so-called "Easterlin paradox" showed a weak correlation between income and increased happiness, fueling a new wave – indeed, a tsunami – of works on economics and happiness: papers, books, and handbooks with theoretical studies and empirical surveys – some of which have been quoted here.[2]

Easterlin's article proved to be a felicitous turn of events, as it reinforced the need for economics to refocus on human ends. As is frequently noted in this book, in the 20th century, economics has considered ends as given, limiting itself to study the best allocation of means to achieve those ends. As Lionel Robbins (1935: 29) argues, "economics is not concerned at all with any ends, *as such*. It is concerned with ends in so far as they affect the disposition of means. It takes the ends as given in scales of relative valuation." However, this approach has some disadvantages, most notably, since there is no real action without ends, if ends are given, economics is not a science of real action but of past actions. Talcott Parsons wisely captured the problems stemming from this attempt back in 1934: "To be sure, an 'end' may refer to a state of affairs which can be observed by the actor himself or someone else after it has been accomplished." Robbins's ends, Parsons concluded, are not ends (1934: 513–4) – they are, if properly construed, a result: "The scale of valuation is not a factor in action but merely a resultant, a reflection" (1934: 516). In the same vein, as has already been quoted, Frank Knight noted (1956: 128–29) that "the end is rarely or never actually given in any strict sense of the word; rather, it is in some degree redefined in the course of the activity directed toward realizing it." He also remarked that "to the extent to which an end is given, it is not really the end in the sense of finality." Ends are not given; they are actually produced in action processes. Means and ends are mutually interactive and determined by one another, and to focus only on the allocation of means, merely a technical proceeding, is a partial undertaking that neglects the most interesting part of human action: decisions concerning ends. Recall that I argued that this approach stems from the modern Humean reduction of practical reason to technical or instrumental reason. As mentioned, economics is currently revisiting ends, and happiness economics illustrates this trend, while showing economists' growing concern with the meaning of life and revealing the need to carefully appraise the strengths and weaknesses of happiness economics. This is a felicitous process according to the theses of this book.

Different concepts of happiness

A problem besieging happiness economics is that a variety of notions of happiness have found their way into this field, with "life satisfaction" and "subjective well-being" (SWB – an indicator used by the World Values Survey) being the primary happiness concepts. Thus a plethora of happiness definitions and metrics has surfaced. In addition, Bruno Frey and Aloys Stutzer (2002: 5) also refer to an "objective" approach that endeavors to capture subjective well-being by measuring brain waves with a so-called *hedonometer* or *hedometer*.

These differences prove to be relevant. They are not just neutral measurements as they underlie different anthropological conceptions of happiness. Although happiness economics has tried to limit itself to being a positive or descriptive theory, it unavoidably commits itself to specific values and has normative implications. The dimensions chosen to define happiness and the weights assigned to each dimension involve a specific conception of mankind and also guide social policies. As argued in Chapter 1, until the 1950s, a positivistic value-free scientific mind-set largely prevailed in economics, but evidence of the involvement of values in scientific research has increasingly pushed it aside. In his recent book, Harvard philosopher Hilary Putnam (2004) elaborates on the *entanglement* of facts and values, present in many human sciences fields of study, using the "collapse of the fact-value dichotomy" to "explain the significance of this issue particularly for economics." He argues that ends are in fact important in economics and can be discussed rationally. Ends cannot be removed from economics because evaluation and description are interwoven and interdependent (Putnam 2004: 3).[3] If this applies to economics, there is no doubt that it also applies to other social sciences. These ideas are not new; the old traditions of hermeneutics and practical reason maintain the essentially normative and ethical character of human sciences. These traditions were overshadowed by positivism in recent centuries, but they have made a comeback in the second half of the 20th century, with practical science being strongly propelled in Germany. In Chapter 1, I mentioned the collective work edited by Manfred Riedel

(1972–1974), entitled *Rehabilitierung der praktischen Philosophie*, which may be deemed a hallmark of this trend that views the practical paradigm as a reaction against the prevailing requirement for value-neutrality in the realm of social sciences. Similar conclusions have been drawn by pragmatists, hermeneutics experts, and critical theorists. Charles Taylor combines the hermeneutical and Aristotelian practical reason approaches, concluding that "these sciences cannot be *wertfrei* [value-free]; they are moral sciences" (1985b: 57). Bent Flyvbjerg provides another example with his (somewhat Aristotelian) "phronetic social science" (see, e.g., 2001) proposal, which has made quite an impact.

Psychology is no exception when it comes to non-neutral data, as Taylor has also noted (1985a: Chapters 5 and 8). So have Brent Slife and Richard Williams (1995) and Frank C. Richardson, Blaine Fowers and Charles Guignon (1999). The very subtitle of Slife and Williams's book, *Discovering Hidden Assumptions in Behavioural Sciences*, points to the need of unveiling underlying assumptions or interpretations. The subtitle of the book by Richardson, Fowers and Guignon, *Moral Dimensions of Theory and Practice*, is also quite revealing. Scientific value-neutrality is itself an ethical stance, and these authors argue for a new interpretative psychology.

Clearly, then, a discussion on the appropriate concept of happiness used in happiness economics is highly relevant for the aims of this book: hedonistic conceptions leave little room for practical reason and freedom. They tend to be restrictive or scientific naturalistic positions rather than liberal naturalistic ones.

Over time, hedonistic notions of happiness have also come under criticism, as efforts have been made to redefine happiness in more *eudaimonic* terms. Both Julia Annas (2001: 127) and Pierluigi Barrotta (2008: 149) critically quote the same passage from Richard Layard's *Happiness: Lessons from a New Science* (2005: 4): "Happiness is feeling good, and misery is feeling bad." Layard shares Bentham's view that happiness is a hedonic reality that can be measured, and, at the same time, he rejects Mill's qualitative dimension of happiness. Additionally, Layard (2007: 162) states that "good tastes are those which increase happiness, and vice versa." Aloys Wijngaards (2012: 103) summarizes his analysis of Layard's concept of happiness, asserting that it "is to be understood in a hedonic sense, based upon a pleasure/pain duality" (see also Atherson 2011: 7, Steedman 2011: 36–39 and Grenholm 2011: 45–48). Nevertheless, this is a rudimentary notion of happiness – enduring hardship is part of true happiness. As Annas suggests, "a life of having all your desires fulfilled without the problems created by human neediness leaves humans with nothing to live *for*, nothing to propel them onwards" (2011: 137). Indeed, true happiness goes beyond life satisfaction.

Nick Begley (2010) has reviewed the current literature on subjective well-being (SWB) surveys and physiological (objective) happiness studies, concluding that these two psychological approaches to happiness are widely regarded as hedonic. Bruni and Porta (2007: xx–xxiv) believe that economic theories trying to indirectly understand the logic of happiness by explaining the

"Easterlin paradox" do not consider the role of sociality as relationality. A quick review of the literature on happiness economics and survey questions to measure SWB reveals that words associated with happiness have hedonic connotations – "tastes," "feelings," "desires," "satisfaction," "pleasure and displeasure."

A recent European survey of "flourishing" – a more comprehensive notion than that of SWB (including positive emotions, engagement, interest, meaning, purpose, self-esteem, optimism, resilience, vitality, self-determination and positive relationships) – reveals SWB shortcomings. This survey's findings (Huppert and So 2009: 6; and Huppert and So 2013, 846–847) are as follows:

> The correlation between flourishing and life satisfaction in the ESS [European Social Survey] data is 0.32. For the population as a whole, 12.2% met criteria for flourishing, and 17.7% had high life satisfaction scores. The percentage who had high life satisfaction and were flourishing was 7.2%. One third of flourishing people did not score high on life satisfaction, and half of the sample population with high life satisfaction did not meet flourishing criteria. Therefore, these two are clearly different concepts, so a single life satisfaction metric is not an adequate substitute for a flourishing measurement. Furthermore, a life satisfaction metric would lack the greater texture of a flourishing measurement, whose elements can also be examined separately according to temporal or social changes.

These findings indicate the need to identify an adequate concept to measure happiness. As noted earlier, although happiness economics seems to be merely descriptive, this description refers to survey questions containing values. Moreover, happiness economics leads to policy-making, thus becoming normative. Therefore, in all fairness, values should be brought to the table and discussed rationally – and this is the task of practical reason. Aristotle developed a kind of practical reasoning about the values (the highest good) contributing to happiness: *eudaimonia*, a notion that fits in nicely with the idea of flourishing.[4]

Fortunately, during the last several decades, the literature on happiness and well-being has assiduously paid attention to this ancient Greek concept of *eudaimonia* (see Huta and Waterman 2014; Huta 2013; Ryff and Singer 2008; Ryff 1989; Keyes and Annas 2009; Fowers 2012a and 2012b; Richardson 2012), considering it a richer concept than the standard notion of happiness. Bruni and Porta (2011: 168–169) explain how the *eudaimonian* conception of happiness provides a satisfactory explanation of the Easterlin paradox. This literature usually quotes Aristotle's *Nicomachean Ethics* as a fundamental source of inspiration. Stemming from this interest, a whole literature on "human flourishing" has arisen, also referring to Aristotle. Indeed, "flourish" is now the standard way of translating *eudaimonia* (see Keyes 2002 and 2007; Frederickson and Losada 2005; Ryff and Singer 2008; Seligman 2011; Hone et al 2014; Huppert and So 2013; Diener et al 2009).

Flourishing, calling and flow

Flourishing, a construct that includes eudaimonic dimensions (but also hedonic dimensions – Aristotle thinks that pleasure, when it is well governed, contributes to *eudaimonia*), is regarded in the above-mentioned literature as a richer way of assessing people's well-being than subjective or objective well-being, commonly known as "happiness." In Aristotle we can distinguish, first, an ultimate or final end of human beings (i.e., *Eudaimonia*); second, ends that are good for the sake of themselves and also good for the sake of the final end (i.e., pleasure, honour and virtue); and, third, merely instrumental means. For this author, *eudaimonia* can only be achieved but through the practice of virtues within the *polis*, because the human being is a political animal. In addition, a minimum of material instrumental means are also necessary for *eudaimonia*. In the above mentioned paper about the relation between flourishing, calling and flow (Mesurado et al 2016), these Aristotelian characteristics of *eudaimonia* are represented in "flourishing" as a psychological construct by including emotional, psychological and social well-being in it. In effect, for Carol Ryff and Burton Singer (2008), a eudaimonic perspective includes happiness, personal growth, giving to others and living in accordance with values.

Though it is a new psychological construct, "flourishing" has been characterized in distinct but related ways (see, for example, Frederickson and Losada 2005: 678 – "To *flourish* means to live within an optimal range of human functioning, one that connotes goodness, generativity, growth, and resilience" Huppert and So 2013: 837 – "a combination of feeling good and functioning effectively"; Seligman 2011: 16ff. – "an arrangement of positive emotion, engagement, meaning, positive relationships and accomplishment"). Though the best-known definition is probably the one provided in Martin Seligman's book *Flourish*'s definition (2011), we prefer Corey Keyes's characterization of flourishing (2002 and 2007) because Keyes's description of flourishing better approximates Aristotle"s *eudaimonia* than does Seligman"s. Keyes includes emotional, social and psychological well-being in his definition of flourishing, whereas Marijke Schotanus-Dijkstra et al (2016) adopt Keyes's characterization of flourishing.

For Aristotle, *eudaimonia* is a process and not a state; it is the act of flourishing. He writes: "we should count happiness [*eudaimonia*] as one of those activities that are choice-worthy in their own right" (*Nicomachean Ethics – NE– X*, 6, 1176b 5). When proposing the famous *ergon* argument for *eudaimonia*, he also states that "happiness, [*eudaimonia*] is something final and self-sufficient – the end of actions [*prakton*]" (*NE* I, 7, 1097b 21–22). That is, *eudaimonia* – flourishing – is an activity and an end of the activity, and as Christine Korsgaard explains, "happiness therefore does after all 'reside' in the performance of our function" (2008: 149). Flourishing is not about the things we own; it is a matter of how we live our lives, whatever the circumstances (see Annas 2011: 129). Living our lives well means developing our capabilities for a worthwhile or useful goal (see Annas 2011: 140). According to Aristotle, "it is thought to be the mark of a man of practical wisdom to be able to deliberate well about what is good and expedient for himself, not in some particular respect, e.g. about what sorts of things conduce to health or to strength, but about what sorts of things conduce to the good life in general" (*NE* VI, 5, 1140a 25–30). He also affirms: "everybody able to live according to his own purposive choice should set before him some object for noble living to aim at – either honor or else glory or wealth or culture – on which he will keep his eyes fixed in all his conduct (since clearly it is a mark of much folly not to have one's life regulated with regard to some end)" (*Eudemian Ethics* I 2 1214b 6–11).

Aristotle's teachings about *eudaimonia* may thus be summarized as follows:

** *Eudaimonia* is the final end of human beings – *Nicomachean Ethics* I, 4.
** The content of this end matches the appropriate function of human nature – *Nicomachean Ethics* I, 7.
** Humans are characterized by Aristotle as simultaneously rational and political – *Politics* I, 2. They are essentially relational because they can only acquire knowledge and accomplish *eudaimonia* within the *polis* (*Politics* I, 2 and *Nicomachean Ethics* I, 2).
** *Eudaimonia* is essentially a relational concept. Given that man is a political animal, *eudaimonia* cannot overlook the common good: individuals must look for the common good in order to achieve their individual good and happiness (*Nicomachean Ethics* I, 2). Human beings flourish when they develop their capabilities, while taking into account the good of others.
** This requires virtues (*Nicomachean Ethics* I, 7). Relational virtues are key drivers of happiness for all people.
** Happiness requires the possession of a certain amount of material goods, provided by market exchanges (*Politics* III, 9; *Nicomachean Ethics* I, 8).
** The market is not an isolated reality with a particular end; rather, its end is subordinated to the ends of both individuals and *polis: eudaimonia* (*Politics* III, 9).

This conception of flourishing naturally connects with "calling." Calling or vocation is an ancient concept with religious roots that has been recently revivified principally by the field of organizational behavior. The starting point was Robert Bellah et al's *Habits of the Heart* (1985) distinction between Job, Career and Calling, which was picked up by Amy Wrzesniewski (see, e.g., Wrzesniewski et al 1997).

One primary characteristic of calling is that people who feel called see their work as socially valuable. They feel it pertains to a greater mission than one that they could perform alone. This distinctive specificity of calling matches Aristotle's conception of the human being as a political animal. For him, this notion goes beyond our contemporary conception of politics. The Aristotelian human being can only achieve *eudaimonia* within the *polis*, looking for the common interest of the whole community: "the best way of life, for individuals severally as well as for states collectively, is the life of goodness" (*Politics* VII, 1, 1323b 40–41). When this good is complete (*teleion*), it is self-sufficient (*autarkes*). However, Aristotle notes, "what we count as self-sufficient is not what suffices for a solitary person by himself, living an isolated life, but what suffices also for parents, children, wives, and, in general, for friends and fellow citizens, since a human being is naturally a political animal" (*NE* I, 7, 1097b 9–12). In a similar vein, Wrzesniewski (2003: 301) affirms: "In Callings, the work is an end in itself, and is usually associated with the belief that the work contributes to the greater good and makes the world a better place."

There has been growing interest in the idea of calling.[5] Bryan Dik and Ryan Duffy characterize calling in the following manner: (a) "a transcendent summons experienced as originating beyond the self"; (b) "to approach a particular life role in a manner oriented toward demonstrating or deriving a sense of purpose or meaningfulness"; (c) "that holds other-oriented values and goals as primary sources of motivation" (2009: 430). A. R. Elangovan et al, in a similar way, define calling as "a course of action in pursuit of pro-social intentions embodying the convergence of an individual's sense of what he or she would like to do, should do, and actually does" (2010: 430), including the possibility of an internal origin of callings (see 2010: 433).

Another characteristic of calling, as Wrzesniewski et al note, is that people feel called to perform "activities that may, but need not be, pleasurable" (1997: 22). This suggests the connection between flourishing and calling with the idea of a flow. Elangovan et al suggest that "the concepts of flow (Csíkszentmi-hályi 1990) and work engagement (Kahn 1990) are temporary episodes of an individual having the 'optimal experience' or expressing his/her 'preferred self' unlike the long-term, stable nature of the callings construct" (2010: 433). Moreover, for Aristotle, the ultimate end – *eudaimonia*/flourishing and calling – is desired for "a complete life; for just as one swallow does not make a summer, nor does one day; and so too one day, a short time, does not make a man blessed and happy" (*NE* I 7 1098a 18–20). During this search man can have times of enjoyment or a lack thereof, and this does not affect his calling or flourishing. That is, though it is natural for flourishing activities to sometimes originate a flow, this is not necessary and they can also contribute to other episodes of a flow that are disconnected from flourishing.

Mihály Csíkszentmihályi has used the term "flow" to designate an optimal enjoyable experience. Flow experiences occur when an individual performs activities in which he/she is an expert; he/she enjoys doing these activities and receiving immediate feedback. This view assumes that individuals have a harmonious set of clearly defined goals and commitments and that they are in control of their lives (1990: 10).

According to Csíkszentmihályi, we achieve happiness indirectly when we perform these kinds of activities by doing our best. Annas (2011: 70ff.) maintains that the characteristics of flow experience, as developed by Csíkszentmihályi, apply in the case of virtue: "the virtuous person experiences enjoyment and satisfaction in her activity and not just in the result" (2011: 82).

Csíkszentmihályi, Kevin Rathunde and Samuel Whalen specifically assert: "Aristotle extolled the enjoyment derived from the achievement of excellence in activity and called it 'virtue.' The form in which this idea is expressed in this volume is that of the *flow model of optimal experience*" (1993: 13). Antonella Delle Fave maintains that the optimal experience or flow "promotes personal growth and skill development in the long run" (2009: 295). However, it should be noted that it is possible to experience flow in maladjusted activities (Delle Fave et al 2011). Thus, we cannot overlap flow with virtue. Virtues may produce flow but not all flows are necessarily virtuous.

Given this panorama, my conclusion is that *eudaimonia*, a normative concept, seems to be the ideal form of happiness which people should aim for. Hence, it is relevant to know what the means are for attaining it and what the actual situations of people in relation to it are.

Measuring flourishing

Keyes (2002: 211–212) views flourishing as featuring traits of emotional, psychological and social well-being (see Keyes 1998). Emotional well-being is conceptualized as the presence or absence of positive feelings about life, thus including a hedonistic perspective on happiness (2002: 208). Psychological well-being is the individual's perception of fulfilment in his or her personal life (2002: 208). Finally, social well-being deals with the relationship between individuals and society – individuals feel they belong to and are accepted by their communities; they perceive themselves as contributing to society (2002: 209). This is an interesting standpoint, since it does not present the hedonistic and eudaimonic perspectives as being opposed, but provides instead an integrative conceptualization of both concepts. In addition, it is not incompatible with Aristotle's thinking, as Aristotle views pleasure as a dimension of *eudaimonia* – albeit not its only or most relevant dimension. In fact, for Aristotle, the political condition – that might be associated with social well-being – is more important than pleasure. Similarly, Keyes (2002) views the contrast between languishing and flourishing as related to psychosocial aspects.

The ties between hedonic and eudaimonic well-being orientations, and between instrumental or end-oriented goals are correctly analyzed in Aristotelian terms and empirically verified by Fowers et al (2010). They state that "flourishing is a pattern of activity in which one finds meaning, purpose, and personal growth through pursuing worthwhile goals in positive, collaborative relationships with others, all of which is inseparable."

Flourishing is a very new concept in psychology, and, as a result, empirical studies do not abound. Nonetheless, in addition to Huppert and So's studies, others may be noted. For example, a recent research on flourishing in students has shown that students reporting high flourishing levels tend to score higher in civic and community engagement dimensions and do more volunteer work than students with low flourishing scores (Graff Low 2011: 559). This underscores the relevance of social dimensions in flourishing.

Two studies (one with undergraduates and another one with adults) by Ethan McMahan and David Estes (2011) revealed correlational analyses indicating that both hedonic and *eudaimonic* dimensions are associated with well-being. However, the more robust associations were found between *eudaimonia* and well-being. Another empirical research study by Veronika Huta and Richard Ryan (2010) showed that, while *hedonia* and *eudaimonia* are distinct dimensions, when combined, they are associated with greater well-being.

Keyes and Annas's study (2009) offers an adequate example of possible collaborations between philosophers and psychologists. After explaining Aristotle's concept of *eudaimonia*, they identify a meeting point between this concept and contemporary psychology, linking happiness with: "*the quality of your life as a whole*, as opposed to just having good feelings, or getting what you want, or enjoying something you are doing" (2009: 198). That is, they look for an aim that surpasses hedonic motivations. They make a distinction between *functioning in life* (eudaimonic) and *feelings toward life* (hedonic) – *functioning* and *feeling*, in short. Based on Keyes (2002 and 2005), they draw data from the Midlife in the United States (MIDUS) national study and report a differential impact on mental illness (2009: 200):

> While 48.5% of the MIDUS sample fit the criteria for high hedonic well-being, only 18% are flourishing, and the other 30.5% with high hedonic well-being but lower eudaimonic well-being have nearly twice the rate of mental illness as flourishing individuals.

This study also detected similar patterns in the American teenage population and in black Setswana-speaking South African adults. It concluded that "most" Americans are happy, but only two out of every ten adults are flourishing. Indeed, Ed Diener et al (2010), using a different flourishing scale (one that does not measure social–psychological well-being), found that flourishing is associated with different dimensions of basic psychological need satisfaction (competence, relatedness and autonomy). In short, these studies show that, though complementary, the hedonic and non-hedonic flourishing dimensions differ, with the latter being more relevant than the former – people can still flourish in the absence of the hedonic dimension. Schotanus-Dijkstra et al (2016: 1363) study a national representative sample of adults in The Netherlands, finding that 78.3 per cent have high hedonic well-being, 38.2 per cent possess high eudaimonic well-being, and 36.5 per cent are flourishers: thus, the connection of flourishing with eudaimonic well-being is stronger than the connection with hedonic well-being. They find that flourishers possess high levels of conscientiousness, are more extroverted, and have lower levels of neuroticism. Yet, a key question remains: what makes people who feel good (or happy) want to flourish?

Flourishing is a more comprehensive concept than subjective well-being. In fact, for Aristotle, it is also more encompassing than the hedonistic or utilitarian concepts of happiness. Hence, it seems reasonable to view flourishing as a more complete category. From an Aristotelian perspective, attention must be paid to emphasizing virtues and the relational dimension in the construction of the psychological notion of flourishing.

Keyes (2005) suggests that the presence of hedonic symptoms and positive functioning is required for a person to be classified as flourishing. We have mentioned that Keyes believes that flourishing combines emotional well-being (positive affect and avowed quality of life), psychological well-being (Ryff's 1989 dimensions: self-acceptance, personal growth, purpose in life, environmental mastery, autonomy, positive relation with others) and social well-being (social acceptance, actualization, contribution, coherence, integration) (2002 and 2007: 98). Thus, he has developed a categorical diagnosis of mental health (the Mental Health Continuum Form) which contains 14 items (2 items about hedonic well-being and 12 items of positive functioning). To be diagnosed as flourishing in life individuals must exhibit high levels on one of the two items of hedonic well-being and high levels on 6 of the 12 items of positive functioning during the past 30 days (Keyes 2005).

Diener et al (2010) has also developed a "flourishing scale" which includes such aspects as relationships, self-esteem, purpose, and optimism. However, though called "flourishing scale," it chiefly covers only psychological well-being. In addition, Huppert and So (2009; 2013) suggest that a measure of flourishing has two features: a core feature which includes positive emotions, engagement-interest, and meaning-purpose; and additional features such as self-esteem, optimism, resilience, vitality, self-determination and positive relationships. More recently Lucy Hone et al (2014) assessed four operationalizations of flourishing: Huppert and So, Keyes, Diener et al and Seligman (for a review of different operationalizations of the eudaimonic aspect of flourishing see Huta and Waterman 2014). When comparing the four proposals, Hone et al (2014: especially 71–72) noted that Keyes's conceptualization is the most complete, including life satisfaction and social well-being. We think that this completeness is related to our theoretical reasons for adopting Keyes's conceptualization: its reliance upon Aristotle's notion of *eudaimonia*.

After that review in our article (Mesurado et al 2016) we decided to develop a new scale to measure flourishing in terms of Keyes's dimensions: social well-being, psychological well-being and emotional well-being, but by reformulating the contents of some of these dimensions, in particular emotional and psychological well-being. Our scale did not use Ryff's conceptualizing of psychological well-being because although this theoretical model has had strong empirical support in different countries (Ryff 2014), a previous study developed in Argentina did not find the same dimensions (Aranguren and Irrazábal 2015). Consequently, psychological well-being should be operationalized as one's perception of the meaning and purpose of life, engagement with personal activities (family and work), and as a stable and general perception of family and work satisfaction. Concerning emotional well-being, Keyes's scale includes two general items to measure it, and we consider it more appropriate to distinguish positive and negative emotions in a continuum. Hence, our scale measures positive and negative emotions during the past two weeks using a semantic differential – for example: happy versus sad; negative versus positive. Finally, social well-being for us means to be an important part of society, to feel close to others, to be engaged with social problems, and to feel that one's work contributes to social progress. Psychological and social well-being would be a more stable perception, while emotional well-being would be operationalized as a state of mind.

The analyses we presented in Mesurado et al (2016) demonstrated that our scale is psychometrically valid, possesses strong internal consistency and reliability for the entire scale, and is adequately reliable for each subscale. The results establish empirical support for the Flourishing Scale and confirm the three-dimensional measurement instrument to assess the facets of Keyes's (2005) conceptualization of flourishing. The emotional, psychological and social forms of well-being seem to be essential to a flourishing life in adults. Moreover, this study demonstrated convergent and discriminant validity between the flourishing scale and two other ways of relating to work: calling and job. We thus found that two dimensions of the flourishing scale, social well-being and psychological well-being, are positively associated with calling.

In addition, two other characteristics of the new scale that show its convergent validity are the correlation found between three dimensions of flourishing and three dimensions of work-flow (namely, absorption, work enjoyment and intrinsic work motivation) and the association between social and psychological well-being with prosocial work motivation. These results are a clear proof that work flow experience constitutes an important element to a flourishing life. Indeed, Anna Strati, David Shernoff and Hayal Kackar (2011) have suggested that "flow experiences are valuable for learning and development because they provide an orientation of engagement and skill-building that carries into the future," and that "because flow states are enjoyable, they motivate individuals to continue developing skills and raising challenges to reenter flow" (2011: 1058). Nakamura and Csíkszentmihályi (2009: 199) believe that "experiencing flow encourages a person to persist in and return to an activity because of the experiential rewards it promises, and thereby fosters the growth of skills over time." Although the experience of flow is not always associated with virtuous actions, it is evident that when a person has a flow experience carried out in positive and productive activities (such as work) it can contribute to the development of a flourishing life.

Conclusion

Happiness economics certainly deserves much praise; but, truth be told, its underlying notion of happiness could use some fine-tuning to help advance its goals. This chapter has tackled criticisms to this new branch of economics by suggesting the use of another philosophical concept, Aristotle's *eudaimonia*, as well as a psychological theory of happiness, a revised version of positive psychology that stresses human beings' relational nature and the close link between happiness and virtues. Particularly, the idea of strong relationality in the realm of human action seems especially important (Slife and Richardson 2008; Richardson 2012), and the newly coined term of "flourishing" takes the spotlight. Flourishing is a more comprehensive and refined activity than just being happy, though flourishing often includes happiness. However, empirical evidence shows that, while most people are happy, they do not always flourish, and happiness is a more modest goal than flourishing. Thus, we propose turning happiness economics into "flourishing economics," with the above-mentioned philosophical and psychological views serving as its foundations. This would indeed be a flourishing economics. Given present-day governments' interest in well-being research for refining their policies and the fact that most studies include only hedonic well-being, Schotanus-Dijkstra et al (2016: 1366) recommend including measures of flourishing to produce a more comprehensive well-being objective. I have also noted the connection of flourishing with calling and flow – a link that strengthens the argument for adopting this particular notion within happiness economics.

In addition to Aristotle, two other closer theoretical economic precedents help make the case for this new approach. While John Maynard Keynes died before the advent of happiness economics, Anna Carabelli and Mario Cedrini have looked at his ideas on happiness, clearly unveiling their meaning (2011: 355) and relevance:

Keynes's notion of happiness related to a good life closer to Aristotle's concept of eudaimonia. Unsurprisingly, Keynes believes that happiness – and goodness – cannot be reduced to pleasure, though they usually (but not always) accompany each other. Nor can they be treated as homogeneous, one-dimensional concepts. Keynes maintains that there exists a plurality of values and ends. Happiness is to him a composition of heterogeneous and incommensurable values, desires and virtues, and his ethics concerns the whole conduct of human life, rather than a simple aspect of well-being.

More recently, Robert and Edward Skidelsky (2012: 120) relied on Aristotle's *eudaimonia* to criticize Layard's views on happiness economics and to support their attempt to introduce changes into this new field.

Concerning the main themes of this book, happiness economics which possesses a hedonistic concept of happiness is principally a restrictive naturalist concept, while a happiness economics which adopts a flourishing concept of happiness leaves ample room for practical reason, liberal naturalism, human intentionality and freedom. In this sense, I think that happiness economics is more inclined to achieve the direction that I have recommended for economics in this book than any of the other currents analyzed in the previous chapters. I believe that we have to promote new developments and studies of happiness economics by using increasingly refined concepts of happiness and the corresponding psychological constructs allowing for empirical research.

Finally, the changes proposed by this new approach come from mixed roots: as explained, happiness was present at the origin and development of economics, and, at the same time, this new notion is clearly influenced by contemporary psychology.

Notes

1 See, for example, Martha Nussbaum (2005) for a comparison of the notions of happiness used by Aristotle, Bentham and Mill.
2 A recent complete survey is George MacKerron's (2012).
3 John Davis (2016) has proposed slight changes to Putnam's arguments in order to apply them to economics. See also the classical paper by Richard Rudner (1953). Besides, there are psychological empirical studies showing how this divide is actually "transgressed": see, for example, Colombo et al (2005). Wilhelm Röpke affirms: "science – above all, moral sciences of which economics is a part – is indeed inseparably mixed up with value judgments, and our efforts to eliminate them will only end in absurdity" (1942: 9).
4 Elizabeth Anscombe (1958: 1) suggests translating Aristotle's *eudaimonia* as flourishing.
5 For a recent review, see Duffy and Dik (2013).

References

Annas, J. (2011). *Intelligent Virtue*. Oxford: Oxford University Press.

Anscombe, G. E. M. (1958). "Modern Moral Philosophy," *Philosophy* 33/1: 1–19.

Aranguren, M. and N. Irrazábal (2015). "Estudio de las Propiedades Psicométricas de la Escala de Bienestar Psicológico de Ryff en una Muestra de Estudiantes Argentinos" ["Psychometric Properties of Ryff's Scales of Psychological Well-Being in an Argentinean Sample"], *Ciencias Psicológicas* 9/1: 73–83.

Aristotle (1954). *Nicomachean Ethics*. Translated and Introduced by Sir David Ross. Oxford: Oxford University Press.

Aristotle (1958). *Politics*. Edited and Translated by E. Barker. Oxford: Oxford University Press.

Aristotle (1971). *Eudemian Ethics*. Translated by H. Rackham. Cambridge, MA: Harvard University Press.

Aristotle (1995). *The Complete Works of Aristotle. The Revised Oxford Translation*, J. Barnes (ed.) 6th printing with corrections. Princeton, NJ: Princeton University Press.

Atherson, J. (2011). "Introductory essay: Developing an overview as context and future." In J. Atherson, E. Graham and I. Steedman (eds.), *The Practices of Happiness*. London and New York: Routledge.

Barrotta, P. (2008). "Why Economists Should Be Unhappy with the Economics of Happiness," *Economics and Philosophy* 24: 145–165.

Begley, N. (2010). "Psychological Adoption and Adaption of Eudaimonia," http://positivepsychology.org.uk/pp-theory/eudaimonia/140-the-psychological-adoption-and-adaptation-of-eudaimoni.html, retrieved March 1, 2012.

Bellah, R. N., R. Madsen, W. M. Sullivan, A. Swidler and S. M. Tipton (1985). *Habits of the Heart*, New York: Harper & Row.

Bentham, J. (1954). *Jeremy Bentham's Economic Writings*, critical edition based on his printed works and unprinted manuscripts by W. Stark. London: The Royal Economic Society and George Allen & Unwin.

Bruni, L. and Porta, P.-L. (2007). "Introduction." In Bruni, Luigino and Pier Luigi Porta (eds.), *Handbook on the Economics of Happiness*. Cheltenham: Elgar.

Bruni, L. and Porta, P.-L. (2011). "Happiness and experienced utility." In J. B. Davis and D. W. Hands (eds.), *The Elgar Companion to Recent Economic Methodology*. Cheltenham and Northampton: Elgar.

Bruni, L. and S. Zamagni (2016). "The Challenges of Public Happiness: An Historical-Methodological Reconstruction," in *World Happiness Report Update 2016*, Special Rome Edition, http://worldhappiness.report/, retrieved July 6, 2016.

Carabelli, A. M. and Cedrini, M. A. (2011). "The Economic Problem of Happiness: Keynes on Happiness and Economics," *Forum of Social Economy* 40: 335–359.

Colombo, M., L. Bucher and Y. Inbar (2015). "Explanatory Judgment, Moral Offense and Value-Free Science," *Review of Philosophical Psychology*, doi:10.1007/s13164-13015-0282-z.

Crespo, R. F. (2006). "The Ontology of the Economic: An Aristotelian Analysis," *Cambridge Journal of Economics*, 30/5: 767–781.

Crespo, R. F. and B. Mesurado (2015). "Happiness Economics, Eudaimonia and Positive Psychology: From Happiness Economics to Flourishing Economics," *Journal of Happiness Studies* 16: 931–946.

Csíkszentmihályi, M., K. R. Rathunde, and S. P. Whalen (1993). *Talented Teenagers. The Roots of Success and Failure.* Cambridge: Cambridge University Press.

Csíkszentmihályi, M. (1990). *Flow: The Psychology of Optimal Experience.* New York: Harper.

Davis, J. B. (2016). "Economists' Odd Stand on the Positive-Normative Distinction: A Behavioral Economics View." In G. DeMartino and D. McCloskey (eds.) *Oxford University Press Handbook on Professional Economic Ethics: Views from the Economics Profession and Beyond.* Oxford: Oxford University Press.

Delle Fave, A. (2009). "Optimal Experience and Meaning: Which Relationship?," *Psychological Topics* 18/2: 285–302.

Delle Fave, A., F. Massimini, and M. Bassi (2011). *Psychological selection and optimal experience across cutures. Social empowerment through personal growth*, Vol. II. Heidelberg, London, New York: Springer.

Diener, E., Wirtz, D., Tov, W., Kim-Prieto, C., Choi, D., Oishi, S. and Biswas-Diener, R. (2010). "New Well-being Measures: Short Scales to Assess Flourishing and Positive and Negative Feelings," *Social Indicators Research* 97: 143–156.

Dik, B. J. and R. D. Duffy (2009). "Calling and Vocation at Work: Definitions and Prospects for Research and Practice," *The Counseling Psychologist* 37/ 3: 424–450.

Duffy, R. D. and B. J. Dik (2013). "Research on Calling: What Have We Learned and Where are We Going?," *Journal of Vocational Behavior* 83/3: 428–436.

Easterlin, R. A. (1974). "Does Economic Growth Improve the Human Lot? Some Empirical Evidence." In R. David and M. Reder (eds.) *Nations and Households in Economic Growth: Essays in Honor of Moses Abramovitz.* New York: Academic Press.

Elangovan, A. R. (Elango), C. C. Pinder and M. McLean (2010). "Callings and Organizational Behavior," *Journal of Vocational Behavior* 76: 428–440.

Flyvbjerg, B. (2001). *Making Social Science Matter.* Cambridge: Cambridge University Press.

Fowers, B. J., C. O. Mollica and E. N. Procacci (2010). "Constitutive and instrumental goal orientations and their relation with eudaimonicv and hedonic well-being," *Journal of Positive Psychology* 5: 139–153.

Fowers, B. J. (2012a). "An Aristotelian Framework for the Human Good," *Journal of Theoretical and Philosophical Psychology* 32/1: 10–23.

Fowers, B. J. (2012b). "Placing Virtue and the Human Good in Psychology," *Journal of Theoretical and Philosophical Psychology* 32/1: 1–9.

Frederickson, B. and M. F. Losada (2005). "Positive Affect and the Complex Dynamics of Human Flourishing," *American Psychologist* 60/7: 678–686.

Frey, B. S. and Stutzer, A. (2002). *Happiness and Economics: How the Economy and Institutions Affects Human Well-Being*. Princeton, NJ: Princeton University Press.

Graff Low, K. (2011). "Flourishing, Substance Use, and Engagement in Students Entering College: A Preliminary Study," *Journal of American College Health* 59/6: 555–561.

Grenholm, C.-H. (2011). "Happiness, welfare and capabilities." In J. Atherson, E. Graham and I. Steedman (eds.), *The Practices of Happiness*. London and New York: Routledge.

Hone, L. C., A. Jarden, G. M. Schofield and S. Duncan (2014). "Measuring Flourishing: The Impact of Operational Definitions on the Prevalence of High Levels of Wellbeing," *International Journal of Wellbeing* 4/1: 69–90.

Hume, D. ([1752] 1970). *Writings on Economics*, edited with an Introduction by Eugene Rotwein. Madison, WI: University of Wisconsin Press.

Huppert, F. A. and So, T. T. C. (2009). *What Percentage of People in Europe Are Flourishing and What Characterises Them?*Cambridge: Well-Being Institute, University of Cambridge, Prepared for the OECD/ISQOLS meeting "Measuring subjective well-being: An opportunity for NSOs?" Florence, July 23/24, 2009, http://www.isqols2009.istitutodeglinnocenti.it/Content_en/Huppert.pdf, retrieved May 1, 2013.

Huppert, F. A. and So, T. T. C. (2013). "Flourishing Across Europe: Application of a New Conceptual Framework for Defining Well-Being," *Social Indicators Research* 110: 837–861, http://link.springer.com/content/pdf/10.1007%2Fs11205-011-9966-7.pdf, retrieved May 1, 2013.

Huta, V. and Ryan, R. M. (2010). "Pursuing Pleasure or Virtue: The Differential and Overlapping Well-Being Benefits of Hedonic and Eudaimonic Motives," *Journal of Happiness Studies* 11: 735–762.

Huta, V. and A. S. Waterman (2014). "Eudaimonia and Its Distinction from Hedonia: Developing a Classification and Terminology for Understanding Conceptual and Operational Definitions," *Journal of Happiness Studies* 15: 1425–1456.

Huta, V. (2013). "Eudaimonia." In S. David, I. Boniwell, and A. C. Ayers (eds.), *Oxford Handbook of Happiness*. Oxford: Oxford University Press.

Kahn, W. A. (1990). "Psychological Conditions of Personal Engagement and Disengagement at Work," *Academy of Management Journal* 33: 692–724.

Keyes, C. L. M. (1998). "Social Well-Being," *Social Psychology Quarterly* 61: 121–140.

Keyes, C. L. M. (2002). "The Mental Health Continuum: From Languishing to Flourishing in Life," *Journal of Health and Social Research* 43: 207–222.

Keyes, C. L. M. (2005). "Mental Illness or Mental Health? Investigating Axioms of the Complete State Model of Health," *Journal of Consulting and Clinical Psychology* 73: 539–548.

Keyes, C. L. M. (2007). "Promoting and Protecting Mental Health as Flourishing: A Complementary Strategy for Improving Mental Health," *American Psychologist* 62: 95–108.

Keyes, C. L. M. and Annas, J. (2009). "Feeling Good and Functioning Well: Distinctive Concepts in Ancient Philosophy and Contemporary Science," *The Journal of Positive Psychology* 4/3: 197–201.

Knight, F. H. (1956). *On the History and Method of Economics.* Chicago, IL: University of Chicago Press.

Korsgaard, C. M. (2008). *The Constitution of Agency: Essays on Practical Reason and Moral Psychology,* Oxford: Oxford University Press.

Layard, R. (2005). *Happiness. Lessons from a New Science.* New York: Penguin.

Layard, R. (2007). "Happiness and Public Policy: A Challenge to the Profession," in J. F. Bruno, and A. Stutzer, *Economics and Psychology. A Promising New Cross-Disciplinary Field.* Cambridge, MA: MIT Press.

MacKerron, G. (2012). "Happiness Economics from 35 000 feet," *Journal of Economic Surveys* 26/4: 705–735.

Malthus, T. R. ([1798] 1914). *An Essay on the Principle of Population.* London: J. M. Dent.

McMahan, E. A. and Estes, D. (2011). "Hedonic Versus Eudaimonic Conceptions of Well-being: Evidence of Differential Associations with Self-reported Well-being," *Social Indicators Research* 103: 93–108.

Mesurado, B., O. Rodríguez and R. F. Crespo, 2016. "Development and Initial Validation of a Multidimensional Flourishing Scale Relating It to Calling, Prosocial Work Motivation and Flow in the Workplace," https://papers.ssrn.com/sol3/papers.cfm?abstract_id=2858417, retrieved October 25, 2016.

Nakamura, J. and Csíkszentmihályi, M. (2009). "Flow theory and research." In S. Lopez and C. R. Snyder (eds.), *Oxford Handbook of Positive Psychology.* Oxford: Oxford University Press.

Nussbaum, M. (2005). "Mill between Aristotle and Bentham." In L. Bruni and P. L. Porta (eds.), *Economics and Happiness.* Oxford: Oxford University Press.

Parsons, T. (1934). "Some Reflections on 'The Nature and Significance of Economics'," *Quarterly Journal of Economics* 48/3: 511–545.

Putnam, H. (2004). *The Collapse of the Fact/Value Dichotomy and Other Essays.* Cambridge, MA: Harvard University Press.

Rasmussen, D. C. (2011). "Adam Smith on Commerce and Happiness: A Response to Den Uyl and Rasmussen," *Reason Papers* 33: 95–101.

Richardson, F. C. (2012). "On Psychology and Virtue Ethics," *Journal of Theoretical and Philosophical Psychology* 32/1: 24–34.

Richardson, F. C., Fowers, B. J. and Guignon, C. (1999). *Re-envisioning Psychology: Moral Dimensions of Theory and Practice.* San Francisco, CA: Jossey-Bass.

Riedel, M. (ed.) (1972–1974) *Rehabilitierung der praktischen Philosophie,* Freiburg: Rombach.

Robbins, L. (1935). *An Essay on the Nature and Significance of Economic Science.* London: MacMillan.

Röpke, W. (1942). "A Value Judgment on Value Judgments," *Revue de la Faculté des Sciences Economiques d'Istanbul* III/1–2: 1–19.

Rudner, R. (1953). "The Scientist qua Scientist Makes Value Judgments," *Philosophy of Science* 20/1: 1–6.

Ryff, C. D. (1989). "Happiness Is Everything, or Is It? Explorations on the Meaning of Psychological Well-Being," *Journal of Personality and Social Psychology* 57/6: 1069–1081.

Ryff, C. (2014). "Psychological Well-Being Revisited: Advances in the Science and Practice of Eudaimonia," *Psychotherapy and Psychosomatics* 83: 10–28

Ryff, C. D. and B. H. Singer (2008). "Know thyself and become what you are: A eudaimonic approach to psychological well-being," *Journal of Happiness Studies* 9/1: 13–39.

Sabetti, F. (2012). "Public Happiness as the Wealth of Nations: The Rise of Political Economy in Naples in a Comparative Perspective," *California Italian Studies* 3/1: 1–31.

Schotanus-Dijkstra, M., M. E. Pieterse, C. H. C. Drossaert, G. J. Westerhof, R. de Graaf, M. ten Have, J. A. Walburg and E. T. Bohlmeijer (2016). "What factors are Associated with Flourishing? Results from a Large Representative National sample," *Journal of Happiness Studies* 17: 1351–1370.

Seligman, M. (2011). *Flourish*. New York: Free Press.

Sen, A. (1987). *On Ethics and Economics*. Oxford: Basil Blackwell.

Skidelsky, R. and Skidelsky, E. (2012). *How Much Is Enough?* New York: Other Press.

Slife, B. D. and Richardson, F. C. (2008). "Problematic Ontological Underpinnings of Positive Psychology: A Strong Relational Alternative," *Theory and Psychology* 18/5: 699–723.

Slife, B. D., and Williams, R. (1995). *What's Behind the Research? Discovering Hidden Assumptions in the Behavioral Sciences*. Thousand Oaks, CA: Sage.

Smith, A. ([1759] 1976) *The Theory of Moral Sentiments*. Oxford: Clarendon Press.

Steedman, I. (2011). "Economic theory and happiness." In J. Atherson, E. Graham and I. Steedman (eds.), *The Practices of Happiness*. London and New York: Routledge.

Strati, A. D., Shernoff, D. J., & Kackar, H. Z. (2011). "Flow." In R. J. R. Levesque (ed.), *Encyclopedia of Adolescence*. Dordrecht: Springer.

Taylor, C. (1985a). *Human Agency and Language. Philosophical Papers 1*. Cambridge: Cambridge University Press.

Taylor, C. (1985b). *Philosophy and the Human Sciences. Philosophical Papers 2*. Cambridge: Cambridge University Press.

Taylor, C. C. W. (1995). "Politics." In J. Barnes (ed.) *The Cambridge Companion to Aristotle*. Cambridge: Cambridge University Press.

Wijngaards, A. (2012). *Wordly Theology. On Connecting Public Theology and Economics*. PhD thesis defended at the Radboud Universiteit Nijmegen, http://hdl.handle.net/2066/93624, retrieved March 1, 2013.

Wrzesniewski, A. (2003). "Finding positive meaning in work." In K. S. Cameron, J. E. Dutton, and R. E. Quinn (eds.), *Positive Organizational Scholarship*. San Francisco, CA: Berrett-Koehler.

Wrzesniewski, A., C. McCauley, P. Rozin and B. Schwartz (1997). "Jobs, Careers, and Callings: People's Relations to Their Work," *Journal of Research in Personality* 31: 21–33.

7   Institutional economics

The study of institutions as key figures in economic life has a long tradition. As in the case of happiness economics, current institutional economics mixes elements drawn from ancient political economy with other taken from modern sciences – especially from sociology. We could sustain that the birth of institutional economics occurred with Thorstein Veblen at the beginning of the twentieth century, though many different ways of approaching institutions can be discerned in economics before Veblen. In this chapter, nonetheless, I will appraise Veblen's ideas and other contemporary institutionalist currents in their consideration or negligence of practical reason and their kind of naturalism following Veblen"s thread of thought. It is important to review different forms of institutionalism because, as explained in Chapter 1, some connections with other social sciences that have reemerged in the last years have been "domesticated" (Davis 2008: 365) by standard economic logic and its instrumental maximizing rationality.

In this chapter, I will first provide a concise review of the history of twentieth century economic institutionalism. Then, before analyzing Veblen's institutionalism, resurging contemporary Veblenian currents and up-to-date theories of institutions, I will briefly consider the basic concepts of institutionalism – agency, habits and institutions – from the perspective of classical practical reason. This last examination will help to discriminate between institutionalist currents fitting with the argument of this book and currents that have been "domesticated" by economic logic.

Economics and institutions

Institutions as "stable, valued, recurring patterns of behavior" (Huntington 1965: 394) are necessary for the functioning of society, the predictability of people's behavior and the construction of social sciences, including economics. Human actions are usually guided by habits and institutions more than by the maximization of motivations. The particular characteristics of human actions may make human behavior difficultly predictable. This is why Aristotle argues:

Our treatment discussion will be adequate if it has as much clearness as the subject-matter admits of; for precision is not to be sought for alike in all discussions, any more than in all the products of the crafts. Now fine and just actions, which political science investigates, exhibit much *variety and fluctuation* (...). We must be content, then, in speaking of such subjects and with such premises to indicate the truth *roughly and in outline*.

(*Nicomachean Ethics* I, 3, 1094b 11–27, emphasis added)

Aristotle identifies two reasons for "inexactness" in practical sciences like politics (or economics – *oikonomikè*): action exhibits "variety and fluctuation" – that is, there are many possible situations and human beings may change their decisions. As a result, Aristotle views human action as being singular. He asserts:

We must, however, not only make this *general statement*, but also apply it to the individual facts. For among statements about conduct, those which are general apply more widely, but those *which are particular are more true*, since conduct has to do with *individual* cases, and our statements must harmonize with the facts in these cases.

(*Nicomachean Ethics* II, 7, 1107a 31–3, italics added)

At first glance, this way of thinking about human action would leave us in an uncertain, unmanageable and unpredictable situation. However, this is where habits and institutions come into play, providing guidelines to act and to roughly anticipate others' behavior.

The notion of institution has been used extensively and was developed in the 20th century.[1] "Habit" (*hexis*) is a classical notion that derives from ancient Greek. The link between habit and institution has been widely acknowledged by contemporary sociology. For Pierre Bourdieu, institutions and habits form a couple, with one influencing the other and vice versa.[2] For Bourdieu "habitus" (the Latin word) constitutes a system of durable dispositions. An institution embodies and creates habits.

Walton H. Hamilton (1919: 309) coined the expression "institutional economics" and affirmed that "the proper subject matter of economic theory is institutions" (1919: 313). He asserted that the term institution "connotes a way of thought or action of some prevalence and permanence, which is embedded in the habits of a group or the customs of people" (1932: 84). For Veblen, the founder of Economic Institutionalism, institutions consisted of "settled habits of common thought to the generality of men" (1919: 239). Institutionalism thus stresses the role of habits and institutions in the motivation of economic decisions and actions. Geoffrey Hodgson defines institutions as "systems of established and prevalent social rules that structure social interactions" (2006: 2). A rule creates a habit that becomes normative, can be codified, and is adopted by a group of people (cf. Hodgson 2006: 6). Following Veblen, Hodgson also notes that "institutions work only because the rules involved are embedded in shared habits of thought and behavior" (2006: 6). He explains that institutions constrain and enable behaviors, create stable expectations, have the potential to change agents' habits of thought and action – "downward causation" – and feature strong self-reinforcing and self-perpetuating characteristics (see Hodgson 2004a, 2004b and 2006).

The old institutionalist economic current, which flourished around the work of Veblen, John Commons and Wesley Mitchel during the early years of the last century, has been continued by some "institutionalist" economists during the interwar period. The distinctive characteristic of this branch of economic institutionalism is its emphasis on the influence that institutions have on individuals. As Hodgson expresses it, "the old institutionalism holds to the idea of interactive and partially malleable agents, mutually entwined in a web of partially durable and self-reinforcing institutions" (2004a: 86). The influence is bi-directional: "individuals create and change institutions, just as institutions mold and constrain individuals" (2004a: 87). Apart from the latter, there are some common characterizations of old institutionalism. Some features that are usually noted include: institutionalists consider that there is no unique logic of choice; they emphasize the role of culture; they are organicists; they believe that habits and institutions influence people more than traditional economic motivations; they stress the unavoidability of normative dimensions of institutions and therefore, that values should be made explicit and be discussed (see Mirowski 1987: 1019–1020 and 1988: 122; Samuels 1991: 108–109 and 1995: 573–575).

Following the lead of Ronald Coase's theory of the firm, Oliver Williamson's 1975 book is generally considered the starting point of "new institutional economics." The distinctive trait of this new institutionalism is its adherence to methodological individualism: "the explanatory movement is from individuals to institutions, taking individuals as primary and given" (Hodgson 2004a: 88). In this sense, this current belongs to mainstream economics, and though it investigates the sociological dimensions of institutions, it considers them as stemming from the behaviour of individuals. As Herbert Simon maintains, quoting Williamson (1975 and 1985), "The so-called 'new institutional economics' does not depart from neoclassical theory in any significant way in its assumptions about the motives of managers or employees of business firms" (2005: 91). Williamson's famous quote "in the beginning there were markets" (1975: 20) disregards that markets do not emerge in a vacuum, but that they suppose a whole society with its rules and customs (see Hodgson 2007: 326). John Davis considers new institutional economics as a "mainstream approach." It "investigates possible social-institutional influences on individuals" but it is still committed to methodological individualism (2003: 101). Roger Frydman (2003: iv) stresses the discontinuity between new institutionalism and the original institutionalism of Veblen and his followers: the former makes a stronger distinction between what is economic and non-economic and displays an economic explanation that is closed in itself.[3]

In effect, in a seminal article about new institutionalism, Williamson (1973: 316) writes:

> As compared with the study of market failures, the analysis of the sources and consequences of internal organizational failures is at a very primitive stage of development. I submit, however, that substantially the same factors that are ultimately responsible for market failures also explain failures of internal organization. If this contention is correct, the study of alternative modes of economic organization can proceed in a symmetrical fashion. Rather than having to devise a separate apparatus for each organizing mode, a common language and conceptual apparatus can be brought systematically to bear across modes.

In contrast, for old institutionalism the functioning of an economy goes beyond market logic; there is more to it than just maximization. Williamson's position, however, has gone unchanged. In fact, in his 2000 article "The NIE [New Institutional Economics]: Taking Stock, Looking Ahead," Williamson states that what old and new institutionalism share is the recognition of the role of institutions and what distinguishes them is that the former insists that institutions can be analysed using the standard tools of economic theory (2000: 595). This "neoclassical spirit" is present in his profuse work. Thus, we cannot consider new institutionalism as a reverse imperialist current despite its emphasis on sociology as it does not consider practical reason.

At the same time, old institutionalism has in some sense been resurrected and renewed with new insights. In 1967, the *Journal of Economic Issues* (*JEI*), sponsored by the recently created Association for Evolutionary Economics, was founded in the United States. The *JEI is* an outlet for scholarly articles with foundations in old institutional economics. In Europe, the European Association for Evolutionary Economics was founded in 1988. It supports the *Journal of Institutional Economics* (*JOIE*). An inspiring leader of this European emergence is Hodgson. He founded the JOIE and is one of its editors. Though it is open to all contributions investigating institutions in economics, this journal has published theoretical and empirical articles with a theoretical background inspired in old institutional thinking. The journal is now sponsored by the "World Interdisciplinary Network for Institutional Research" organization, which holds international symposia and conferences on institutionalism every year. Apart from Hodgson, there are many economists, philosophers and sociologists who have an interest and develop work on institutions: John Searle, Margaret Gilbert, Richard Langlois, Malcolm Rutheford, Jack Vromen, Robert Sugden, Viktor Vanberg, Dani Rodrik, Daron Acemoglu and James Robinson, to mention only a few.

Frank Hindriks and Francesco Guala (2015a) have recently proposed a framework to unify three contemporary theories of institutions: rule-based, equilibrium-based, and constitutive rules theories. This proposal has caused a fertile reflection on the fundamental underpinnings of a theory of institutions, fueling a fruitful discussion about their definition, nature, characteristics, emergence, persistence, and evolution. The discussion includes papers by Masahiko Aoki, Ken Binmore, Geoffrey Hodgson, John Searle, Vernon Smith, Robert Sugden (all 2015), as well as Hindriks and Guala's reply (2005b).

The rules-based account points to a definition of institutions as "integrated systems of rules that structure social interactions" (Hodgson 2015: 501). For the equilibrium-based account, rules and institutions are the fruit of interactions among individuals, underscoring the process aspect of institutions: an adjustment of individual behaviors that leads to the establishment of an institution and its evolution. Searle's (2005) constitutive rule account points to a collective acceptance of obligations. In Aristotelian terms, the first account concerns the definition of institutions, the second one refers to their action of efficient causes, and the third one focuses on their final cause.

Rules-based theories have their roots in traditional sociology – Hindriks and Guala mention Max Weber and Talcott Parsons – while an equilibrium-based theory is associated with game theory, and, finally, Searle's constitutive rule approach draws from continental philosophers like Kant (see, for example, Searle, 2015: 512). Philosophy consistently lies beneath social theories and sometimes surfaces, but, mostly, it underlies and permeates them – consciously or not – Hindriks and Guala (2015b) mention David Hume. Sugden (2015) and Smith (2015) explicitly and approvingly mention David Hume and Adam Smith. Aoki mentions Hegel, Binmore takes an evolutionary stance, and Hodgson (2015) turns to Aristotle, stressing the predominance of inner ontological capacities over outcomes. These philosophical links facilitate the discernment of the relation of these theories to scientific naturalism and practical reason. In the present chapter I will appraise Veblen's ideas and the theories unified by Hindriks and Guala from this philosophical point of view. However, before analyzing these theories, I will briefly describe the implications of the classical concept of practical reason for the basic concepts of institutionalism: agency, habits and institutions.

Agency, habits and institutions in light of classical practical reason

Aristotle, as explained in Chapter 2, regarded human action as voluntary and rational in a *broad* sense, making a distinction between two of its dimensions: a practical or immanent dimension and an instrumental, "poietical," or technical dimension. He correlatively distinguished between practical and poietical (or technical) reason as guiding these dimensions of human action (*Metaphysics* IX, 8). Practical reason is related to the immanent aspect of human actions; that is, to the effect that the action has on the agent who decides and acts. Even if an action is directed at a result outside of the agent, it also bears an impact on the agent himself. Poietical or technical reason drives the action's results. While practical reason asks how one should act to find one's own fulfilment, technical or poietical reason asks what means and actions are required to achieve a desired external result. Aristotle (*Metaphysics*, IX, 8, 1050a 35) believed that, while some actions are purely practical, like seeing and theorizing, there are no purely technical actions because all human action leaves some mark on people's inner self. In other words, actions feature immanent and transient aspects. While practical reason deals with ends and means to the extent that it impacts ends, technical reason is exclusively a rationality of means. Max Weber's value-rational, affectual and traditional motives are a part of Aristotle's practical reason (Weber, 1978: 24–5).[4] This is why I sustain that, for Aristotle, human action is rational in a *broad* sense – values, emotions, habits, as well as instincts drive human decision and action, with reason being present to some extent. Aristotle views "agency" as this immanent practical aspect of human action.

Aristotle prioritizes this practical dimension of actions, because it is related with the end of actions, that is, with its immanent character: there is no choice of means without a desired end (*NE* VI, 2, 1139a30 to 1139b2). In other words, the most relevant aspect of human action is its immanent dimension, not its external result.

Instrumental reason deals with "how" to achieve an end, and practical reason tackles "why" we seek this end. Within the framework of the first question – a technical one – we may consider how to *best* allocate means in order to achieve a specific end: this is a matter of instrumental maximizing rationality, generally used by standard economics. An exclusive consideration of this aspect of human action is reductive. As Amartya Sen states, "this narrow view of rationality as self-interest maximization is not only arbitrary; it can also lead to serious descriptive and predictive problems in economics (given the assumption of rational behaviour)" (2002: 23).

In sum, Aristotle's concept of agency stresses a dimension of human action that goes beyond mere instrumental behavior, which is its immanent quality. However, given the variable and dynamic character that this aspect introduces into human action, doubts have arisen about the possibility of prediction. Fortunately, habits provide an important dose of stability and guidance in one's own and others' actions. It is a virtuous circle of actions generating habits and habits facilitating actions. In effect, concerning the origin of habits, Aristotle indicates: "Habits are born of similar activities. So we have to engage in behavior of the relevant kinds, since the habit formed will follow upon the various ways we behave" (*Nicomachean Ethics* II, 1, 1103b21–25). All types of habits, ethical virtues, vices and skills are ingrained by habituation: they can be relatively unconscious (Lear 1988: 186). However, habit creation also involves a cognitive component (Lockwood 2013: 22) – we learn by practice: it is not something merely mechanical or automatic (see Burnyeat 1980: 73). As nicely put by Aristotelian scholar Julia Annas, with habits (specifically virtues and skills) "the agent becomes more intelligent in performance rather than routinized" (2011: 4). Consider this quotation from Annas (2011: 13–14), as it provides a good example:

When we see the speed with which a skilled pianist produces the notes we might be tempted to think that constant repetition and habit have transformed the original experience, which required conscious thought, into mere routine. But this is completely wrong. The expert pianist plays in a way not dependent on conscious input, but the result is not mindless routine but rather playing infused with and expressing the pianist's thoughts about the piece. Further, the pianist continues to improve her playing. The way she plays exhibits not only increased technical mastery but increased intelligence [...] If practical skills become routine they ossify and decay.

Obviously, given these characteristics of habits, Aristotle rules nature out as their origin, stating in *Nicomachean Ethics* that "none of the excellences of character comes about in us by nature, for no natural way of being is changed through habituation" (II, 1, 1103a19–21). However, habits do have a basis in our nature because we are naturally capable of acquiring them, which also indicates that habits are not infallible or unexceptionable. As a result, though habits point us towards a specific behavior, we can always choose to act against our habits. That is, the characteristics of agency, the immanent free dimension of human action, applies to habits.

Habits produce character, which is a kind of second nature. Aristotle starts the second book of *Nicomachean Ethics* with the following statement: "Excellence of character results from habituation" (II, 1, 1103a17–18). Habits may create a sense of stability. This is right, but it is a dynamic rather than a fixed stability that enables people to react to changing or different situations in dissimilar, adequate ways. As Lockwood remarks in his work about Aristotle's views on habits, "although *héxeis* [habits] are distinguished from other mental states by their enduring, permanent or entrenched nature, their permanence is paradoxically dynamic or kinetic rather than static" (2013: 24). In the same vein, Jonathan Lear notes, "habits, in Aristotle's view, do not merely instil a disposition to engage in certain types of behaviour: they instil a sensitivity as to how to act in various circumstances" (Lear 1988: 166). Thus, it is not necessary to learn a complete set of rules on how to act in different occasions. Once developed, habits indicate how to act. As Annas (2011: 73) explains:

> we are engaged in an activity which is not simple enough to be routine, but not such as to require self-conscious figuring out what to do. We respond to the situation in a way that has already been educated by practice and so can be direct and unselfconscious, but it is still intelligent in responding to feedback, and so consists of more than simple repetition.[5]

Concerning institutions, then, Aristotle posits that there is also a reinforcing virtuous circle linking human actions, habits, and institutions. For Aristotle, the community is ontologically prior to the individual because human beings can only flourish in a community and not alone. Communities, with their rulers and educators, laws and education, try to instill in citizens the habits that make them flourish, according to every individual community's shared values. For him, the final causes of institutions are ontologically their first causes – though chronologically the last – as they trigger the working of the efficient causes leading to them. Some of these final causes are ingrained in human nature, and are then specified in conventions, while others are conventionally defined by people. In any case, on account of human freedom, final causes are objectives that are not automatically given, rather they are tasks to be performed. They possess a normative status and have to be accepted by an institution's members. Additionally, for Aristotle, language plays a crucial role in all human interactions, as well as in the creation of institutions. Let us remember that for Aristotle the human being is the animal possessing *logos*, which is language and reason (*Politics* I, 2, 1253a 10).

With this in mind, we are now ready to appraise Veblen's ideas and other current theories of institutions found in the discussion raised in Hindriks and Guala's paper from an Aristotelian standpoint.

Thorstein Veblen

I could have treated Veblen in Chapter 4, which addresses evolutionary economics or I had the choice to do so in this chapter given that his theory of institutions is evolutionary. I decided to mention him in the present chapter considering that he is a leading figure of old economic institutionalism.

I have mentioned the role of habits in Veblen's institutionalism which is a topic that has been extensively studied. Nevertheless, as Felipe Almeida (2015) notes, the role of instincts in Veblen's thought has been generally neglected. Veblen starts his book *The Instinct of Workmanship and the State of the Industrial Arts* affirming:

> For mankind as for the other higher animals, the life of the species is conditioned by the complement of instinctive proclivities and tropismatic aptitudes with which the species is typically endowed. Not only is the continued life of the race dependent on the adequacy of its instinctive proclivities in this way, but the routine and details of its life are also, in the last resort, determined by these instincts. These are the prime movers in human behaviour, as in the behaviour of all those animals that show self-direction or discretion. Human activity, in so far as it can be spoken of as conduct, can never exceed the scope of these instinctive dispositions, by initiative of which man takes action. Nothing falls within the human scheme of things desirable to be done except what answers to these native proclivities of man. These native proclivities alone make anything worthwhile, and out of their working emerge not only the purpose and efficiency of life, but its substantial pleasures and pains as well.
>
> (Veblen [1914] 1918: 1)

This is an idea that he had even expressed earlier: "Like other animals, man is an agent that acts in response to stimuli afforded by the environment in which he lives" (1898a: 188). Veblen maintains that consciousness and intelligence have a role in human behavior, but he then states that "instinct also governs the scope and method of intelligence in all this employment of it. Men take thought, but the human spirit, that is to say the racial endowment of instinctive proclivities, decides what they shall take thought of, and how and to what effect" ([1914] 1918: 6).

All possible variations between the behavior of individuals has to do with differences in the social environment, differences in individual instincts and, consequently, in the different ways in which individuals react. That is, Veblen's notion of instinct goes beyond a mere inner impulse, considering that sociability (habits and institutions) mediates the relation between human's inner impulses and good, and that instincts are the result of this relation (see Almeida 2015: 230). Veblen quotes pragmatist and early behaviorist books such as William James's *Principles of Psychology*, William McDougall's *Introduction to Social Psychology* (both stressing the role of instincts) and Jacques Loeb's *Comparative Physiology of the Brain and Comparative Psychology* (who sustained a physicalist reductionism). Rutherford (2001: 175) also notes the influence of John B. Watson on Veblen, and Hodgson (1998: 417; 1999: 16; 1993: 125) notes the influence that Peirce had on him.[6]

Hodgson (1993: Chapter 9; and 1998) examines the historical background of Veblen's writings and shows how in the period between 1896 and 1898 he shifted from a Spencerian to a Darwinian view of evolution. In effect, in the quoted paper of 1898, Veblen already affirms: "By *selective necessity* he is endowed with a proclivity for purposeful action" (1898a: 188) and "Like other species, man is a creature of habits and propensities. He acts under the guidance of propensities which have been imposed upon him by the *process of selection* to which he owes his differentiation from other species" (1898a: 5, my emphasis). This article was written the same year as his "evolutionary manifesto" (as Hodgson 1999: 97 calls it) "Why is Economics not an Evolutionary Science?" (1898b).

However, Veblen's "neo-Darwinism" is not strictly Darwinian. Hodgson (1998: 421–422) argues that under the possible influence of C. Lloyd Morgan, who promoted the idea of an emergent level of socio-economic evolution which is not exclusively explicable in biological terms, Veblen believed that evolution occurs at the level of the social system, not mainly at the biological level. As discussed in Chapter 4 on evolutionary economics, Veblen speaks about teleology but, Hodgson notes, "while Veblen consistently regarded the human agent as purposeful, he never reconciled the notion of purposeful behaviour with mechanical causality. The separation of the Aristotelian final and efficient types of causes remained, but Veblen was disposed to the latter notion of causality" (1998: 423; see also 1999: 150). For Philip Mirowski (1987: 1022; and 1988: 123) the non-teleological, mechanical and materialist side clearly prevails. Samuels also stresses the non-teleological characteristic of Veblenian Darwinism (1995: 580). However, Hodgson remarks, "it would be a mistake to suggest that Veblen denied the reality of purposeful behavior" (1998: 423; see also 1997: 27). The problem is that this purposeful behavior has to be considered in the context of Veblen's idea of a cumulative causal evolutionary sequence (see Veblen 1900: 266; 1919: 176–177; and Hodgson 1998: 426). He criticizes Marx's personal and teleological position contrasting it to Darwin's:

> in the Darwinian scheme of thought, the continuity sought in and imputed to the facts is a continuity of cause and effect. It is a scheme of blindly cumulative causation, in which there is no trend, no final term, no consummation. The sequence is controlled by nothing but the *vis a tergo* of brute causation, and is essentially mechanical.
>
> (Veblen 1907: 304; 1919: 436)

Serhat Kologlugil (2016) offers a useful study which clarifies Veblen's Darwinism. After characterizing Darwin's evolutionary theory, he shows how Veblen applies Darwin's key concepts and principles to the explanation of human behavior and life in human societies. Their evolution is a question of "cumulative causation," not of teleological process, as Darwin also claims about the biological realm. However, Veblen does not fall into biological reductionism because he thinks that there is an interaction between instincts, habits, institutions, and material and technological conditions. Kologlugil thinks that "gene-culture coevolution theory," a theory born in the 1960s, which includes culture as a variable in evolutionary processes, can be accommodated to Veblen's thought. For this theory there is a mutual influence between biological – genetic – and cultural evolution. Hence, this theory, as Kologlugil also argues, "clearly subscribes to Universal Darwinism" (2016: 652). As Marlies Schütz and Andreas Rainer (2016: 738) conclude, whereas Joseph Schumpeter (as explained in Chapter 4) relied on sociology and history, Veblen relied on "evolutionary sciences" (1898b: 374) such as anthropology, psychology and biology.

The evident conclusion is that the tensions within scientific-liberal naturalism, determinism-free will, and practical-technical reason are also present in Veblen. However, given the weight of the biological elements in Veblen's thinking and his non-teleological stance, I consider that for him the balance is inclined towards the first elements of these pairs.

Contemporary economic theories of institutions

In the introduction of this chapter I mentioned that Hindriks and Guala (2005a) presented a proposal to unify three contemporary theories of institutions – rule-based, equilibrium-based, and constitutive rule theories. In this section I will assess whether these three theories and their proposal leaves room for practical reason.

Rule theory

The rule-based account particularly points to a widely shared definition of institutions. Coming back to Hodgson's definition, institutions are "systems of established and prevalent social rules that structure social interactions" (2006: 2). He adds that a rule is a habit that has become normative, can be codified, and has been adopted by a group of people (cf. Hodgson 2006: 6). Hodgson also notes that "institutions work only because the rules involved are embedded in shared habits of thought and behaviour" (2006: 6).

I think that this account is compatible with classical ideas of practical reason about agency, habits and institutions. The rule theory and Aristotle's views share the following elements:

1 the links between actions, habits and institutions;
2 the normative character of the system of rules that constitute an institution;
3 the creation of stable behaviors resulting from institutions.

The rule account does not include some of the philosophical underpinnings and characteristics considered by Aristotle, such as the teleological nature of institutions and the role of language in their origin and functioning. However, the rule account is not a philosophical but a sociological theory and therefore should not be expected to explicitly include these features.

Equilibrium theory

According to the equilibrium account, institutions are equilibria of strategic games. This position relies on instrumental rationality, leaving practical rationality aside (see Colman 2004: 287; Bicchieri 2014: 216, 229).[7] Like the previous account, this theory might be compatible with Aristotelian ideas, but it possibly only captures – at most – a partial instance of the Aristotelian process. In Aristotle's market case, for example, buyers and sellers may be expected to eventually reach equilibrium after their interaction. However, for Aristotle, market equilibrium requires more than this, as practical reason comes into play to determine the actual need for the good in demand. This is an essential trait of the Aristotelian market. If practical reason were absent, equilibrium would only be achieved by chance. The same applies to the case of the *pólis*: the Aristotelian *pólis* is not a kind of liberal equilibrium of individual goals. If there is not a common end as well as a conscious reasoning and search for the specific way to accomplish it, a *pólis* will not emerge. In sum, the equilibrium account involves a kind of process that differs greatly from Aristotle's view of practical reason. Searle (2015: 512) clearly elaborates on this:

> You cannot do an equilibrium analysis of institutional facts of the sort that they [Hindriks and Guala 2015a] propose, because the equilibria are

insufficient to generate the deontology – rights, duties, obligations, etc. – that is the defining trait of institutional facts.

He adds that Hume already made the same mistake, and remarks that an inadequate notion of rationality is involved in this account (Searle 2015: 514).

Constitutive rules theory

Aristotle's ideas on practical reason concerning agency, habits and institutions fit very nicely with Searle's (2005) constitutive rules account. In his article "What Is an Institution?" (2005), Searle introduces three basic notions that he considers necessary to explain social and institutional reality:

1 collective intentionality as the basis of all societies;
2 the assignment of functions to objects; and
3 the collective assignment of a certain status function to objects and/or persons (2005: 6–8).

For Searle, an institution is a set of status functions that stem from a system of constitutive rules (2005: 10). It creates desire-independent reasons for action (2005: 11) – that is, deontic obligations that are the glue of every society. For Aristotle the deontological duties that emanate from societies are synergic with an individual's well-being because he is a political animal. Searle stresses that the relevance of language is crucial for the constitution of institutional facts: institutions and their deontic power cannot emerge and persist without language (2005: 12ff.).

Additionally, constitutive rule theory cannot be reduced to the "rules-in-equilibrium" account proposed by Hindriks and Guala (2015a). The essential intentional and deontic character of rules cannot be narrowed down to the equilibrium of individual strategic behaviors because, as already said, these behaviors are ruled by instrumental rationality.

Summing up, the constitutive rules theory of institutions and Aristotle's views share the following elements:

1 the idea of a common underlying end in Searle's collective intentionality;
2 the normative and uniting character of reasons that constitute an institution;
3 the role of language in the emergence and persistency of institutions.

The conclusion is that the constitutive rule theory makes room for practical reason in its impact on agency, habits and institutions. Consequently, in accordance with Searle's general posture about rationality, explained in Chapter 2, his theory is against scientific naturalism. Searle sustains the existence of intentions, of desire-independent reasons (i.e., reasons that create desires, of values and ends, as part of the natural world thus adhering to a broader naturalism than a scientific physically closed naturalism).

Conclusion

The time has come for assessing economic institutionalism in relation to practical reason. In this chapter I appraised Veblen's ideas and recent theories of institutions in economics as being unified and explained by Hindriks and Guala from this philosophical point of view. However, before analyzing these theories, I briefly described the implications of the classical concept of practical reason on the basic concepts of institutionalism – agency, habits and institutions.

Given the close link of original institutional economics with evolutionary theories, the conclusion about the latter in Chapter 4 also applies to institutionalism in its relation with evolution: as long as evolutionary ideas do not affect the possibility of free will or, in other words, do not imply that human behavior is deterministic, they can contribute a useful basis for understanding human actions.

In this sense, it seems that there is a tension in Veblen's thought given that he wants to consider human purposefulness but, at the same time, proposes a neo-Darwinian theory where ultimately all human behavior – habits, institutions, and culture – seems to be deterministically caused. I argue, however, that we need a non-deterministic balance between biological and non-biological elements. I think that Hodgson (1999: 126) expressed it well:

> Biology may establish links with, but should not deny the autonomy of, the social sciences. With this conceptualization it is possible to articulate a relationship between economics and biology in which each play their part, but the domination of one by the other is excluded.

Old Institutionalism stresses the role of agency, habits and institutions in the motivation of economic decisions and actions. In this chapter I developed an Aristotelian approach to these concepts which is completely compatible with the consideration of practical reason. For Aristotle, the community is ontologically prior to the individual, because human beings can only flourish in a community and not alone. Communities instill in citizens the habits that make them flourish. These habits facilitate the corresponding actions of people who simultaneously self-govern themselves. These connections are grounded in philosophical theories of human action, human habits and communities and notions about the interactions between them. I think that these philosophical theories offer additional support to Institutionalism's ideas about the relation among agency, habits and institutions, and may help to clarify contemporary discussions about the nature of institutions. This approach is ignored by neoclassical theory. Agency is absent in its mechanical view of human action, reduced to its instrumental maximizing dimension, while habits and institutions, when present, are also regarded in a mechanical way. As a result, neoclassical theories can only offer a very limited and often misguided explanation of economic decisions and actions. Moreover, another conclusion is that institutionalist theories that ultimately reduce explanations of human behavior to neoclassical theories of rationality *ipso facto* leave practical reason aside.

Notes

1 See Alain Guery (2003) for a history of this notion. He does not mention Giambattista Vico, who used the term "institution" in his 1725 *Scienza Nuova* to refer to its nature and evolution. Guery stresses the ancient use of the term as possessing a dynamic character.
2 See, for example, his 1994 work. Other major thinkers on institutions include Emile Durkheim, Talcott Parsons, Anthony Giddens, Douglass North, Jonathan Turner, Rom Harre, John Searle, Raimo Tuomela, and Margaret Gilbert. See the review in the article by Seumas Miller (2011).
3 See Jean-Jacques Gislain (2003) for a history of the emergence of the topic of institutions in economics. Also see Rutherford (1995) for an effort in setting bridges between old and new institutionalisms.
4 For Weber, actions intended to allocate means to attain agents' ends are instrumentally rational, while value-rational actions are determined by a conscious belief in the intrinsic value of a specific behaviour. Affectual actions are driven by individuals' affects and feelings, and traditional actions stem from ingrained habits. Weber argued that, although one specific motive often prevails, actions are also ruled by various types of motives.
5 This supposes a different classification of habits and routines that are common in sociology: habits belong to the individual, routines to the organization.
6 On the possible Veblen-behaviourism connection, see José Edwards (2016).
7 A recent symposium on Rational Choice Theory has understood it as including decision theory, game theory and social choice theory (Okasha and Weymark 2016: 171).

References

Almeida, F. (2015). "The psychology of early institutional economics: The instinctive approach of Thorstein Veblen"s conspicuous consumer theory," *EconomiA* 16: 221–234.
Annas, J. (2011). *Intelligent Virtue*. Oxford: Oxford University Press.
Aoki, M. (2015). "Why is the equilibrium notion essential for a unified institutional theory? A friendly remark on the article by Hindriks and Guala," *Journal of Institutional Economics* 11/3: 485–488.
Aristotle (1943). *Politics*. Translated by B. Jowett. New York: Random House.
Aristotle (1954). *Nicomachean Ethics*. Translated and Introduced by Sir David Ross. Oxford: Oxford University Press.
Aristotle (1958). *Politics*. Edited and translated by E. Barker. Oxford: Oxford University Press.
Aristotle (1995). *The Complete Works of Aristotle. The Revised Oxford Translation*, J. Barnes (ed.). Princeton, NJ: Princeton University Press, 6th printing with corrections.

Aristotle (1999). *Nicomachean Ethics.* Translated by T. Irwin. Indianapolis and Cambridge: Hackett.

Bicchieri, C. (2014). "Norms, Conventions, and the Power of Expectations." In N. Cartwright and E. Montuschi (eds.) *Philosophy of Social Science. A New Introduction.* Oxford: Oxford University Press.

Binmore, K. (2015). "Institutions, rules and equilibria: a commentary," *Journal of Institutional Economics* 11/3: 493–496.

Bourdieu, P. (1994). *Raisons pratiques. Sur la théorie de l'action.* Paris: Éditions du Seuil.

Burnyeat, M. F. (1980). "Aristotle on Learning to Be Good." In A. Oksenberg Rorty (ed.) *Essays on Aristotle's Ethics.* Berkeley and Los Angeles: University of California Press.

Colman, A. J. (2004). "Reasoning about strategic interaction. Solution concepts in game theory." In K. I. Manktelow and Man Cheung Chung (eds.) *Psychology of Reasoning,* Hove and New York: Psychology Press (Taylor & Francis).

Davis, J. B. (2003). *The Theory of the Individual in Economics.* London and New York: Routledge.

Davis, J. B. (2008). "The turn in recent economics and the return of orthodoxy," *Cambridge Journal of Economics* 32: 349–366.

Edwards, J. (2016). "Behaviorism and control in the history of economics and psychology," *History of Political Economy* 48: Supplement 1, 170–197.

Frydman, R. (2003). "Presentation," *Cahiers d'économie Politique/Papers in Political Economy* 1/2003 (44): i–xv.

Gislain, J.-J. (2003). "L'émergence de la problématique des institutions en économie," *Cahiers d'économie Politique/Papers in Political Economy* 1/2003 (44): 19–50.

Guery, A. (2003). "Institution, histoire d'une notion et de ses utilisations dans l'histoire avant les institutionnalismes," *Cahiers d'économie Politique/Papers in Political Economy* 1/2003 (44): 7–18.

Hamilton, W. H. (1919). "The Institutional Approach to Economic Theory," *American Economic Review* 9/1: 309–318.

Hamilton, W. H. (1932). "Institution." In E. R. A. Seligman (ed.), *Encyclopaedia of the Social Sciences, vol. 8.* London: MacMillan, https://archive.org/stream/ency clopaediaoft030467mbp#page/n105/mode/2up.

Hindriks, F. and F. Guala (2015a). "Institutions, rules, and equilibria. A unified theory," *Journal of Institutional Economics* 11/3: 459–480.

Hindriks, F. and F. Guala (2015b). "Understanding institution: replies to Aoki, Binmore, Hodgson, Searle, Smith, and Sugden," *Journal of Institutional Economics* 11/3: 515–522.

Hodgson, G. M. (1993). *Economics and Evolution. Bringing Life Back to Economics.* Cambridge: Polity Press.

Hodgson, G. M. (1997). "Economics and Evolution and the Evolution of Economics." In J. Reijnders (ed.), *Economics and Evolution.* Cheltenham: Edward Elgar.

Hodgson, G. M. (1998). "Thorstein Veblen's evolutionary economics," *Cambridge Journal of Economics* 22: 415–431.

Hodgson, G. M. (1999). *Evolution and Institutions. On Evolutionary Economics and the Evolution of Economics.* Cheltenham: Edward Elgar.

Hodgson, G. M. (2004a). "Institutional economics: from Menger and Veblen to Coase and North." In J. B. Davis, A. Marciano and J. Runde (eds.), *The Elgar Companion to Economics and Philosophy.* Cheltenham: Edward Elgar.

Hodgson, G. M. (2004b). "Reclaiming Habit for Institutional Economics," *Journal of Economic Psychology* 25: 651–660.

Hodgson, G. M. (2006). "What Are Institutions?," *Journal of Economic Issues* XL/1: 1–25.

Hodgson, G. M. (2007). "The Revival of Veblevian Institutional Economics," *Journal of Economic Issues* XLI/: 325–340.

Hodgson, G. M. (2015). "On defining institutions: rules versus equilibria," *Journal of Institutional Economics* 11/3: 497–505.

Huntington, S. P. (1965). "Political Development and Political Decay," *World Politics* 17/3: 386–430.

Kologlugil, S. (2016). "Thornstein Veblen's Darwinian framework and gene-culture coevolution theory," *European Journal of the History of Economic Thought* 23/4: 641–672.

Lear, J. (1988). *Aristotle: The Desire to Understand.* Cambridge: Cambridge University Press.

Lockwood, T. C. (2013). "Habituation, Habit, and Character in Aristotle's *Nicomachean Ethics.*" In T. Sparrow and A. Hutchison (eds.) *A History of Habit: From Aristotle to Bourdieu.* Langham: Lexington Books.

Miller, S., (2011), "Social Institutions," *Stanford Encyclopedia of Philosophy,* http://plato.stanford.edu/entries/social-institutions/, retrieved January 20, 2015.

Mirowski, P. (1987). "The Philosophical Bases of Institutional Economics," *Journal of Economic Issues* 21/3: 1001–1038.

Mirowski, P. (1988). *Against Mechanism.* Totawa: Rowman and Littlefield.

Okasha, S. and J. A. Weymark (2016). "An Introduction to the Symposium on Rational Choice and Philosophy," *Economics and Philosophy* 32/2: 171–173.

Rutherford, M. (1995). "The Old and the New Institutionalism: Can Bridges Be Built?," *Journal of Economic Issues* XXIX/2: 443–458.

Rutherford, M. (2001). "Institutional Economics: Then and Now," *American Economic Review* 15/3: 173–194.

Samuels, W. J. (1991). "Institutional Economics." In D. Greenaway, M. Bleaney and I. Stewart (eds.), *Companion to Contemporary Economic Thought.* London: Routledge.

Samuels, W. J. (1995). "The present state of institutional economics," *Cambridge Journal of Economics* 19: 569–590.

Schütz, M. and A. Rainer (2016). "J. A. Schumpeter and T. B. Veblen on economic evolution: the dichotomy between statics and dynamics," *European Journal of the History of Economic Thought* 23/5: 718–742.

Searle, J. R. (2005). "What is an institution?," *Journal of Institutional Economics* 1/1: 1–22.

Searle, J. R. (2015). "Status Functions and Institutional Facts. Reply to Hindriks and Guala," *Journal of Institutional Economics* 11/3: 507–514.

Sen, A. (2002). *Rationality and Freedom.* Cambridge, MA: The Belknap Press of Harvard University.

Simon, H. A. (2005). "Darwinism, altruism and economics." In K. Dopfer (ed.), *The Evolutionary Foundation of Economics.* Cambridge: Cambridge University Press.

Smith, V. (2015). "Conducts, rules, and the origins of institutions," *Journal of Institutional Economics* 11/3: 481–483.

Sugden, R. (2015). "On 'common-sense' ontology: A comment on the paper by Frank Hindriks and Francesco Guala," *Journal of Institutional Economics* 11/3: 489–492.

Veblen, Th. (1898a). "The Instinct of Workmanship and the Irksomeness of Labor," *American Journal of Sociology* 4(1898–99): 187–201, https://archive.org/stream/jstor-2761796/2761796#page/n3/mode/2up, retrieved May 16, 2016.

Veblen, Th. (1898b). "Why Is Economics not an Evolutionary Science?," *The Quarterly Journal of Economics* 12/4: 373–397.

Veblen, Th. (1900). "The Preconceptions of Economic Science. III," *Quarterly Journal of Economics* 14/1: 240–269, re-edited in *The Place of Science in Modern Civilization and Other Essays.* New York: B.W. Huebsch.

Veblen, Th. (1907). "The Socialist Economics of Karl Marx and his Followers II: The later Marxism," *Quarterly Journal of Economics* 21/1: 299–322, re-edited in *The Place of Science in Modern Civilization and Other Essays.* New York: B. W. Huebsch.

Veblen, Th. ([1914] 1918). *The Instinct of Workmanship and the State of the Industrial Arts.* New York: B. W. Huebsch (first edition by MacMillan).

Veblen, Th. (1919). *The Place of Science in Modern Civilisation and Other Essays.* New York: B. W. Huebsch.

Weber, M., (1978). *Economy and Society.* Edited by G. Roth and C. Wittich. Berkeley and Los Angeles: University of California Press.

Williamson, O. E. (1973). "Markets and Hierarchies: Some Elementary Considerations," *American Economic Review* 63/2: 316–325.

Williamson, O. E. (1975). *Markets and Hierarchies: Analysis and Anti-Trust Implications: A Study in the Economics of Internal Organization.* New York: Free Press.

Williamson, O. E. (1985). *The Economic Institutions of Capitalism: Firms, Markets, Relational Contracting.* London: MacMillan.

Williamson, O. E. (2000). "The new institutional economics: taking stock, looking ahead," *Journal of Economic Literature* XXXVIII: 595–613.

8   The capability approach

In Chapter 1 I explained how Amartya Sen distinguishes two different origins of economics in his book *Ethics and Economics*. One is the ethics-related tradition that goes back to Aristotle, which he supports (Sen 1987: 2–4). For him (1987: 4), "This 'ethics-related view of social achievement' cannot stop the evaluation short at some arbitrary point like satisfying 'efficiency'. The assessment has to be more fully ethical, and take a broader view of 'the good'." Sen also highlights the engineering-related tradition that focuses on logistic aspects associated with instrumental rationality, and thinks that both perspectives must be combined because they are complementary. In this sense we can affirm that Sen's approach, the capability approach, comes from within economics. This point of view has been expressed, for example, by Hilary Putnam (2004: 48):

> If we are to understand Sen's place in history, the reintroduction of ethical concerns and concepts into economic discourse must not be thought as an *abandonment* of "classical economics"; rather it is a *reintroduction* of something that was everywhere present in the writings of Adam Smith.

Nevertheless, given that Sen's proposal involves the renewal of philosophical thinking, long excluded from economics, it can also be considered a "reverse imperialist" current that is influenced by ethics. Consequently, these two origins of change, from outside and from within economics, are synergic.

Sen's capability approach explicitly considers practical reason, human agency, freedom and ends in economics. In Sen's approach, the tensions between determinism and freedom, scientific and liberal naturalism, instrumental and practical reason disappear. Instead, other tensions pertaining to the practical field appear.

By focusing on capabilities, Sen reinserts the notion of ends into economics: capabilities are themselves ends, purposes, freedoms. For Sen, a crucial aspect of human well-being – understood in a broad sense that goes beyond utility – is human "agency." Agency is related to the quality of life, but it also includes others' goals and the possibility of commitment to actions that do not benefit the agent himself. Human agency entails freedom: freedoms are "capabilities" of performing actions that Sen calls "functionings." The French philosopher Paul Ricoeur equates Sen's use of the term "agency" with the "capacity to act," a power that goes beyond the capacity to choose (2005: 141–146). Capabilities and functionings compose a good life. Capabilities, for Sen, are seen as a better way of assessing well-being than utility or income.[1]

Sen's approach involves a broad perspective that considers the person in his/her individuality, as a socially-shaped unique, reflective and free agent. This leads to an enriched evaluation of well-being, equality, development and all the areas in which it may be applied. The focus is not on means (e.g., income), but on ends (e.g., the satisfaction of the aspirations and ultimate goals of different people). This acknowledgment of human heterogeneity and of the heterogeneity of objectives implies broadening the informational basis for evaluation and considering the plurality of different human situations. Notwithstanding the foregoing, this plurality does not mean that we accept capricious ambitions, desires and behaviors. For Sen, the free agent must be responsible and not only consider his own concerns but others' as well.

Capabilities according to Sen are heterogeneous and incommensurable. They can only be compared. Decisions about capabilities are thus prudential and go beyond calculations. They are ruled by practical reason. Sen's criticism of contemporary economics points to its lack of concern for values. Accordingly, he asserts, "rationality includes the use of reasoning to understand and assess goals and values" (2002: 46), that is, theoretical and practical reasoning.

In this chapter, I will present Amartya Sen's capability approach (CA) and highlight how it creates a role for practical reason in the social sciences, and specifically in economics. Sen focuses his attention on the capabilities of persons, which are their ends or purposes. He maintains that dealing with capabilities requires the use of practical reason. In Chapter 2, I defined practical reason as human reason exercised in the task of directing people's decisions, choices, and actions. Practical reason tries to answer questions such as "what should I intend?," "how should I behave?" Hence, practical reasoning involves discursive thinking about what we should do: it looks for ends and reasons and appraises the impact of means upon them. As also explained in Chapter 2, sciences studying and applying practical reason are called practical sciences.

The use of practical reason to deal with the practical realm is therefore a strength of the CA. At the same time, however, it is considered a weakness by some critics. The particularities of the subject matter of practical science – unpredictability, fluctuation and context-dependency of human behavior – make practical sciences inexact. Given this, practical sciences cannot provide general recipes: this is the shortcoming noted by critics when accusing the CA of being inoperative. The more universal and operative a science is, the less practical it is (in the sense of being adapted to particular cases). Conversely, the more practical a science is, the less universal and operative it is. However, practical reason helps for making practical decisions: in this sense it is highly operative. Confronted with this tension, Sen favors the practical side. He forcefully defends the heterogeneity of human beings, situations, and objectives. Consequently, he does not want to establish a hierarchical ordering of capabilities. This obviously undermines universal recommendations.

In section 1 of this chapter I will present the CA, specially focusing on one of its contributions, which is to explain development and the removal of poverty in a more qualitative manner than is usually the case in economics. Section 2 will deal with two problems in Sen's CA: first, the definition of specific capabilities given their plurality; second, how to choose among capabilities given their incommensurability, and thus the issue of whether there is a hierarchy of capabilities. I will show that these problems emerge in part from Sen's conception of practical reason that is more Kantian than classical. The conclusion is that Sen's CA is decidedly close to the ideal suggested in this book, which entails considering practical reason, freedom, intentionality, and a "liberal naturalist" approach.

Introducing the capability approach

The capability approach (CA) is a broad framework for the evaluation or assessment of individual well-being – as well as the development of entire countries, socio-economic circumstances and social arrangements – for the purpose of implementing social and economic policies. The CA has a highly interdisciplinary character. Such character facilitates the multidimensional nature of the objectives to be achieved, that is, outcomes (functionings) and freedoms (capabilities). Sen's CA has promoted wide-ranging research and the development of different versions of the CA. These different versions raise difficult questions as to what the specific constitutive ends of a good life are or what the concrete content of the CA is. Here the philosophical roots of the CA manifest themselves.

A presentation of Sen's CA must include an explanation of the meaning of some key concepts: "well-being," "agency," "functioning" and "capability."[2] It also requires discussing three related topics stressed by the approach: first, the multidimensionality of ends and the differences among persons, and thus, the need for a multidimensional evaluation of situations (such as poverty, inequality, and development); second, the problem of incompleteness regarding the ordering of ends; and, third, the consequent need for practical reason to deliberate about ends, either through personal reflection at the individual level or through public discussion at the social level.

Sen proposes a fourfold classification for assessing human advantage that stems from the intersection of two different distinctions. According to him, on the one hand, we can draw a distinction between the assessment of the person's well-being and the person's agency. On the other hand, we can distinguish between the assessment of achievement and the freedom to achieve. Hence, we have four possibilities (see Table 8.1):

Table 8.1 Sen's four possibilities for assessing human advantage

	Well-being	*Agency*
Achievement	1. Well-being Achievement	2. Agency achievement
Freedom to achieve	3. Well-being freedom	4. Agency freedom

1   assess the achievement of well-being;
2   assess the achievement of agency;
3   assess the freedom to achieve well-being; and
4   assess the freedom of agency. These different kinds of evaluation apply to different situations (Sen 1993: 35–36; 2009: 287).

Let us take a look at these possibilities more closely. For Sen, on the one hand, well-being is a state of a person that goes beyond material welfare or the "standard of living" (Sen 1993: 37). This obviously means that his understanding of the concept of well-being goes beyond material wealth or opulence (1999a: 19). On the other hand, agency includes other-regarding concerns that do not operate through our personal well-being, that is, it also embraces purely non self-serving purposes. Then, although agency is related to the quality of life, it also includes others' goals and a commitment to actions that do not benefit the very agent himself.

Having defined these two possible types of evaluative objectives, namely evaluation of well-being and evaluation of agency, Sen distinguishes between the evaluation of their achievement and the opportunity that people may have of achieving them (because we can have opportunities and not exercise them). Summing up, we can evaluate human advantage in terms of the achievement of well-being, in terms of the achievement of agency, in terms of the well-being freedom and in terms of agency freedom. Although these different kinds of evaluation are generally suitable for different aims, the spirit of Sen's exposition is that the most complete evaluations are those that involve freedom and agency. He (2009: 289) asserts that "while the former [well-being freedom] may be of more general interest to public policy [...], it is the latter [agency freedom] that can, arguably, be seen as being of primary interest to the person's own sense of values." Hence, agency freedom has special relevance for Sen. The concept of "agency freedom" "refers to what the person is free to do and to achieve in pursuit of whatever goals or values he or she regards as important" (1985: 203). This concept goes beyond a concept of "well-being-freedom" – that is, the freedom to achieve that what the person believes is conducive to her well-being; agency, as mentioned, is open to the values of others.

Sen also calls achievements "functionings" and freedoms "capabilities." "A functioning is an achievement of a person: what he or she manages to do or to be" (Sen 1999a: 7). Functioning is an overarching concept that includes what a person is, does and has. Functioning is a fact, not a possibility. It includes freedom as part of the state of the person (e.g., 1999a: 44–45). Sen also distinguishes elementary and complex functionings. Functionings such as being adequately nourished, being in good health, escaping morbidity and mortality, having mobility are elementary. Functionings such as achieving self-respect, being socially integrated, being happy, taking part in the life of a community are complex (Sen 1993: 31 and 36–37). Sen realizes that these goals are heterogeneous.

The plurality of functionings depends not only on their variety but also on the differences between persons. For Sen, each person is unique and has his/her personal set of functionings. Causal relations (derived from functionings) are *person-specific* (1985: 196). This is one of his most important points of departure from other approaches, namely the basic heterogeneity of human beings: "Human beings are thoroughly diverse" (1992: 1). This centrality of the human person speaks to us of a highly humanistic approach.

Functionings are related to capabilities. While the combination of functionings reflects the person's actual achievements, the capability set represents the person's "real opportunities" (1992: 31; see also 2009: 231ff.), the possibilities or freedom to achieve (1999b: 75). Sen used this concept for the first time in 1979. He introduced it in his Tanner Lecture – "Equality of What?" in order to present an alternative approach to the evaluation of equality that was distinct from the Utilitarian and Rawlsian views. In that lecture he spoke of "basic capability equality," regarding "a person being able to do certain things" (1980: 217) – as he recalls in 1993 (1993: 30, footnote 1), as a particular approach to well-being (1993: 30). He then considered basic capabilities as a refinement of Rawls's concentration on primary goods to evaluate equality (an element of "goods fetishism"). His aim was to produce the most complete possible form of evaluation. We have to pay attention to "what a person *can* do rather than what he *does* do" (1980–1981: 209). He then added the concept of functionings and redefined the capabilities of a person in relation to them, as the "set of functioning vectors within his or her reach" (1985: 201). He realized that both concepts were intimately related, "because the extent of the capability set is relevant to the significance and value of the respective functionings" (1985: 202). Sen also noted that "many capabilities may be trivial and valueless, while others are substantial and important" (1987b: 108). In 1989 (54) he explained that valuable capabilities are quite diverse and that they vary from elementary freedoms such as being free from hunger and undernourishment to complex abilities such as achieving self-respect and social participation. In his 1993 (41, note 32) paper, however, he says, in retrospect, that while he had used the expression "basic capabilities" in his Tanner Lecture (1980), he did not qualify capabilities as basic or complex in ensuing papers. He provided a more formal treatment of these concepts in *Commodities and Capabilities* published in 1985 (1999a: 6–11).

We then have a plurality of different dimensions for evaluating functionings and capabilities, and the heterogeneity between persons. We are different, and we are free. Given these characteristics of human beings we need to choose and therefore reflect upon our choices. Thus, for Sen the agent is a free and reflective being. He asserts:

> I am using the term agent [...] in its older – and "grander" – sense as someone who acts and brings about change, and whose achievements can be judged in terms of her own values and objectives.
>
> (Sen 1999a: 19)

> The people have to be seen [...] as being actively involved – given the opportunity – in shaping their own destiny, and not just as passive recipients of the fruits of cunning development programs.
>
> (Sen 1999b: 53)

For Sen, then, well-being is only one of the motives that guide people's choices. Agency means a responsible autonomy, an other-regarding way of deciding and acting. It may even lead to acts that decrease our well-being to the benefit of other persons (1999a: 9). Additionally, as Davis (2002: 483–4) has emphasized, Sen recognizes the role of community and groups influencing personal behavior and even individual identity. However, this emphasis on agency does not imply a neglect of the consideration of well-being. This is still very important in matters of public policy.[3] Yet concerning issues of personal behavior, the agency aspect is central (1985: 208). A first central characteristic of this agent is its freedom:

> The capability of a person refers to the various alternative combinations of functionings, any one of which (any combination, that is) the person can choose to have. In this sense, the capability of a person corresponds to the *freedom* that a person has to lead one kind of life or another.
>
> (Nussbaum and Sen 1993: 3, italics in the original)

> The *capability* of a person reflects the alternative combination of functionings the person can achieve, and from which he or she can *choose* one collection.
>
> (Sen 1993: 31, my emphasis)

Hence it is clear that freedom is a key notion in Sen's CA. Following Isaiah Berlin (cf. e.g. Sen 1992: 41), Sen distinguishes between negative freedom (to not be interfered with) and positive freedom (to be able to pursue a goal), and claims the necessity of both. Sen conceives of development as a process of expanding real freedoms (1999b: 3, 37, 53 and 297). Human capability is an expression of freedom (Sen 1999b: 292). As David Crocker puts it, "capabilities add something intrinsically and not merely instrumentally valuable to human life, namely, positive freedom" (Crocker 1995: 159; see also 183). Positive freedom is what people are actually able to do or to be, "to choose to live as they desire" (Berlin quoted by Sen 1992: 67). This notion of freedom goes beyond the classical liberal conception of freedom. In Chapter 12 of *Development as Freedom*, entitled "Individual Freedom as Commitment," Sen links freedom with a conscious commitment to disinterested actions, among other objectives. He also speaks about substantive or constitutive freedom (1999b: 33 and 36), and relates freedom to responsibility. This notion of freedom corresponds to Sen's rich notion of agency. As Sen remarks, positive freedom entails taking into account the person's concept of the good (1985: 203). It is freedom to achieve whatever the person decides (1985: 204). This pivotal role of the agent is clear also in Sen's *Inequality Reexamined* where he speaks of "a person's capability to achieve functionings that he or she *has reason to value*" (1992: 4–5, my emphasis). Thus, his conception of freedom assumes an agent who has the intellectual capacity to valuing and choosing. He adds:

> This open conditionality [of the responsible agent] does not imply that the person"s view of his agency has no need for discipline, and that anything that appeals to him must, for that reason, come into the accounting of his agency freedom. The need for careful assessment of aims, objectives, allegiances, etc., and of the conception of the good, may be important and exacting.
>
> (Sen 1985: 204)

That is, freedom is not a completely open or capricious notion: its claims have to be carefully appraised. Sen maintains that because we have freedom, we must also have reasons to value the things we choose. This is one reason why practical reason is needed as a key element in Sen's conception. Freedom moves within the frame of a rationale known or defined by practical reason: "freedom must depend on reasoned assessment" (Sen 2002: 5). This reflects the person's freedom to choose from different possible lives and the real opportunities that the person has (1992: 40 and 83). The idea is more refined in *Development as Freedom* where he refers to "the freedom to achieve actual livings that one can have reason to value" (1999b: 73). Moreover, in *Rationality and Freedom* (2002), as its title expresses, these two concepts are closely linked. The organization of the volume points to this objective: they "all relate in different ways to the two principal themes highlighted in the introductory essay, namely the demands of rationality and the role and relevance of freedom" (2002: 46). Reason intervenes in the form of reflecting on and deliberating about what to do, "to understand and assess goals and values" (2002: 46): this is practical reason. In sum, another central characteristic of Sen's notion of agency is its emphasis on reason and the person's capacity for reflection.

As noted, an interesting aspect of capabilities is their ambiguity in both their definition and their election, given the particularities of persons and their situations. Sen positively appraises this feature because it reflects and respects freedom and the differences between persons (1993: 33–34). For Sen, asserting that there is an ambiguity and fuzziness regarding capabilities is not a weakness but a strength. This further implies that it is a mistake to look for complete orderings of capabilities (1992: 49). Sen calls this "the fundamental reason for incompleteness" (1992: 49). Indeed, this reflects arguments Sen has previously made that we can only arrive at and use partial orderings of preferences. As Davis (2012: 169–170) has put it, Sen:

> has devoted years of demanding and exacting work to a critique of the theoretical adequacy of systems of complete choice orderings, often essentially using a kind of *reductio ad absurdum* impossibility logic against them, but more importantly arguing, contrary to a largely unexamined transcendentalist conviction, that incomplete and partial choice orderings can indeed be rational (and may in fact be the very heart of rationality).

This incompleteness applies both at the individual and social levels. Sen allows that maximization is an important dimension of human action: "a person can accommodate different types of objectives and values within the maximizing framework" (2002: 37). However, Sen's concept of maximization differs from the one used in standard economics. For him, maximization neither requires nor implies completeness of preferences (cf. Sen 1997: 746 and 763; 2000: 483, 486–487; 2002: 158ff., 563–565; 2004c: 49). According to Sen, maximization is more like Simon's concept of satisficing (Sen 1997: 768). Thus, incompleteness and the need for partial choice orderings reinforce the need for using a type of reasoning such as the one practical reason involves. Applied to our specific subject, Sen (2002: 622) comments:

> The recognition that the ranking of opportunity and of freedom would tend to be incomplete may cause disappointment to those who want to rank nothing unless it is possible to rank every opportunity set against every other. I have argued here that this expectation does less than justice to the diversity and reach of freedom in general and opportunity in particular. Admitting incompleteness does not make the use of a reasoned partial ordering "imperfect" in any sense. Indeed, the incompleteness may sometimes have to be asserted, rather than conceded.

The kind of decisions that the agent has to make thus entails a broader use of reason than merely instrumental reason. Sen asserts that "rationality cannot be just an instrumental requirement for the pursuit of some given – unscrutinized – set of objectives and values" (1999a: 39). It should also scrutinize these objectives and values. It includes the use of reason to understand and assess goals and values (1999a: 46), that is, practical reason.

We have thus arrived at the intended central message of this chapter: Sen reintroduces the use of practical reason into economics in the CA. Practical reason determines what capabilities we choose at the personal and social levels. Three important characteristics of the CA thus appear to be inter-linked: incompleteness, multidimensionality and practical reason. The next section about the "problems" in the CA will confirm this statement.

Some problems in Sen's capability approach

Clark (2005: 5–6) suggests that the strengths of the CA may also be considered its weaknesses: Sen"s views about the differences among human persons lead to problems in the identification and evaluation of capabilities – as Sen himself recognizes. He also notes the extreme exigency of the infor-mational requirements of the CA. These weaknesses in the CA culminate in the criticism expressed by Robert Sugden: "it is natural to ask how far Sen's framework is operational" (1993: 1953).

Sen (1993: 32–33) distinguishes between two different evaluation exercises, first choosing the objects of value – functionings and capabilities – composing the "evaluative space," and, second, determining the relative values of those objects. The first evaluation exercise is where an identification problem arises. Here I will consider it from the perspective of Sen's debate with Martha Nussbaum about lists of essential capabilities. Concerning the second evalua-tion exercise, the problem is the incommensurability of capabilities that leads to an absence of hierarchies or orderings of capabilities within the evaluative space. For Sen, these problems are overcome by practical reason. I will ana-lyze them in turn: first the difficulties involved in the identification of cap-abilities – the discussion about lists – and then the difficulties involved in determining their relative weights – the incommensurability of capabilities and the absence of hierarchies among them.

Identification of valuable capabilities: The debate over lists of capabilities

In the debate between Nussbaum and Sen about the capabilities to be sought, Nussbaum argues in favor of a particular list of capabilities that all individuals ought to have, while Sen prefers to leave the matter open (see e.g., Sen 1993; Sen 2004a; Nussbaum 2003). The problem, then, is as follows: should we have a list of specific capabilities to guide public policy or should we only shape a general framework to be filled in later on any given occasion? Sen's answer favors the second alternative. This is consistent with the context-dependent character of practical matters highlighted in the introduction of this chapter. He therefore reacts against Nussbaum's proposal for defining a list of capabilities as follows:

> I accept that this would indeed be a systematic way of eliminating the incompleteness of the capability approach. I certainly have no great objection to anyone going on that route. My difficulty with accepting that as the *only* route on which to travel arises partly from the concern that this

view of human nature (with a unique list of functionings for a good human life) may be tremendously overspecified [...] [T]he use of the capability approach as such does not require taking that route, and the deliberate incompleteness of the capability approach permits other routes to be taken.

(Sen 1993: 47)

Hence, Sen does not define a list of needed capabilities because he maintains that this would involve an over-specified view of human nature. His view is compatible with different views about the human person and the good. This is consistent with his emphasis on human heterogeneity.

Given that this discussion began with Nussbaum's claims, let us explain briefly what her position is. While for Sen, freedom is the central capability, for Nussbaum the central capabilities are practical reason and affiliation (sociability). For Nussbaum these two capabilities are "architectonical." They suffuse and organize "all the other functions – which will count as truly human functions only in so far as they are done with some degree of guidance from both of these" (Nussbaum 1993: 266). For her, these two elements are a core part of human nature (see especially Nussbaum 1995a). Freedom, practical reason and sociability are complementary: since we are free we need to use practical reason in a social context. However, for Sen the priority belongs to freedom (without discarding practical reason), while for Nussbaum it belongs to practical reason (without discarding freedom). However, at the same time, for Sen, as already quoted, "freedom must depend on reasoned assessment" (Sen 2002: 5).

For Nussbaum, the role or proper function of government is "to make available to each and every member of the community the basic necessary conditions of the capability to choose and live a fully good human life, with respect to each of the major human functions included in that fully good life" (Nussbaum 1993: 265). Hence, the task of the government cannot be fulfilled without an understanding of these functionings. According to Nussbaum, capabilities are internal and have to be developed or exercised as concrete functionings; they also depend on external conditions which she calls external capabilities. The role of government, then, is "deep [good lives of all the people, one by one] and broad [the totality of the functionings needed]" (Nussbaum 1987: 7, 29; and 1990: 209): this role is to provide the external opportunities to all the people, to avoid institutions that could block capabilities and to encourage people, through education and through the family, to look for internal capabilities (Nussbaum 1987: 20ff.; 1990: 214). She consistently affirms: "The legislator's total task will be to train internal capabilities in the young, to maintain those in the adult, and simultaneously to create and preserve the external circumstances in which those developed capabilities can become active" (Nussbaum 1987: 25). Nussbaum's government, then, seems to be more paternalistic than Sen's.

One important characteristic of Nussbaum's list is that it has to be complete. She asserts with respect to ten capabilities she lists: "These ten capabilities [...]

all are part of a minimum account of social justice: a society that does not guarantee these to all its citizens, at some appropriate threshold level, falls short of being a fully just society, whatever its level of opulence" (2003: 40; cf. also 1990: 225–226; and 1987: 7). They are necessary for each and every person, and all of central relevance. Nussbaum thus argues:

> Sen needs to be more radical than he has been so far in his criticism of the utilitarian accounts of well-being, by introducing an objective normative account of human functioning and by describing a procedure of objective evaluation by which functionings can be assessed for their contribution to the good human life.
>
> (Nussbaum 1987: 40; and 1988: 176)

Notwithstanding Nussbaum and Sen's disagreement, two things should be noted that might make this disagreement apparent. First, although Nussbaum criticizes Sen for having a "thin" notion of the good compared to her own "thick vague conception of the good,"[4] she proposes a rational debate about shared ethical experiences – for example, of justice or injustice – with the aim of determining the central human capabilities (Nussbaum 1993: 3; and 1995a *passim*). She argues that this consensual character of the debate does not undermine objectivity (1993: 251). This is what she regards as the work of practical reason. Second, although Nussbaum proposes lists of central human capabilities,[5] she always qualifies it by saying that she considers "the list as open-ended and subject to ongoing revision and rethinking" (2003: 42), or as "just a list of suggestions, closely related to Aristotle"s list of common experiences" (1993: 265).

Besides, Sen's reluctance towards producing a unique list of functionings for a good human life has also to be "moderated" (Sen 1993: 47; 2004b: 77). Sen does not dismiss the possibility of there being "a universal set of 'comprehensive' objectives shared by all" (1995: 269). He only argues that it is unnecessary to define a complete ordering to arrive at a comparison of capabilities (1995: 269). Thus Sen is not against lists. Moreover, he clearly thinks that we need lists. He asserts that "there can be substantial debates on the particular functionings that should be included in the list of important achievements and the corresponding capabilities. This valuational issue is inescapable" (1999b: 75).

On some occasions, Sen has defended particular functionings or capabilities as necessary or basic. In *Development and Freedom* (1999b), in "Elements of a Theory of Human Rights" (2004b), and in *The Idea of Justice* (2009), he asks where human rights come from. He says that they are primarily ethical demands that by nature may go beyond legislation (2004b: 319). He emphasizes their universality (2004b: 320; 2009: 373), that they have an inescapable non-parochial nature, and that they are meant to apply to all human beings (2004b: 349).

In 1995, David Crocker compared Nussbaum's list of capabilities with the capabilities that Sen has considered as basic or necessary. In *Development as*

Freedom Sen includes nourishment (1999b: 19 and Chapter 7), health (19), surviving from mortality (21; and Sen 1998), tradition and culture (31), employment (94), political participation (16, 31 and Chapter 6), and literacy (19). Only a few of Nussbaum's capabilities are not included by Sen – for example, "being able to have opportunities for sexual satisfaction," "being able to live with concern for and in relation to animals, plants, and the world of nature," and "being able to laugh, to play, to enjoy recreational activities." In sum, it turns out that in fact there is not an insurmountable distance between Nussbaum's list and the capabilities that Sen regards as necessary, and that practical reason has a vital role in ascertaining them.

However, a tension remains in Sen's line of thinking, between refusing to set a fixed and complete list and asserting the commonsense defense of some basic capabilities. I think that this tension connects with Sen's conception of practical reason and with his ideas about personal identity. In *Reason before Identity* (1999c) Sen devotes a whole section to the question "Discovery or Choice?" (1999c: 15–19). Sen's view of identity derives from his answer to the question "discovery or choice?" posed by the communitarian Michael Sandel. Sandel says we discover our identities while Sen says we choose them. He softens this view by saying that our choices are not unrestricted (1999c: 17) and that sometimes we also make discoveries, but he adds: "choices have to be made even when discoveries occur" (1999c: 19). The tension here is manifest. John Davis (2008) argues that for Sen having an identity is the most important capability. Given that for Sen identity is constructed through the choices an individual makes, it must be central to the development of all other capabilities of the individual. This concept of identity correlates with a conception of practical reason. In Chapter 2, I explained the differences between the classical and the Kantian conceptions. For Kant, like for Sen, freedom has priority over practical reason, determining the way of acting, and consequently practical reason is constructivist: it constructs our own identity.[6] This is necessary for Kant because he does not recognize the possibility of a metaphysical or theoretical knowledge of human nature.

Some Sen commentators also speak about a metaphysical deficit in his view consisting of an insufficient conception of human nature. Crocker (1992: 588) asserts that neither Sen nor Nussbaum are trying to ground their ethical proposals in a metaphysics of nature or in an account of a transhistorical human essence. Des Gasper (1997: 288ff; 2002: 442, 447, 449, 450) complains about Sen's "thin" conception of the person. He also notes that Sen's theory lacks an elaborated theory of the good (2002: 441). Sabina Alkire and Rufus Black (1997) propose we complete the "deliberately incomplete approach" of Sen with John Finnis's principles of practical reason. Séverine Deneulin (2002), in a positive way, argues that the policies undertaken according to the CA need to be guided by a perfectionist conception of the human good. Ananta Giri (2000) complains about the lack of a creative and reflective self in Sen.[7] Benedetta Giovanola, (2005) proposes expanding Sen's conception of the human person in Marxian terms. The very diversity of orientations of these proposals for overcoming Sen's incomplete definitions speaks to us about the difficulties of arriving at a conception of the human being. However, a minimum conception would help to provide a fundament to a basic guide for social and economic policy and would consequently improve the operative character of the CA.

Heterogeneity and incommensurability

For Sen, the evaluative space is composed of ends that are values in themselves that are sought as the achievements for the kind of life chosen. He does not directly attach – as opposed to derivatively – importance to the *means* of living or *means* of freedom (for example, real income, wealth, opulence, primary goods, or resources). For him, these easily measured variables are not part of the evaluative space (Sen 1993: 33).

Otherwise, Sen and Nussbaum (Nussbaum and Sen 1987: 25; Sen and Williams 1982: 19) argue that capabilities are incommensurable, because ends of different character cannot be quantitatively appraised: "Capabilities are clearly non-commensurable since they are irreducibly diverse" (Sen 2009: 240). Incommensurable or non-commensurable means that there is no common measurement unit to quantitatively compare these things, e.g., capabilities. This position is opposite to the Utilitarian view in which "utility" is a common measure that comprehends all kind of ends. Instead, for Sen "we cannot reduce all the things we have reason to value into one homogeneous magnitude" (2009: 239). Once quantitative comparisons are discarded, the only possible remaining comparisons are qualitative ones: "reflected evaluation demands reasoning regarding relative importance, not just counting" (Sen 2009: 241). Reflected evaluation is the task of practical reason.

The key to the problem is that capabilities are heterogeneous and so there is no common (quantitative) measure with which to evaluate them. In the "Annexe," co-written with John Foster, to the enlarged edition of *On Economic Inequality,* Sen asserts that "functionings are robustly heterogeneous" (Foster and Sen 1997: 203). In the same vein, more recently, in *Development as Freedom,* he has argued for pluralism of capabilities and against homogeneous magnitudes: "heterogeneity of factors that influence individual advantage is a pervasive feature of actual evaluation" (1999b: 76–7). Nussbaum also maintains incommensurability: she speaks about "heterogeneity and noncommensurability" (2003: 34; see also 1990: 219).

However, despite incommensurability, we still have to make decisions that involve choosing the proportions of each capability we seek, both at the personal and social levels. If that were impossible, the CA would be totally inoperative. Once we have defined the different weights that we are willing to assign to each capability, the problem of evaluation is only technical and informational, and could in principle be overcome by various means (statistics, surveys and indexes).[8] But the real problem is the definition of these weights. "The focus has to be related to the underlying concerns and values, in terms of which some definable functionings may be important and others quite trivial and negligible" (Sen 1993: 32). Moreover, as soon as the role of freedom in Sen's CA is considered, the limits between elementary and complex capabilities become blurred.

Sen does not propose a general solution to this problem. He maintains that this overall exercise can be performed only in cases in which the list and the weights of the different capabilities on the list are determined through reasoned evaluation (practical reason). As noted, he embraces this situation. He says that there is no "magic formula" (1999b: 79; and 1999a: 32) and that "there is no 'royal road' to geometry." He adds: "It is not clear that there is any royal road to evaluation of economic or social policies either" (Sen 1999b: 85). That is, there are no general recipes applicable for all cases, but only the possibility of evaluation through practical reason in each situation. He maintains in *Development as Freedom*:

> it is of course crucial to ask, in any evaluative exercise of this kind [partial orderings extended by specifying possible weights], how the weights are to be selected.[9] This judgmental exercise can be resolved only through reasoned evaluation. For a particular person, who is making his or her own judgments, the selection of weights will require reflection, rather than any interpersonal agreement (or consensus). However, in arriving at an "agreed" range for *social evaluation* [...], there has to be some kind of rational "consensus" on weights, or at least on a range of weights. This is a "social choice" exercise and it requires public discussion and a democratic understanding and acceptance.
>
> (Sen 1999b: 78–79)

It is clear here that he is speaking of the exercise of practical reason on different levels, both personal and social. As noted, this goes against general recipes, and has been criticized because it rules out automatically operative solutions. Sen answers these criticisms:

> The connection between public reasoning and the choice of weighting of capabilities in social assessment is important and to emphasize. It also points to the absurdity of the argument that is sometimes presented, which claims that the capability approach would be usable – and "operational" – only if it comes with a set of "given" weights of the distinct functionings in some fixed list of relevant capabilities. The search for given, pre-determined weights is not only conceptually ungrounded, but it also overlooks the fact that the valuations and weights to be used may be reasonably influenced by our own continued scrutiny and by the reach of public discussion. It would be hard to accommodate this understanding with inflexible use of some pre-determined weights in a non-contingent form.
>
> (Sen 2009: 242–243)

Thus, the CA is in fact operative, but in the specific sense of leaving all the work to practical reason. In my book published in 2013 (Chapter 6), I put as an example of the exercise of practical reason the determination of the weights assigned to the dimension of the Human Development Index. This example can be replicated in the case of many economic indexes in which a political or prudential decision is involved to define the dimensions used and the weight assigned to them.

Conclusion

The CA has three essential characteristics: the heterogeneity of persons and their capabilities; the incompleteness of the ordering of those capabilities; and the consequential need for practical reason or public discussion to deliberate about our capabilities and their hierarchy. This situation stems from human freedom and diversity, and can be managed by reflective agents exercising practical reason. We should add that institutions are a way of giving a material embodiment to the outcomes of practical reason thus stabilizing the relevant causal relationships.

We conclude that this new economic current, the capability approach, puts a strong emphasis in considering practical reason. Consequently, we also conclude that the capability approach corresponds to a "liberal naturalist" view of economic reality. We have finally arrived at a current that effectively adopts practical reason and that escapes from the physicalist contemporary predominant worldview. In this case, the change comes mainly from within economics, given that Sen considers that the assessment of the good by practical reason is an intrinsic characteristic of the ethics-related origin of economics.

We have, however, still noticed a tension in Sen's line of thinking, which stems from his chiefly Kantian notion of practical reason: he does not want to define a minimum content of human identity, and consequently does not want to predefine a list of capabilities, but at the same time he supports a common sense set of basic goods or capabilities, but without grounding them in a theory of the good. The adoption of a classical notion of practical reason would provide him the possibility of discovering a minimum content of human identity bringing a foundation to his common sense list of capabilities.

Notes

1 This chapter draws on Chapters 3 and 4 of my book published in 2013.
2 For a survey of Sen's position, see, e.g., Sen (1993); Robeyns (2005); and Walsh (2000 and 2003).
3 "It is sometimes desirable", asserts Severine Deneulin, "that functionings and not capabilities constitute the goal of public policy. In some areas, it is sometimes more important to have people function in a certain way than it is to give them the opportunity to function in a certain way. It is sometimes more important to focus on the human good (functionings), rather than on the freedom and opportunities to realize that human good (capabilities)" (Deneulin 2002: 506).

4 Nussbaum (1990: 205, 217 – an outline sketch – 234 and 237).
5 Nussbaum (1990: 219–225; 1992: 216–220; 1993: 263–265; 1995b: 76–79; 2000: 78–80; 2003: 41–42; 2006: 392–401).
6 On the Kantian character of Sen's conception of practical reason, see Petri Rasanen (2012). Herlinde Pauer-Studer (2006) argues that Sen's position on practical rationality and identity can be considered as a middle position between Humeanism and the Kantian line.
7 Sen's concept of commitment (1977; 2002) seems, however, to entail a reflective self (see Davis 2008).
8 About the information and interpretation problems, see Sen (1999a: 26–32).
9 Sen develops the issue of how to do with partial orderings in many writings. A complete order, he maintains, is not necessary. It is a special case within the general case of partial orderings. See, e.g., Sen (1985: 198–199; 1997: Annexe; 1999a: 22–32 and *passim*).

References

Alkire, S. and R. Black (1997). "A Practical Reasoning Theory of Development Ethics: Furthering the Capabilities Approach," *Journal of International Development* 9/2: 263–279.
Clark, D. (2005). "The Capability Approach: Its Development, Critiques and Recent Advances," GPRG-WPS-032, Global Poverty Research Group, Economic and Social Research Council.
Crespo, R. F. (2013). *Theoretical and Practical Reason in Economics. Capacities and Capabilities*. Dordrecht: Springer.
Crocker, D. A. (1992). "Functioning and Capability: The Foundations of Sen's and Nussbaum"s Development Ethic," *Political Theory* 20/4: 584–612.
Crocker, D. A. (1995). "Functioning and Capability. The Foundations of Sen's and Nussbaum's Developments Ethics, Part II." In M. C. Nussbaum and J. Glover (eds.), *Women, Culture and Development*. Oxford: Clarendon Press.
Davis, J. B. (2002). "Capabilities and Personal Identity: Using Sen to explain personal identity in Folbre's 'structures of constraint' analysis," *Review of Political Economy* 14/4: 481–496.
Davis, J. B. (2008). "The conception of the socially embedded individual." In J. B. Davis and W. Dolfsma (eds.), *The Elgar Companion to Social Economics*. Cheltenham: Edward Elgar.
Davis, J. B. (2012). "The idea of public reasoning." *Journal of Economic Methodology* 19/2: 169–172.
Deneulin, S. (2002). "Perfectionism, Paternalism and Liberalism in Sen and Nussbaum's Capability Approach," *Review of Political Economy* 14/4: 497–518.
Foster, J. and A. Sen (1997). "On Economic Inequality after a Quarter Century." In A. Sen (ed.) *On Economic Inequality*, enlarged edition. Oxford: Clarendon Press.
Gasper, D. (1997). "Sen's capability approach and Nussbaum's capabilities ethic," *Journal of International Development* 9/2: 281–302.
Gasper, D. (2002). "Is Sen's Capability Approach an Adequate Basis for Considering Human Development?," *Review of Political Economy* 14/4: 435–461.
Giovanola, B. (2005). "Personhood and Human Richness: Good and Well-Being in the Capability Approach and Beyond," *Review of Social Economy* LXIII/2: 249–267.
Giri, A. K. (2000). "Rethinking Human Well-being: A Dialogue with Amartya Sen," *Journal of International Development* 12: 1003–1018.

Nussbaum, M. C. (1987). "Nature, Function, and Capability: Aristotle on Political Distribution," *WIDER Working Paper* 31, Helsinki.

Nussbaum, M. C. (1988). "Nature, Function and Capability: Aristotle on Political Distribution," *Oxford Studies in Ancient Philosophy*, suppl. vol.: 145–184.

Nussbaum, M. C. (1990). "Aristotelian Social Democracy." In R. B. Douglass, G. M. Mara, and H. S. Richardson, *Liberalism and the Good*. New York and London: Routledge.

Nussbaum, M. C. (1992). "Human Functioning and Social Justice: In Defense of Aristotelian Essentialism," *Political Theory* 20/202: 202–246.

Nussbaum, M. C. (1993). "Non-Relative Virtues: An Aristotelian Approach." In M. C. Nussbaum and A. Sen (eds.) *The Quality of Life*. Oxford: Oxford University Press and United Nations University.

Nussbaum, M. C. (1995a). "Aristotle on human nature and the foundations of ethics." In J. E. J. Altham and R. Harrison (eds.) *World, Mind, and Ethics. Essays on the ethical philosophy of Bernard Williams*. Cambridge: Cambridge University Press.

Nussbaum, M. C. (1995b). "Human Capabilities, Female Human Beings." In M. C. Nussbaum, and J. Glover (eds.), *Women, Culture and Development*. Oxford: Clarendon Press.

Nussbaum, M. C. (2000). *Woman and Human Development. The Capabilities Approach*. Cambridge and New York: Cambridge University Press.

Nussbaum, M. C. (2003). "Capabilities as Fundamental Entitlements: Sen and Social Justice," *Feminist Economics* 9/2–3: 33–59.

Nussbaum, M. C. (2006). *Frontiers of Justice*. Cambridge, MA, and London: The Belknap Press of Harvard University Press.

Nussbaum, M. C. and A. Sen (1987). "Internal Criticism and Indian Rationalist Traditions," WIDER Working Paper 30, Helsinki.

Nussbaum, M. C. and A. Sen (1993). "Introduction," in M. C. Nussbaum and A. Sen (eds.), *The Quality of Life*. Oxford: Oxford University Press and United Nations University.

Pauer-Studer, H. (2006). "Identity, commitment and morality," *Journal of Economic Methodology* 13/3: 349–369.

Putnam, H. (2004). *The Collapse of the Fact/Value Dichotomy and Other Essays*. Cambridge, MA, and London: MIT Press.

Rasanen, P. (2012). "Kantian Basis of Amartya Sen's Idea of the Reasoned Scrutiny of Thinking," *SATS, Northern European Journal of Philosophy* 12: 178–197.

Ricoeur, P. (2005). *The Course of Recognition*. Cambridge, MA, and London: Harvard University Press (*Parcours de la Reconnaissance*, Editions Stock, 2004, translated by David Pellauer).

Robeyns, I. (2005). "The Capability Approach: a theoretical survey," *Journal of Human Development* 6/1: 93–114.

Sen, A. (1977). "Rational Fools: A Critique of the Behavioral Foundations of Economic," *Philosophy & Public Affairs* 6/4: 317–344.

Sen, A. and B. Williams (1982). "Introduction: Utilitarianism and Beyond." In A. Sen and B. Williams (eds), *Utilitarianism and Beyond*. Cambridge: Cambridge University Press.

Sen, A. (1980). "Equality of What?," The Tanner Lecture on Human Values Delivered at Stanford University, May 22, 1979. In S. M. McMurrin (ed.), *Tanner Lectures on Human Values*, vol. I. Cambridge and Salt Lake City: Cambridge University Press and University of Utah Press.

Sen, A. (1980–1981). "Plural Utility," *Proceedings of the Aristotelian Society* NS LXXXI: 193–215.

Sen, A. (1985). "Well-Being, Agency and Freedom. The Dewey Lectures 1984," *The Journal of Philosophy* 82/4: 169–221.

Sen, A. (1987a). *On Ethics and Economics.* Oxford: Basil Blackwell.

Sen, A. (1987b). *The Standard of Living.* In G. Hawthorn (ed.) *The Standard of Living.* Cambridge: Cambridge University Press.

Sen, A. (1989). "Development as Capability Expansion," *Journal of Development Planning* 19: 41–58.

Sen, A. (1992). *Inequality Reexamined.* Cambridge, MA: Harvard University Press.

Sen, A. (1993). "Capability and Well-being." In M. C. Nussbaum and A. Sen (eds.), *The Quality of Life.* Oxford: Oxford University Press and United Nations University.

Sen, A. (1995). "Gender Inequality and Theories of Justice." In M. C. Nussbaum and J. Glover (eds.), *Women, Culture, and Development: A Study of Human Capabilities,* Oxford: Clarendon Press.

Sen, A. (1997). "Maximization and the Act of Choice," *Econometrica* 65/4: 745–779.

Sen, A. (1999a). *Commodities and Capabilities.* New Delhi: Oxford University Press, Indian edition (first edition, 1985).

Sen, A. (1999b). *Development as Freedom.* New York: Alfred A. Knopf.

Sen, A. (1999c). *Reason before Identity. The Romanes Lecture for 1998.* New Delhi, Oxford, New York: Oxford University Press.

Sen, A. (2000). "Consequential Evaluation and Practical Reason," *The Journal of Philosophy* 97/9: 477–502.

Sen, A. (2002). *Rationality and Freedom.* Cambridge, MA: The Belknap Press of Harvard University Press.

Sen, A. (2004a). "Dialogue. Capabilities, Lists, and Public Reason: Continuing the Conversation," *Feminist Economics* 10–3: 77–80.

Sen, A. (2004b). "Elements of a Theory of Human Rights," *Philosophy and Public Affairs* 32/4: 315–356.

Sen, A. (2004c). "Incompleteness and Reasoned Choice," *Synthese* 140/1–2: 43–59.

Sen, A. (2009). *The Idea of Justice.* Cambridge, MA: The Belknap Press of Harvard University Press.

Sugden, R. (1993). "Welfare, resources, and Capabilities: A Review of Inequality Reexamined by Amartya Sen," *Journal of Economic Literature* 31: 1947–1962.

Walsh, V. (2000). "Smith After Sen," *Review of Political Economy* 12/1: 5–25.

Walsh, V. (2003). "Sen After Putnam," *Review of Political Economy* 15/3: 315–394.

9   The Civil Economy approach

In addition to the capability approach considered in the previous chapter, this chapter deals with another perspective which also adopts practical reason as a rationality governing economic behavior, featuring a liberal naturalist approach to economic reality.

If you Google the words "civil economy," you will surely get thousands of entries. This term generally puts more emphasis on social embeddedness of actual economies rather than on contractual arrangements underlying standard neoclassical economics as the way to achieve a "human economy" that makes people happy.

Here, I will specifically address a current approach to the idea of a civil economy based on an old Italian school of thought about market economy as inserted in civil society. This perspective contrasts the usual utility maximization and market competition principles with the search for the common good and cooperation. In this case, we can also assert that the proposed changes come partially from within economics, through recapturing ideas of ancient Italian political economists. The Civil Economy proposal believes in the self-organization of civil society with the support of intermediate (between the state and individuals) organizations or institutions to achieve a healthy economic coordination. It also upholds that a close, relational character of personal identity – linked to forms of reciprocity guided by non-instrumental rationality – enables the emergence of a united and friendly society.

This inherently interdisciplinary approach draws on economics, history, philosophy, and sociology to explain the current market *ethos* and to argue for a change that will enable a "humane" social order. Consistent with this interdisciplinary approach, it tries to avoid dualisms, especially between economics and morality, therein finding a way to accomplish its goal. It does not adopt a fatalist stance, viewing today's market *ethos* prevalence as an unavoidable negative fact while trying to mitigate this reality by "moralizing" the market. Instead, it maintains a positive perspective, considering the role of the market as inseparable from the community, as part of the effort by civil society to work as a team for the common good. This idea is very well expressed in the title to Luigino Bruni and Robert Sugden's article (2008): "Fraternity. Why the market needs not to be a morally free zone." According to Bruni and Sugden, "a market relationship between individuals can be perceived simultaneously as a mutually beneficial exchange and as a genuinely social interaction" (2008: 36), they are genuine social relations *in themselves* (2008: 61).

In the Civil Economic approach, markets are not ethically neutral, they are either civil or not. If civil, they are designed to produce the common good, create values and work, and take care of people and the environment. "Civil Economy" is sometimes understood as related exclusively to the third sector (non-profit organizations). The approach expounded here, however, relates to the whole economy. It is not a specific economic theory but a paradigm of thought and action.

Supporters of this perspective such as Italian economists Stefano Zamagni and Bruni trace their proposal back to 15th- to 18th-century markets in Italy, and explain why this market conception disappeared in the 19th century. They consequently advocate the reinstitution of a modern form of civil economy, with economic interactions being, at the same time, moral, fraternal and mutually beneficial. This might sound unrealistic. However, the 2005 *World Happiness Report* contains a chapter on "Human values, civil economy, and subjective well-being" that includes a review of the empirical evidence relevant to the dimensions stressed in the idea of a civil economy (Bechetti et al 2015: 138–144). In this chapter, I will first delve into the historical and intellectual roots of this approach and I will then introduce its contemporary developments. This is the book's final chapter; as chapters progressed, the analyzed approaches have come close to the ideal suggested: a liberal naturalist economics which considers practical reason. This will be the conclusion at the end of the chapter.

1 Historical and intellectual roots of Civil Economy: from Aristotle to Genovesi and Dragonetti

We have to go back to Aristotle to find the original roots of the Civil Economy approach. As Bruni and Zamagni (2007: 27) note, "on the level of ideas, its origin are to be found in Aristotle's *politeia* and Cicero"s reflections on civic virtues" (see also Bruni 2012: 24–33). They carefully show how these ancient authors, especially Aristotle, have influenced the civic humanist tradition. In Chapters 6 and 7 I briefly expounded some of Aristotle's ideas about civil society – the *polis*. At the beginning of *Politics* (I, 2), Aristotle describes the human person as a rational animal – *lógou dè mónov ánthropos héxei tôn zóon:* "man alone of the animals is furnished with the faculty of language [or reason]" – and as a *zóon politikòn* – "political [social] animal." This characterization has profound significance. Aristotle claims that, through speech, human beings can both know and express what is good and what is evil, morally just and unjust, as well as what is technically expedient and inexpedient – that is, the Greek word *logos* goes beyond mere language; it has a wide range of meanings including knowledge. As a result, this passage has produced the famous definition of man as a rational animal. At the same time, "it is an association of [a common perception of] these things [known] which makes a family and a *polis*" (*Politics* I, 2, 1253a 18). For Aristotle, rationality and political communities are closely intertwined: he cannot conceive one without the others. People develop their rationality or capacity for theoretical (metaphysical), practical (ethical) and technical knowledge in the realm of the family and the political community. How, then, does Aristotle view the relation between these two realities: human individuals and communities?

In *Politics* I, 1–2, Aristotle presents two strong metaphysical theses: first, the natural character of the *polis* and, second, human beings' political nature – *hóti tôn phýsei he pólis estí kai hóti ánthrôpos phýsei politikòn zôon* (*Politics*, I, 2 1253a 2–3). From a metaphysical standpoint, clearly, given their substantial nature, human beings take precedence over the city, which is an association of individuals. Then, how should we interpret the following statement by Aristotle? *Kaì próteron dé tê phýsei pólis hè oikía kaì ékastos hemôn estín* – "and the *polis* is prior by nature to the house and to each one of us" (1253a 19). Aristotle recognizes the temporal priority of the parts of the *pólis* when he explains that a household stems from the union of a man and a woman, a clan stems from the union of many households, and a *polis* stems from a group of clans. However, he adds: *télos gàr aúte ekeínon, he dè phýsis télos estín* – "for it [the *polis*] is the end of the [former] and the nature is the end" (1252b 31–2). Thus, individuals, households and clans have the *polis* as their final end, and, in Aristotle's system, the final end ("the reason for the sake of which") is the first cause of every reality.

For Aristotle, though it may be chronologically last, the end is ontologically first. Adding the thesis that human beings' end is *eudaimonía* or *eû zên* (happiness as personal fulfilment or flourishing as a result of a good life; *NE* I, 7) to the thesis that the human being is political, he concludes that human beings can only achieve their end within the *polis*. The *polis* exists "for the sake of a good life" (*eû zên*, 1252b 30), and the end of the *pólis* is and "includes" (*NE* I, 2, 1094b 7) the end of human beings. The happiness of the *polis* (*eudaimonía*) is the same as individuals' happiness: "It remains to discuss whether the felicity of the state is the same as that of the individual, or different. The answer is clear: all agree that they are the same" (*Politics* VII, 2, 1324a 5–8). This explains why "for even if the good is the same for a city as for an individual, still the good of the city is apparently a greater and more complete good to acquire and preserve" (*NE* I, 2, 1094b 8–9; see also *NE* VIII, 9, 1160a 9–30).

This good of both *polis* and individuals is to achieve a good life that leads to happiness (i.e., flourishing or fulfilment): "the best way of life, for individuals severally as well as for states collectively, is the life of goodness" (*Politics* VII, 1, 1323b 40–41). When this good is complete (*téleion*), it is self-sufficient (*autarkeías*). However, Aristotle notes, "what we count as self-sufficient is not what suffices for a solitary person by himself, living an isolated life, but what suffices also for parents, children, wife, and, in general, for friends and fellow citizens, since a human being is a naturally political animal" (*NE* I, 7, 1097b 9–12).

This idea is also expressed in the following passage from Aristotle's *Politics*:

> The end [*télos*] and purpose of a *polis* is the good life, and the institutions of social life are means to that end. A *polis* is constituted by the association of families and villages in a perfect and self-sufficing existence; and such an existence, on our definition, consists in a life of true felicity and goodness [*tò zên eudaimónos kaì kalôs*].
>
> (*Politics* III, 9, 1280b 29–35)

Thus, the task of the political community and its practical science – Politics – political organization and society's authorities is to drive and support the good actions that enable all citizens to live this life of true flourishing and goodness – that is, a life of virtues: "the political philosopher is the architect of the end that we refer to in calling something bad or good" (*NE* VII, 11, 1052b3–4).

The idea of a common end underlies these notions. Indeed, in *Politics* III, 6 and 7, Aristotle refers to a "common interest" (*koinê symphéron*), noting, for example, that "governments which have a regard for the common interest are constituted in accordance with strict principles of justice [general or legal]" (1279a 17–18). In a nutshell, Aristotle views the common interest as *eudaimonía* for all citizens, who are political animals, and, thus, *eudaimonía* is only achievable within the *polis*; for him, the common good is the end of a just *polis*.

This concept is clearly normative and leads to political action, to an influence of the community over and upon citizens via its politicians. Aristotle, indeed, states that "legislators make the citizens good by forming habits in them, and this is the wish of every legislator" (*NE* II, 1, 1103b3). In Aristotle's world, there is a community that embodies values and finds ways of instilling these values in people. By encouraging and discouraging, training and teaching, educators create habits in young and adult people. Laws also foster the development and consolidation of habits.

Aristotle considers friendship (*philia*) as the key to the unity of the *polis*. He devoted two books of his *Nicomachean Ethics* to it – it is the virtue most extensively developed by him. As Bennett Helm notes, *philia* is not merely personal friendship: it "extends not just to friends but also to family members, business associates, and one's country at large" (Helm 2013: 2). For Aristotle, it is friendship, and not contract, which unites society; friendship is necessary for happiness (*NE* IX, 9). Friendship, Aristotle states, "would seem to hold cities together, and legislators would seem to be more concerned about it than about justice" (*NE* VIII, 1, 1155a 24–25), because if there is friendship between men we do not need justice (*NE* VIII, 1, 1155a 26–27). Specifically about "civil happiness," he comments (*NE* IX, 1, 1163b 34–37):

In all friendships between dissimilars it is, as we have said, proportion that equalizes the parties and preserves the friendship; e.g. in the political form of friendship the shoemaker gets a return for his shoes in proportion to his worth, and the weaver and all other craftsmen do the same. Now here a common measure has been provided in the form of money, and therefore everything is referred to this and measured by this.

This passage is related to Aristotle's *Nicomachean Ethics* chapter (V, 5) on reciprocal exchange, where he claims that "it is by proportionate requital that the city holds together" (1133b 35). Aristotle set out his theory of the market as a matter of reciprocity, not as a simple *do ut des*. Reciprocity includes a form of exchange that implies taking the other into account as an *alter ego*.

Bruni and Zamagni (2007: Chapters 2–4) show how these Aristotelian ideas have strongly influenced the civil humanist tradition that they pick up: the mutual interaction between virtues, especially friendship, constituting a community – a civil society – sharing a common good which is its final end and, finally, how this kind of life and its results drive to *eudaimonia*. The vision of civil society is built upon these classical ideas.

Aristotle gained renewed influence in the fourteenth century. Francis of Assisi, founder of the Franciscan Order, predicated *agape*, the Christian Evangelical concept of unconditional love, a notion that was not present in Aristotle. However, the Franciscan fraternity, as Bruni (2012: Chapter 4) notes, falls into a paradox: while focused on detachment, it positively appraises commerce. Bruni explains that the Franciscan *agape* lay at the heart of the movement in its early stages, but it later evolved into a form of *philia*, close to the Aristotelian notion. In fact, *philia* (or friendship) was, as already mentioned, the root of community union for Aristotle. The market works well in a setting grounded on good faith and the reliability of Christian *fides*.

Bruni (2006: 24ff.) also addresses another movement that was contemporary with the former and which draws on Aristotelian ideas: "civic humanism," a discourse that emerged in Italy during the 15th century – *il Quattrocento* – particularly in Florence. Bruni characterizes its basic element as a "reawakening to the necessity of a civic or political life for a fully human life" (2006: 25). He mentions thinkers such as Coluccio Salutati, Poggio Bracciolini, Leonardo Bruni, Leon Battista Alberi, San Bernardino di Siena, and Matteo Palmieri. They also emphasize the social value of wealth, and praise the spirit of initiative and the development of commerce as contributing to the common good of society. Zamagni (2005a: 4–6) points to three "pillars" of the market economy sustained by these authors: division of labor, the important position that the notion of development and consequently accumulation occupy in economic activity, and freedom of enterprise.

This movement, however, had a short life span. Bruni and Zamagni (2007) and Bruni (2012) concentrate on some thinkers who changed this way of thinking. They first turn to Niccolò Machiavelli. Influenced by the conflicts of his age, he initiated a new line of thinking based on a pessimistic conception of human nature. For him, the way towards social and political unity was not friendship and reciprocity, but fear. Under the power of the Prince, we need other means than virtue to achieve social harmony (see Bruni and Zamagni 2007: 57–60). Bruni (2012: 75–82) then explains that Martin Luther's reform also leaned in this direction: Christian *fides* and *philia* were no longer the foundations of the market's *ethos* and were replaced by the modern contract. Luther's conception of the church was egalitarian, but, while he viewed individuals as having a direct relationship with God, given the conflictive consequences of sin, relations with others had to be mediated by the political power. Finally, Bruni and Zamagni (2007: 60–65) and Bruni (2012: Chapter 6) address Thomas Hobbes and John Locke. Hobbes followed in this line of thinking, and, instead of the natural *polis*, he promoted an artificial state to control naturally asocial individuals – the *Leviathan*. Locke's views drew closer to classical notions, because the contract is not substitutive (as in Hobbes) but subsidiary to natural sociability. For Hobbes, Bruni (2012: 98) explains, there are not "I" and "You," but "I" and "non-I." Individuals are alone, as is the case in contemporary societies (see Bruni 2006: 30–39). Bruni calls them "uncivil philosophers" who conceived a "society regulated simply by the working of interests and just laws, where there is no place and no role for civil virtues or, more generally, for genuine and not fully instrumental relations" (2006: 40).

In this new social framework of modernity, market relations become increasingly anonymous, depersonalized, so that we need minimal institutions to guarantee alignment of individuals' desires with the common good. The invisible hand only works within an institutional environment, under the rule of law. "It is not from the benevolence of the butcher," Smith points out: the market does not operate on benevolence. For Smith, indifference and the impersonal character of market relations are civilizing, leaning towards the common good. Markets do not shun – quite the opposite, in fact – friendship, but they are not its place. Markets' neutral relations increasingly pervade all fields of human life, dehumanizing them.

At the same time, a different view about markets emerged in Italy, once again going back to Aristotle: the tradition of Civil Economy – an economy based on civil virtues. Bruni and Zamagni have written extensively about the 18th-century Neapolitan philosopher and economist Antonio Genovesi (1713–1769), who revisits the classical tradition of the *polis* based on *philia* as the root of true happiness, as I have already explained in this chapter. In 1752, the first chair in economic matters, "Cattedra di commercio e meccanica" was instituted in Naples and Genovesi took up this position. The expression "civil economy" is present in the title of his main economic treatise: *Lezioni di commercio o sia di economia civile* (1765–1767), referring to the classical Aristotelian conception linking society"s common good, virtues and happiness (Bruni 2006: 50 and 66). In fact, Genovesi quotes Aristotle 50 times in *Lezioni* (Bruni and Zamagni 2016a: 72)

Genovesi upholds that economic activity is a manifestation of civil life and virtue. He claims that the market is built on *philia*. For Genovesi, reciprocity, mutual assistance and fraternity are typical elements of human sociability, while the market is part of the civil society and, as such, it requires individuals' love for the common good and public trust (*fede publica*, public faith) to operate properly (see Bruni and Sugden 2000: 35ff.; and Bruni 2006: 68–72). In his view, civil trust is closely associated with friendship, which is also civil, and with reciprocity and happiness. We cannot be happy without making others happy. Civil virtues are embodied in trade, which allows individuals to satisfy their needs in a spirit of reciprocity – *philia* is the foundation of civil life, including the market. Following the Italian tradition, Genovesi maintains that economics is a science of "Pubblica Felicità" or "public happiness" (see Bruni and Zamagni 2016a: 67ff.). Whereas Smith views civil life as characterized by interest, Genovesi believes it is characterized by mutual assistance, which is more than mutual benefit. For Smith, the market entails civilization but not friendship, non-instrumental reciprocity and fraternity (see Bruni and Sugden 2008). While Smith sees trust as emerging from self-interest, Genovesi believes that uninterested trust is a condition of economic development (see Bruni and Sugden 2000: 40ff.). The market according to Genovesi, notes Bruni, "works properly only if based on civil virtues, that is, if it is conceived as a form of friendship" (2006: 77) – that is, conceived as reciprocal assistance (Bruni and Sugden 2000: 42). Virtue, for Genovesi, is "an economic resource" (Bruni and Sugden 2000: 38).

Another important representative of the school of Civil Economy is Giacinto Dragonetti, who developed a theory on human action based on rewards which are regarded not as an ex-ante motivation or incentive but as an ex-post recognition. This difference is significant because it shows that Dragonetti is not relying on a utilitarian motivation but drawing from the Aristotelian tradition of virtue ethics. Rewards are granted for actions that require efforts that go beyond private interests and are intended for the common good. People pursue the intrinsic value of their actions rather than the rewards themselves. Dragonetti is not against self-interest, but for making it compatible with virtue or finding a way to reconcile them. In fact, given that market and trade are conditions for public happiness (as also stated by Aristotle), they are proper rewards for virtues. Bruni writes, "Dragonetti regards commerce as part of the system for the reward of virtue. It is virtuous to satisfy other people's needs, and by facilitating mutually advantageous transactions the market rewards virtue" (2012: 149). In a recent book, Bruni and Zamagni (2016b) devote a chapter to Amintore Fanfani, a well-known twentieth century Italian politician and professor of History of Economic Thought, who can also be considered as pertaining to the line of Civil Economy thinkers.

2 From Aristotle to the present

This brief historical and intellectual itinerary provides a core notion of Civil Economy: conceiving the market as a civil fraternity. Following Genovesi, mutual assistance goes beyond mutual benefit but is not incompatible with it.

Moreover, without its moral contents, the market does not work effectively. In this context, fraternity does not mean altruism but viewing market activities as a shared task, as collective action. This approach – a shared intention "we" approach – differs from the standard self-centered approach in economics. Quoting Bruni (2012: 165):

> The conventional way of conceiving market relations is characterized today within economic (and social) theory by two great contra-positions: the market vs the social and self-interest vs altruism. The conceptual framework of modern and contemporary economic theory doesn't offer a way of conceiving relationships between individuals *simultaneously* as a mutually advantageous exchange where no part wishes to act altruistically or to renounce to a slice of economic benefit *and* as a genuinely social interaction whose moral value is determined by its social content. I strongly believe that the absence of such a possibility has the effect of limiting our understanding *both* of the market *and* of human relations in general.

Bruni interestingly applies these ideas to the "market of care." He holds that workers in this market deserve to get a fair salary, considering that demands placed on workers in the name of their calling are abusive. Bruni also looks at the possibility of an "agapic market" with unconditional reciprocity (which he distinguishes from the reciprocity of contract and the reciprocity of *philia* 2008: x). This kind of market is obviously intrinsically richer than the *philia*-based market but, at the same time, it is highly dangerous. It is an extraordinary driver of innovation, but, by dismissing results in an all too idealistic conception, we may undertake undeserving enterprises. However, Bruni is willing to take risks: "when *agape* encounters history it opens up new possibilities, it enhances the degrees of freedom, changing it forever" (2012: 201). For these ideas to become operative, we need rewards institutionally supported by a framework of fair laws and institutions. We need both educated citizens and civil institutions, which takes us back to Aristotle's view on the source of virtue: education (in the sense of *paideia*, shaping virtuous characters) and laws. Zamagni, for his part, applies Civil Economy ideas to explain the logic of the cooperative enterprise (2005a), to the "tragedy of the commons" (Zamagni 2014a; and Bruni and Zamagni 2016b, Chapter 7), to the problems arising from the relations between the economy and the environment, to intergenerational fairness and sustainable development (Zamagni 2014b), showing how Civil Economy contributes to overcoming the related problems. Bruni and Zamagni (2007: 200–201) note that current mechanisms for controlling uncertainty block individual creativity and, consequently, economic development. In this context, a civil economy infuses a different spirit, contributing to surpass these difficulties. Concerning unemployment, they stress the need to expand the demand for quality, for non-monetarized activities (2007: 210–215). The spirit of civil economy also fosters socially responsible companies and consumers (Bruni and Zamagni 2016b, Chapter 9).

Supporters of Civil Economy stress the relational dimension of the human being and the relational character of some fundamental goods: friendship, mutual love and political commitment (Bruni 2012: 31). These goods do not have a market price, but they have a use value (Bruni and Zamagni 2007: 160). People's well-being is not limited to material needs but also includes expressive and relational goods. Bruni (2013: 174–175) explains:

> The category of relational goods was introduced into the theoretical debate nearly simultaneously by four authors: philosopher Martha Nussbaum (1986), sociologist Pierpaolo Donati (1986), and economists Benedetto Gui (1987) and Carole Uhlaner (1989). Benedetto Gui (1987: 37) defined relational goods as "non-material goods, which are not services that are consumed individually, but are tied to interpersonal relations." Carole Uhlaner (1989: 254) was on the same track when she defined them as "goods that can only be 'possessed' by mutual agreement that they exist after appropriate joint actions have been taken by a person and non-arbitrary others." These two economists call "relational goods" those aspects of relationships that cannot be either produced or consumed by one individual, because they depend on the types and the motivations of interactions with others, and they can be enjoyed only if shared reciprocally.[1]

Bechetti et al (2008) find that relational goods have significant and positive effects on self-declared life satisfaction, implying that a more intense relational life enhances life satisfaction and that happier people have a more lively social life. According to Zamagni (2005b), reciprocity, for example, entails deep relational aspects. *A* reciprocates *B* in a way that is not comparable to economic exchange. In reciprocity, not only the goods exchanged matter, but also the persons involved in the exchange.

Bruni (2008: x and ff.) proposes a theory of reciprocity that encompasses different forms of this phenomenon. As mentioned before, he distinguishes the reciprocity of contract or "cautious" reciprocity, which pertains to market exchanges; the reciprocity of *philia* or "brave" reciprocity, which is unconditional to some extent, and the completely unconditional reciprocity, which provides an intrinsic reward. Relying on game theory, he argues that these three forms are complementary and that the unconditional form is necessary. He sentences, "civil cooperation is impossible with *only* unconditional behavior, but a fully civil life is impossible, at least in the long run, *without* people able in certain moments and contests to practice also forms of unconditional behaviour" (2008: xi).

Referring to what Bruni calls "reciprocity of *philia*," I have previously argued (2008) that reciprocity does not require exactness but only a certain equilibrium in regard to the things reciprocated. In addition, reciprocity may be fulfilled by returning something of a different kind that may be heterogeneous and incommensurable with the thing received. The reason for this "uneven response" of reciprocity is that, in these situations, the exchange of means aims to manifest some values that are ends of the persons involved. Hence, consideration of reciprocity supposes a reinsertion of ends into economics. Reciprocity entails giving rather than obtaining something. This giving looks for ends that are beyond the nature of the goods exchanged. In other words, the person who gives seeks an end which is different from obtaining the thing she will receive in the way of reciprocity. Moreover, giving is independent from receiving: receiving cannot be regarded as a condition for giving. From this perspective, the "exchanged" goods – more properly, the reciprocated goods – only count as subjective signs of some connected ends. Thus, the rationality governing reciprocal actions is not a means-ends rationality (i.e., an instrumental rationality), but an ends rationality (i.e., a practical rationality which can compare incommensurable ends).

In an earlier article Alvin Gouldner (1960: 172) highlighted the "heteromorphic" character of reciprocity. With this term he referred to the fact that the things exchanged may be concretely different. However, he adds, they should be equal in *value*. Evidently, he is stressing the same issue highlighted above: reciprocity entails a correspondence in ends while means may be different. Gouldner remarks: "there may be occasions when questions as to whether the individual's return is appropriate or sufficient" (1960: 177). These questions, he adds, "arise by virtue of the absence of common yardsticks in terms of which giving and returning may be compared" (1960: 178). He is now addressing the other point: incommensurability. Zamagni (2005: 16) notes:

> The relation of reciprocity requires some form of balancing between what one gives and what one expects to obtain, or expects to be given to some third party, a balancing, however, that is not expressed in a definite magnitude (i.e. in a relative price), since it may vary according to the intensity with which moral sentiments such as sympathy, benevolence, the feeling of solidarity are put into practice by the agents involved in the relation.

This balancing is made by practical reason.[2]

Zamagni (2014a: 17) thus assigns three main theses to the idea of a civil economy. First, he does not accept a separation of economics from ethics and politics. Second, a civil economy is concerned with the design of institutions fostering the civil progress of society. Third, the three principles of market order – exchange of equivalents, redistribution and reciprocity – must be simultaneously at work: we cannot admit trade-offs between them. In this kind of economy, markets should be able to produce and to equitably distribute wealth, to make room for non-profit economic subjects – people who want to reciprocate, to trust, to give – and to citizen consumers interested not only in the quality of the final product but also in how it is produced (Bruni and Zamagni 2007: 166).

Accordingly, Bruni and Sugden (2013) have reclaimed virtue ethics for economics. As I have already mentioned in this chapter, virtues, particularly friendship, is necessary to achieve a united community and its corresponding civil economy.[3] In my book (Crespo 2014: 57–59), I present a set of "economic virtues" such as prudence, justice, friendship, generosity, industriousness, competence, order, initiative, community service, reliability, temperance, continence, and frugality. Bruni and Sugden independently but similarly propose another list of "market virtues," which they do not claim to be complete: "universality, enterprise and alertness, respect for the tastes of one's trading partners, trust and trustworthiness, acceptance of competition, self-help, non-rivalry, and stoicism about reward" (2013: 143). They argue that they are grounded on reciprocity and mutual benefit and that they are closely associated with virtues of civil society. The *telos* or goal of markets, they propose, is to "facilitate mutually beneficial voluntary transactions" (2013: 153), and they show how the previous list of virtues fits this goal (2013: 153–160).[4] In this way, they conceive the market not as a merely instrumental tool, but as a practice possessing an intrinsic value (see also Bruni 2014: 283). Consequently, they recognize a practical dimension of it. In this sense, we can assert that this approach deliberately considers practical rationality, freedom and intentionality, and that it is accordingly normative.

Conclusion

I finished this book analyzing an old and a new economic current that satisfies the ambitions that I have desired for economics: to become a liberal naturalist science – namely, a science that considers human beings as free, motivated by ends that they can know and decide upon due to their practical reason; a science that consequently is concerned with ends using this dimension of reason.

Civil economy has ancient roots going back to Aristotle and a rebirth in the Italian tradition of civil humanism. In the latter case, it has been recently rescued by economists as Bruni and Zamagni. The orientation to community and, within it, of its members towards the common good recommended by the Civil Economy approach supporters reveals that it is a teleological perspective like the one proposed by Nagel and McDowell in their view of a different naturalism, not a materialist one, as explained in the second chapter of the book. Nagel favors the consideration of mind, consciousness, meaning, intentionality and value as fundamental parts of nature that cannot be reduced to matter (2012: 15, 20, 44). McDowell wants to "bring practical reason back into nature" (2002: 184). Both support a teleological view of human action.

Taking elements from ancient traditions of philosophy, social thinking, and economics, and applying them to contemporary economic problems using the tools of economics, civil society economists arrive to a conception of economics that takes into account the plethora of motivations behind economic reality. They show how the market can be considered as a natural civil network when friendship and reciprocity are present. Practical reason lies behind reciprocity because the latter does not consist in a strict exchange but in an interchange in which not only is the good exchanged but also the exchangers are taken into account: it is grounded on a relational theory of rationality (Bruni and Sugden 2000: 44), which is a practical rationality. Bruni and Zamagni explicitly assert that economics belongs to the field of practical reason (2016b: Epilogue). At the same time, this does not imply a kind of altruist relation between market participants. The Aristotelian idea of justice as reciprocity (*Nicomachean ethics* V, 5) is picked up by the Civil Economy approach supporters. As Bruni and Sugden (2008: 41) express it, "it is both a mutually beneficial exchange, in which neither partner makes a sacrifice for the benefit of the other, *and* a genuinely social interaction, carrying moral value by virtue of this social content."

In addition, the Civil Economy approach shows how changes from within and changes from outside economics may interact improving the scope and reach of economic analysis. Ideas from outside economics have and can operate on economics by enlarging its vision in a more humane way. From within economics, these ideas are deeply rooted in a specific economic tradition.

This is the last new current in economics analyzed in this book. The path traversed began with currents that are predominantly physicalist and has finished with currents that can be understood as liberal naturalist. In the final concluding chapter I will present my overall balance of the reverse imperialist currents in relation to new currents arising within economics.

Notes

1 The Aristotelian root of the expression "relational" is deeper than, for example, Martha Nussbaum's (1986: Chapter 12) use of it. However, this does not neglect the relevance of the "relational goods" considered by her – friendship, love, and political commitment – and how important possessing them are for *eudaimonia*. This root, i.e., the foundation of relational goods, is the intrinsic relational character of the human being as a "political animal."

2 For the fundaments and characteristics of relational goods and reciprocity, see Bruni and Zamagni (2007: 163–175).

3 Virtue ethics is currently a widely held ethical theory. Deontological ethics focuses on duties, consequentialism and the consequences of actions, while virtue ethics emphasizes virtues and personal character. Some authors argue that virtue ethics is unilateral because of its emphasis on the subjective aspects of the ethical relation (an "agent-centered" ethics). However, Aristotle's virtue ethics also considers the goodness of acts themselves and their consequences. Virtue ethics is a rational ethics, while the prevailing approach among Modern philosophers, starting with Hume, turned human ends into an irrational matter, addressing ethical problems with consequentialist, sensist, emotivistic, or voluntarist criteria. In her renowned article "Modern Moral Philosophy" (1958), Elizabeth Anscombe criticized this approach and paved the way for virtue ethics rehabilitation. A plethora of authors have ventured into this field since then, with the work by Peter Geach (1977), Philippa Foot (1978) and MacIntyre (1984) marking significant milestones in virtue ethics. Also especially noteworthy is Julia Annas's (2011) very interesting and recent book.

4 Langrill and Storr maintain that "if markets are to function well, they must be peopled by virtuous beings" (2012: 352). They speak of virtues such as honesty, courage, justice, love, commitment, integrity and trust. On Aristotelian virtues as a way to cope with uncertainty; see Yuengert (2012: 75–77 and 90–91). About modern virtues and their relation with classical virtues and economics, see McCloskey (2006 and 2010).

References

Annas, J. (2011). *Intelligent Virtue*. Oxford: Oxford University Press.

Anscombe, G. E. M. (1958). "Modern Moral Philosophy," *Philosophy* 33/124: 1–19.

Becchetti, L., A. Pelloni and F. Rossetti (2008). "Relational Goods, Sociability, and Happiness," *Kyklos*, 61/3, 343–363.

Bechetti, L., L. Bruni and S. Zamagni (2015). "Human values, civil economy, and subjective well-being," in J. Helliwell, R. Layard and J. Sachs (eds.), *World Happiness Report 2015*, pp132–151, http://worldhappiness.report/wp-content/uploads/sites/2/2015/04/WHR15.pdf, retrieved June 2, 2015.

Bruni, L. (2006). *Civil Happiness. Economics and Human Flourishing in Historical Perspective*. London and New York: Routledge.

Bruni, L. (2008). *Reciprocity, Altruism and the Civil Society: In Praise of Heterogeneity*. London and New York: Routledge.

Bruni, L. (2012). *The Genesis and the Ethos of the Market*. Houndmills and New York: Palgrave MacMillan.

Bruni, L. (2013). "Relational Goods A new tool for an old issue," *Ecos*, 3/2: 173–178.

Bruni, L. (2014). "The telos of the market and civil economy," *Studies in Emergent Order* 7: 273–287, https://cosmosandtaxis.files.wordpress.com/2014/05/sieo_7_2014_bruni.pdf, retrieved June 2, 2016.

Bruni, L. and R. Sugden (2000). "Moral canals: trust and social capital in the work of Hume, Smith and Genovesi," *Economics and Philosophy* 16/1: 21–45.

Bruni, L. and R. Sugden (2008). "Fraternity. Why the market needs not to be a morally free zone" *Economics and Philosophy*, 24/1: 394–419.

Bruni, L. and R. Sugden (2013). "Reclaiming Virtue Ethics for Economics," *Journal of Economic Perspectives*, 27/4: 141–164.

Bruni, L. and S. Zamagni (2007). *Civil Economy: Efficiency, Equity, Public Happiness*. Oxford, Bern, Berlin, Bruxelles, Frankfurt am Main, New York, Wien: Peter Lang.

Bruni, L. and S. Zamagni (2016a). "The Challenges of Public Happiness: A Historical-Methodological reconstruction," in *World Happiness Report 2016*, Special Rome Edition, pp67–87, http://worldhappiness.report/wp-content/uploads/sites/2/2016/03/HR-V2Ch3_web.pdf, retrieved July 20, 2016.

Bruni, L. and S. Zamagni (2016b). *Civil Economy: Another Idea of the Market*. New York: Agenda Pub.

Crespo, R. F. (2008). "Reciprocity and Practical Comparability," *International Review of Economics*, 55/1–2: 13–28.

Crespo, R. F. (2014). *A Re-assessment of Aristotle's Economic Thought*. London: Routledge.

Donati, P. (1986). *Introduzione alla sociologia relazionale*. Milan: Franco Angeli.

Foot, P. (1978). "Virtues and Vices," in P. Foot (ed.), *Virtues and Vices and Other Essays In Moral Philosophy*. Berkeley and Los Angeles: University of California Press.

Geach, P. (1977). *The Virtues*. Cambridge: Cambridge University Press.

Gouldner, A.W. (1960). "The Norm of Reciprocity: A Preliminary Statement," *American Sociological Review*, 25/2: 161–178.

Gui, B. (1987). "Eléments pour une définition d'"économie communautaire," *Notes et documents*, 19–20: 32–42.

Helm, B. (2013). "Friendship," *The Stanford Encyclopedia of Philosophy*, http://plato.stanford.edu/entries/friendship/, retrieved May 31, 2016.

Langrill, R. and V. H. Storr (2012). "The moral meaning of markets," *Journal of Markets & Morality* 15/2: 347–362.

MacIntyre, A. (1984). *After Virtue.* Notre Dame, Indiana: University of Notre Dame Press, second edition.

McCloskey, D. N. (2006). *The Bourgeois Virtues: Ethics for an Age of Commerce.* Chicago, IL, and London: University of Chicago Press.

McCloskey, D. N. (2010). *Bourgeois Dignity: Why Economics Can't Explain the Modern World*, Chicago, IL and London: University of Chicago Press.

McDowell, J. (2002). "Two Sorts of Naturalism." In J. McDowell (eds.), *Reason, Value, and Reality.* Cambridge, MA: Harvard University Press.

Nagel, T. (2012). *Mind and Cosmos.* Oxford and New York: Oxford University Press.

Nussbaum, M. C. (1986). *The Fragility of Goodness: Luck and Ethics in Greek Tragedy and Philosophy.* Cambridge: Cambridge University Press.

Uhlaner, C. (1989). "Relational Goods and Participation: Incorporating Sociality into a Theory of Rational Action," *Public Choice* 62: 253–285.

Yuengert, A. M. (2012). *Approximating Prudence: Aristotelian Practical Wisdom and Economic Models of Choice.* London: Palgrave-Macmillan.

Zamagni, S. (2005a). "A Civil-Economic Theory of the Cooperative Enterprise," https://www.uvic.ca/research/centres/cccbe/assets/docs/speakers/Zamagni_Theory_of_Cooperative_Enterprise.pdf, retrieved May 31, 2016.

Zamagni, S. (2005b). "Why happiness and capabilities should stay together," Paper presented at the Conference on Happiness and Capabilities, University of Milano-Bicocca, 16–18 June 2005.

Zamagni, S. (2014a). "Common goods and the civil economy," *Revista Cultura Económica* 32/87: 8–25, http://www.uca.edu.ar/uca/common/grupo103/files/1-Zamagni_ce87.pdf, retrieved June 1, 2016.

Zamagni, S. (2014b). "The influence of virtuous human life in sustaining nature," in *Sustainable Humanity, Sustainable Nature: Our Responsibility Pontifical Academy of Sciences*, Extra Series 41, Vatican City, Pontifical Academy of Social Sciences, Acta 19, www.pas.va/content/dam/accademia/pdf/es41/es41-zamagni.pdf, retrieved June 1, 2016.

10 Conclusion

The aim of this book has been to identify whether new "reverse imperialist" and other new economics currents have broadened the standard economic notion of rationality, adding practical reason – the use of reason to decide about ends – to instrumental maximizing rationality – an optimal allocation of means to ends – and whether these currents concomitantly escape from the contemporary prevailing physicalist world view. In this respect, the book also intends to shed light on the present state and possible future of economics. Changes can stem predominantly from the influence of other sciences on economics, or from the rehabilitation of old elements of classical political economy, building upon today's standard economics. That is, changes can come from outside or from within economics. We have seen in the preceding chapters that these two kinds of changes can be complementary.

First, I have established the theoretical framework used to analyze these new currents. After highlighting how a metaphysical worldview has shaped the principles, development, methodology, and contents of science in every period of time, I argued that today's worldview is physicalist. I explained why in this book I consider physicalism as synonymous to materialism and of a form of naturalism called "restricted or scientific naturalism." This view entails a narrow notion of reality in the sense that all existent things can be reduced to or explained by the world's physical nature. It is also determinist, as, while we sometimes do not know the specific cause of each thing or event, we subscribe to the thesis that everything has a necessary cause. I also argued that this determinism is not fully accepted – especially in the social sciences – because of a tension produced by ideas such as hazard, free will, intentionality, novelty, creativity, teleology and the like.

Following John McDowell, I have made a distinction between "liberal naturalism" and "restricted or scientific naturalism." Similar ideas are held by Thomas Nagel, Mark Bedau and other thinkers. For these scholars, there are not only physical realities but also natural realities, like human thinking, free-will, and values, which make room for practical reason and final causes. Adopting practical reason goes hand in hand with recognizing free-will, human action intentionality and a teleological notion of human behavior. The consideration of these dimensions of human reality by a theory or science is a clear sign that physicalism has been overcome. Further, I also explained in detail why I adopted the Aristotelian notion of practical reason, leaving aside Kantian and Humean views.

I then argued why economics should be developed under the umbrella of liberal naturalism, including a place for free will and practical reason. Instrumental rationality puts freedom into brackets; it describes a deterministic way of acting and places the content of preferences in a black box. I explained the 20th century's development of economics as follows: narrowing the point of view – instrumental rationality – and broadening the human scope encompassed from that standpoint leads to an increasing scientific naturalization of economics called "economic imperialism," because it imposes this narrow economic rationale on other social sciences. The alleged results of this reductive logic (Rational Choice Theory or Expected Utility Theory) have been falsified in many experiments carried out by behavioral economists.

Reverse imperialist currents reverse this process: they import rationality notions from other social sciences – psychology, evolutionary sciences, neurosciences, sociology, ethics and politics – to understand economic action. At the same time, other new currents within economics "revive" these elements from classical political economy, which employed a richer and more varied set of motivations for human action. This is why I think that these new movements both from outside and inside are highly promising: they go in what I view as the right direction, supplementing instrumental rationality with other forms of rationality. Indeed, we are coming back to the four Weberian motivations for action: instrumental, value-rational, traditional and affective.

However, there are two threats to the continued development of this process. The first threat is standard economics' possible "domestication," as John Davis characterizes it, of these additional forms of rationality using instrumental rationality. Ludwig von Mises ([1933] 1978: 78–93) did it with Max Weber's rationality types: he reduced the four Weberian motivations to the first one, instrumental reason. The second threat is the possibility that the "exporting" sciences are already contaminated by the scientific naturalist worldview. This is the reason why I think that a philosophical analysis from the adopted point of view is relevant: we need to ascertain whether these new currents mean change or continuity, and whether they can be "purified" in the latter case. The first two chapters of this book have developed these arguments.

In the chapters that followed, each new current has been analyzed. Concerning currents influenced by psychological theories, Chapter 3 dealt with early 20th-century consumer theory. Contrary to other accounts, my conclusion is that this development features a tension between trying to sustain freedom and a demand for rigor in a positivist view of science. As regards Herbert Simon and Gerd Gigerenzer, the conclusion was that, notwithstanding their attention to the psychological limitations of human nature and its social elements, the tensions between scientificity vs. volition and free will, and instrumental vs. practical reason seem to favor the first components in these pairs, and they can be construed as predominantly physicalist. The conclusion regarding Modern Behavioral Economics (Daniel Kahneman and Amos Tversky) is that it does not include practical reason and it is principally physicalist. Finally, I warn against the insertion of psychological elements into economics in a physicalist way, which leads to "liberal paternalism." This proposal intends to guide people to behave in a standard economic way. The psychological notions underlying Simon, Gigerenzer and Kahneman's proposals are predominantly physicalist, and Modern Behavioral Economics has ultimately domesticated them, which was not hard to do, as physicalism and instrumental rationality share a strong affinity.

In Chapter 4, I reflected upon evolutionary economic theories. Though also a supporter of evolutionary ideas, I did not deal with Thorstein Veblen's thought, saving it for the chapter on institutionalism. A positive characteristic of the authors studied in this chapter is that they have not been completely influenced by biological evolutionary theories. Schumpeter developed his evolutionary ideas outside of evolutionary biology. In the cases of Richard Nelson, Geoffrey Hodgson, and Ulrich Witt, Darwinian ideas, evolutionary psychology and biology are all present, but the notion of novelty and free will run contrary to the scientific naturalism of the former. While I noticed an economic domestication of psychological inputs (that share a physicalist inclination) in Modern Behavioral Economics, I found that evolutionary economics combines scientific naturalism with ideas like the recognition of human freedom and novelty.

Chapter 5 focused on neuroeconomics. It first analyzed the metaphysics underlying the philosophy of neurosciences. Though predominantly materialist, some tensions remain in this field. Neuroeconomics deals with these tensions, solving them in a materialist way. The materialist approach of neurosciences and neuroeconomics reveals that both are contemporary disciplines. However, while neuroeconomics is an almost completely restrictive naturalist current, a tension between physicalism and the recognition of human freedom can be seen both in the philosophy of neurosciences and in neuroeconomics.

In Chapter 6, I dealt with happiness economics, which brings notions from social psychology and ethics into economics. Nonetheless, given that happiness and ethics were also concerns of the old political economics, in this case we find a mixture of insights coming from outside economics and other old elements coming from inside it. Still, this new current hinges on a hedonistic concept of happiness – hedonism not always found in classical economists – and is predominantly physicalist. However, I presented a new version of happiness economics, introducing the notion of "flourishing," which is based in practical reason, human intentionality and freedom. In fact, it shares some of Amartya Sen's ideas. This version is liberal naturalist, and, as a result, I think that it is more likely that this current follows the path that I have recommended for economics in this book.

After discussing the implications of the classical notion of practical reason for the basic concepts of institutionalism – agency, habits and institutions – Chapter 7 assessed Veblen's ideas and contemporary institutional theories from this perspective. Veblen adopted evolutionary ideas, albeit not without tension: he wants to consider human purposefulness, but, at the same time, he introduces a neo-Darwinian theory, with human behavior, habits, institutions, and culture seemingly deterministically caused. Concerning contemporary institutional theories, the conclusion is, first, that, in the equilibrium account, institutions are equilibria of strategic games, a position that adopts instrumental rationality, leaving practical rationality aside. Second, the constitutive rule theory makes room for practical reason in its analysis of agency, habits and institutions, which means that this theory opposes scientific naturalism. Therefore, institutional economics can – depending on the concepts of agency, habits and institutions adopted – follow the line suggested in the book.

Chapters 8 and 9 explore currents that incorporate practical reason most fully and are not physicalist: Amartya Sen's capability approach, and Luigino Bruni and Stefano Zamagni's conception of civil economy. In these cases there are no imports from other sciences because they explicitly argue that economics contains essential ethical elements. That is, the change in economics comes predominantly from within, particularly from its classical conception. We have finally arrived at currents that effectively adopt practical reason and escape from the contemporary, predominantly physicalist worldview. Sen's capability approach explicitly contemplates practical reason, human agency, freedom and ends in economics. The tensions between determinism and freedom, scientific and liberal naturalism, instrumental and practical reason disappear in Sen's approach, which views the person as a unique, reflective and free agent shaped by society. It acknowledges human heterogeneity and the heterogeneity of objectives. According to Sen, capabilities are diverse and incommensurable, while decisions about them go beyond calculations; they are ruled by practical reason. Sen's criticism of contemporary economics points to its lack of concern for values. In sum, the capability approach hinges on three key principles: the heterogeneity of people and their capabilities, the incompleteness of any order for those capabilities, and, thus, the need for practical reason or public discussion to deliberate about our capabilities and their hierarchy. This rationale stems from human freedom and diversity and can be managed by reflective agents using practical reason. I conclude that the capability approach strongly emphasizes practical reason, effectively relying on a "liberal naturalist" view of economic reality. In the corresponding chapter I suggest that some difficulties of operationalization of Sen's approach are related to his specific conception of practical reason.

Bruni and Zamagni's civil economy draws from classical Italian thinkers who were concerned about the insertion of the market into civil society and were aligned with the latter's pursuit of the common good. They view the market as not only an instrumental tool but also as a practice with inherent value, hence recognizing its practical dimension. Indeed, this approach deliberately considers practical rationality, freedom and intentionality, and, thus, it is a liberal naturalist current.

My final view of the contribution of reverse imperialist and other new economic currents to the desired direction suggested in this book for economics is on the whole positive. Though some of them remain prevalently physicalist, I think that incorporating inputs from other sciences, especially from other social sciences, or bringing elements from classical political economy back to life is the right way forward for economics. Biology and neurology are relevant because our biological constitution has an important influence on our behavior. Psychology and sociology add motivations for economic actions that are particularly human. Ethical, institutional and political concerns are often present in human actions. All these motivations lie behind economic actions. A complete explanation of them should take all these drivers into account. All these motivations were present at the beginning of economics. As Dimitris Milonakis and Ben Fine (2009: 19) assert, Smith's approach was pluralistic, "encompassing philosophical, psychological, social, historical and economic elements." There is a fruitful complementarity between changes driven from both outside and inside economics.

It should be stressed that rationality is *per se* normative, and normativity often bear an ethical content. Hence, economics cannot but employ practical reason, which is the use of reason to discover and decide on the ends of human action. All the currents analyzed can improve our explanations of economic affairs, individual economic decisions, and the design of economic policies, including those currents that are more physicalist, once "stripped" from their predominantly materialist orientation. I believe that all these currents should be integrated into a unique economic science that assimilates insights from biology, neurosciences, psychology, sociology, politics and ethics. Practical reason is a unifying faculty that can and should rule this integration.

References

Milonakis, D. and B. Fine (2009). *From Political Economy to Economics*. London and New York: Routledge.

Mises, L. von ([1933] 1960). *Epistemological Problems of Economics*. Princeton, Toronto, New York, London: D. van Nostrand (trans., G. Reisman).

Index

Indicators in **bold** refer to tables.

 **Taylor & Francis eBooks**

Helping you to choose the right eBooks for your Library

Add Routledge titles to your library's digital collection today. Taylor and Francis ebooks contains over 50,000 titles in the Humanities, Social Sciences, Behavioural Sciences, Built Environment and Law.

Choose from a range of subject packages or create your own!

Benefits for you

» Free MARC records
» COUNTER-compliant usage statistics
» Flexible purchase and pricing options
» All titles DRM-free.

Benefits for your user

» Off-site, anytime access via Athens or referring URL
» Print or copy pages or chapters
» Full content search
» Bookmark, highlight and annotate text
» Access to thousands of pages of quality research at the click of a button.

 REQUEST YOUR **FREE** INSTITUTIONAL TRIAL TODAY **Free Trials Available** We offer free trials to qualifying academic, corporate and government customers.

eCollections – Choose from over 30 subject eCollections, including:

Archaeology	Language Learning
Architecture	Law
Asian Studies	Literature
Business & Management	Media & Communication
Classical Studies	Middle East Studies
Construction	Music
Creative & Media Arts	Philosophy
Criminology & Criminal Justice	Planning
Economics	Politics
Education	Psychology & Mental Health
Energy	Religion
Engineering	Security
English Language & Linguistics	Social Work
Environment & Sustainability	Sociology
Geography	Sport
Health Studies	Theatre & Performance
History	Tourism, Hospitality & Events

For more information, pricing enquiries or to order a free trial, please contact your local sales team: www.tandfebooks.com/page/sales

 Routledge Taylor & Francis Group | The home of Routledge books

www.tandfebooks.com

9780367667818